POETRY
From Statement to Meaning

Poetry

FROM STATEMENT TO MEANING

JEROME BEATY
EMORY UNIVERSITY

WILLIAM H. MATCHETT
UNIVERSITY OF WASHINGTON

New York   OXFORD UNIVERSITY PRESS   1965

W. H. AUDEN
"Lay your sleeping head, my love": copyright 1940 by W. H. Auden. Reprinted
from *The Collected Poetry of W. H. Auden* by permission of Random House,
Inc., and from *The Collected Shorter Poems* by permission of Faber and Faber Ltd.
Four lines from "Letter to Lord Byron": reprinted from *Letters from Iceland*,
copyright 1937 by Wystan Hugh Auden, by permission of the author and Faber
and Faber Ltd.

PETER BEILENSON
Five haiku and one prose paragraph: reprinted from *Japanese Haiku*, copyright
1955, 1956 by the Peter Pauper Press, by permission of the Peter Pauper Press.

LOUISE BOGAN
"Women": copyright 1954 by Louise Bogan. Reprinted from *Collected Poems
1923–53* by Louise Bogan, by permission of Farrar, Straus & Giroux, Inc.

For
Shawn, David, Katherine, Stephen, and Andrew

Contents

POETRY
From Statement to Meaning

Introduction

Readers who begin to take an interest in poetry often bring with them (and sometimes, unfortunately, retain) three related assumptions: that a poem is to be read for its "message," that this message is "hidden" in the poem, and that it is to be found by treating the words as "symbols" which naturally do not mean what they say but "stand for" something else. To such people, reading poetry is like breaking open fortune cookies to find the words of wisdom.

If these assumptions were completely false, they could be easily disproved, or even disregarded; but each is a partial truth masquerading as a whole truth. For example, most serious poems are likely to involve ideas, implicit or explicit, which may be discussed separately as "messages," moral affirmations, philosophical assertions, or whatever the reader may wish to call them ("Love alters not," "Beauty is truth, truth beauty," "The Grave's a fine and private place," "All things remain in God"). However, the reader who takes such a statement to be "the point of the poem" will entirely miss the experience of reading poetry and perhaps even the experience with which the poem deals, will distort the poems he reads to fit his preconceptions, and will arrive at logically untenable critical judgments.

The reader who wants only the simple and portable idea from a poem, who reads *Macbeth,* for example, to discover that "what it says" is "Thou shalt not kill," is surely being satisfied too soon with too little. Though he might not deny the idea, the poet is likely to have been concerned with something else — perhaps with an individual experience of the importance of an idea that had grown stale and abstract, perhaps with an experience qualifying the idea, or perhaps with an experience to which the idea was merely incidental. It is even possible that the poet never framed in his own mind the specific "central idea" that the reader finds most obvious. If a reader seeks only messages, he is likely to twist any poem until he finds one, propounding with solemnity some moral principle he perceives in "One, Two, Buckle My Shoe." If he esteems only messages, he will evaluate poems rather strangely. He will not be able to like very many love poems, even those of Shakespeare or Herrick, for very few contain "messages of importance" unless he twists them into evidence for his own preconceptions. He will not be able to sympathize with poets whose thinking does not agree with his own: if religious, he cannot admire the Epicurean poetry of Wallace Stevens; if an atheist, he cannot admire George Herbert. But even such a reader will find undeniably good ideas in poems that he cannot bring himself to value very highly. Finally, how does the message-hunter respond when he finds poems that have almost identical "messages" but differ greatly in quality? Both these poems, for example, tell us a Christian believes death will be conquered:

Time and Death

I saw old Time, destroyer of mankind;
Calm, stern, and cold he sate, and often shook
And turn'd his glass, nor ever car'd to look
How many of life's sands were still behind.
And there was Death, his page, aghast to find   5
How tremblingly, like aspens o'er a brook,
His blunted dart fell harmless; so he took
His master's scythe, and idly smote the wind.
Smite on, thou gloomy one, with powerless aim!
For Sin, thy mother, at her dying breath   10
Wither'd that arm, and left thee but a name.
Hope clos'd the grave, when he of Nazareth,
Who led captivity his captive, came
And vanquish'd the great conquerors, Time and Death.

[Death Be Not Proud]

Death be not proud, though some have called thee
Mighty and dreadfull, for thou art not soe;
For those whom thou think'st thou dost overthrow
Die not, poore Death; nor yet canst thou kill mee.
From rest and sleepe, which but thy pictures bee,   5
Much pleasure, then from thee much more must flow,
And soonest our best men with thee doe goe,
Rest of their bones and soules deliverie.
Thou art slave to Fate, Chance, kings, and desperate men,
And dost with poyson, warre, and sicknesse dwell,   10
And poppie or charmes can make us sleepe as well,
And better than thy stroake; why swell'st thou then?
One short sleepe past, wee wake eternally,
And death shall be no more: Death, thou shalt die.

Can anyone maintain that, since the ideas are so similar, the first of these poems, by William Henry Whitworth, is the equal of the second, by John Donne?

"Of course," some readers are bound to say, "it is not *just* the idea that makes the poem, it is the beauty of its language and form." They quote Pope's description of the good poem — "What oft was thought, but ne'er so well expressed"; or they describe a poem as if it were a sugar-coated pill — a pleasant way to swallow the medicine of ideas. If they hold these opinions very superficially, it is not difficult to show them they do not really believe what they say; few of the words in "Death Be Not Proud," for example, are as "beautiful" as the words in most popular songs, if, as is usual, we mean by "beautiful words" those which merely call up pleasant associations, words like "moon" and "June."

There are, however, two undeniable facts behind the sugar-coated-pill theory. The first is that the "idea" of a poem often boils down to a commonplace. This being true, the message-hunter is contradicted; if the idea is a commonplace, the quality of the poem must lie somewhere apart from that idea (which may even suggest that a good poem cannot be boiled down). The second fact is that an idea is better expressed in a good poem than in a bad one. Much of what follows will attempt to qualify this latter statement of fact through defining and demonstrating certain propositions:

that to express an idea "better" is actually to change it;

that there is a larger gap between the extracted idea and the poem in a good poem than there is in a poor one (or, put another way, that a fine poem cannot be summarized in any words other than those of the poem itself);

that a poem is more than the idea it contains, not because it is also beautiful or well-expressed but because it is itself more concrete, more specific, more real to the senses than any abstract statement that can be abstracted from it, and is indeed concerned with another kind of truth.

If what a poem says is not a message, what is it? The reader is still apt to feel that the meaning is somehow "hidden" in the poem. Somehow the words mean more than they say, for, in discussion, he often discovers that he has not seen what is said to be on the page. How does anyone find this meaning? What does he look for?

He does not look *for* anything; he looks *at* the poem. With closest attention, he looks at it and listens to it. Consider this well-known poem by Robert Frost:

Stopping by Woods on a Snowy Evening

Whose woods these are I think I know.
His house is in the village though;
He will not see me stopping here
To watch his woods fill up with snow.

My little horse must think it queer   5
To stop without a farmhouse near
Between the woods and frozen lake
The darkest evening of the year.

He gives his harness bells a shake
To ask if there is some mistake.   10

> The only other sound's the sweep
> Of easy wind and downy flake.
>
> The woods are lovely, dark and deep,
> But I have promises to keep,
> And miles to go before I sleep,
> And miles to go before I sleep.

15

The reader who believes that all this poem "says" is that a man stops by woods one evening to watch the snow fall, and nothing more, surely misses some of the power of the poem. In a poetry class, he might be asked, for example, what the owner of the house, the horse, and the promises contribute to the poem. (That the details of a poem must be "accounted for" in one's reading of the poem might at first shock him.) The discussion of the poem that followed such questions would be sure to astound him. First of all, the group might try to establish why the poet (or the "I" of the poem) stopped; in abstract terms it could only be to enjoy the beauty of the scene ("The woods are lovely, dark and deep"). There might be the suggestion that this is a special kind of beauty — the transformation of the familiar — which would explain the poet's mentioning that he knew, or thought he knew, the owner. Why is it important that the owner will not see the poet watching the woods fill up with snow? Surely he would not object merely on the grounds of trespassing. Perhaps because the owner, like the horse, would "think it queer" for someone to sit out in the cold and watch the snow. And that brings up the horse. He is the practical one; there is no sense to stopping far from a farmhouse on a cold dark night; his "protest" — the jangling harness bells — is the only sound interrupting the soft silence of the scene. Then there is another interruption — the recollection of the promises, the obligations, probably, of everyday affairs — and the practical recognition of the miles there are yet to go. So the "meaning" of the poem somehow involves a conflict between the enjoyment of beauty and the practical pressures of everyday life. But someone at this point would be bound to bring up the last clause, "before I sleep," and that forces a re-examination of the abstraction "beauty." It is obvious that the poet is not speaking about beauty in general, but about this particular kind of experience: the woods are not only "lovely" but "dark and deep." (This is the kind of distinction we had in mind before when we said that poetry was concrete and "ideas" abstract, so that poems could not be reduced to ideas.) There is a definite suggestion in the poem that "sleep" is somehow allied to this experience in the woods; it offers, of course, an escape also from everyday pressures, but there seems to be an even more complete identification (remember "dark and deep"), so that the beauty of this moment and the beauty of sleep are united. (Someone is even likely to say this is suggested in the sleepy repetition of the next to the last line.)

These are tentative suggestions — actually the kind of thing you would be more likely to hear in a class, where everyone is simply trying to explain why the poem moved him or how it moved him, than to see in cold print, where one is trying to "prove" what the poem "really means." An instructor would have all he could do to prevent your writing in your notebook: " 'Stopping by Woods on a Snowy Evening' by Robert Frost — practical considerations of society (neighbor), comfort (no farmhouse, frozen lake, darkest evening), and obligation (promises) interrupt those moments of solemn beauty which in their loveliness, unpracticality (dark), and depth are like the freedom of the unconscious in sleep."

Though it may be a fuller summary of the "meaning" or effect of the poem than the mere statement that it is about a man who stops to watch the snow, it is likely to be at least as misleading. A reader hearing such a discussion, however, who himself has neither seen nor, perhaps, even felt these elements in the poem, and, having heard of them still doesn't see "how you get that out of the poem," is likely to confuse sensitivity with ingenuity. When the meaning of poem after poem escapes him, whatever the reason, he comes to feel that the process of writing a poem must be one of attempting to disguise an otherwise obvious meaning in a tangle of artificial words, and that reading a poem consists in conjecturing as grandiosely as possible as to the "real meaning" of those words. He becomes a symbolmonger, fearing simplicity and embroidering ridiculous or irrelevant interpretations — for symbolmongering is merely the most desperate way of attempting to wrench into the light some meaning or other when none is apparent. One student, for example, identified the owner of the woods in this Frost poem as God; his house in the village as the church; the speaker as an atheist whose horse, the common man, is wiser than he is and knows that God is omnipresent.

Such a student must be reminded that a poem is, among other

things, an instrument of verbal communication, like a recipe or a telegram. What a poem communicates, if successful, is something more than most prose passages convey (including a prose paraphrase of the poem itself) — not because there is a special language of poetry, but because poetry exploits more consistently the full potentialities of the language it shares with prose. Poems are not written to conceal meanings but to express them exactly, not to be solved like riddles but to be encountered as they are. When the meaning of a poem is obscure to a reader, when he fails to understand what he has read, there has been a failure of communication. This failure may have a variety of causes — a general inadequacy of the poet, a flaw in the individual poem, historical developments such as changes in definitions of certain words — but by far the most common causes of failure must be attributed not to the poet or the poem or to the nature of poetry but to the reader. And not to the reader's lack of intelligence or sensitivity, necessarily, but rather to false preconceptions, misleading partial truths, carelessness, or application of some false or inadequate method in his reading of poems. In this volume we hope to help the reader surmount some of the obstacles which may stand between him and the experience of poetry; we hope, more positively, to present an approach that will allow him to develop his sensitivity to poetry through developing his sensitivity to the language of particular poems.

We begin where most readers should feel at home: in the world of prose statement. Frequently, however, the reader who has trouble with poetry has, though he is not aware of it, the same trouble with prose. He is not aware of it because he has managed to get along, reading most prose with an eye only for its general sense and with little awareness of the modifiers which create the precise statement. Content with a vague impression, he fails to realize that he is missing much of what he reads. His trouble with poetry is, however, more immediately obvious to him because poetry, being more concise, withholds even a vague impression; it *demands* the precise attention that prose only *deserves*.

Our first problems, then, are common to prose and poetry. In fact, we go about understanding the poetry by asking the reader first to turn the poem into prose, that is to paraphrase the "prose statement" of the poem. This process should serve two purposes: it shows him what, on the most literal level, the poem "says" and it shows him how much of the full meaning of the poem even the best and fullest para-

From Statement to Form

I

Prose Statement

This discussion of poetry is based on two related assumptions: that poetry usually goes beyond prose statement to something that might be called "poetic meaning," and that poetry makes prose statements before transcending them — that is, makes prose statements and something more. The purpose of this first chapter is to suggest a procedure for delimiting the prose statement of poems so that the reader may go more accurately beyond statement to meaning, beyond prose to poetry.

An obvious example of the relationship of poetry to prose may be seen in the poetic line itself. Perhaps the most sophisticated as well as the most naïve reader first recognizes a poem as a poem by its appearance on the printed page: it is not, like prose, printed in blocks of paragraphs but in shorter, less regular lines, beginning usually with capitals but sometimes ending without so much as a comma. A perceptive reader soon learns that this division into lines is not arbitrary, that lines are units which, through rhythmic regularity and variation (the breaking of regularity), create effects or provide emphases (and thus meanings). However, it is equally important to recognize that if a poem has lines it also has sentences; if it has meaning added to the statements of the sentences, it has no meaning contrary to or less than that of the same sentences had they appeared in prose. It is possible to miss a great deal in a poem by failing to consider it as a group of poetic lines; but it is also possible to miss a great deal in a poem by failing to read it as a group of prose sentences.

So it is that many people read and remember the opening lines of one of Wordsworth's sonnets as:

> The world is too much with us late and soon;
> Getting and spending, we lay waste our powers:

The words and the word order are exactly right, but the relationships — here represented by punctuation — are wrong, because these readers instead of reading by sentences have read by lines, ignoring punctuation, and so have distorted the meaning. The poem actually begins:

> The world is too much with us; late and soon,
> Getting and spending, we lay waste our powers:

We can emphasize the structure and prose meaning by printing syntactical divisions thus:

> The world is too much with us;
> late and soon, getting and spending, we lay waste our powers:

What this chapter proposes, then, is that *for the time being* you read poems almost as if they were arranged in sentences and paragraphs. This will, we hope, serve two purposes: you will learn to determine the prose statement of the poem, and, by considering the differences between the way the prose might be arranged and the way the poetry in fact is arranged, you will begin to gather some idea of what poetry gains through form. You should, that is, come to see how a poem, because of its arrangement, can say more than prose in the same words, and how its words and word order cannot be altered without change of meaning.

REORDERING

One of the most disturbing things about poetry to those who are not used to reading it is that, even if one ignores lines and reads by sentences, many poems still do not make immediate sense. Even reading by sentences does not help one very much in understanding Shakespeare's "Sonnet 146":

> Poore soule, the center of my sinfull earth,
> Thrall to these rebbell powres that thee array,
> Why dost thou pine within and suffer dearth,

> Painting thy outward walls so costlie gay?
> Why so large cost, having so short a lease,   5
> Dost thou upon thy fading mansion spend?
> Shall wormes, inheritors of this excesse,
> Eate up thy charge? is this thy bodie's end?
> Then, soule, live thou upon thy servant's losse,
> And let that pine to aggravat thy store;   10
> Buy tearms divine in selling hours of drosse,
> Within be fed, without be rich no more:
>> So shalt thou feed on Death, that feeds on men,
>> And Death once dead, ther's no more dying then.*

Few inexpert readers of poetry will fully grasp the prose statement, much less the entire meaning, of this poem upon first reading: there will be those, however, who will think (or "know") that they know what it says; others will think (or "know") that they do not know what it says; some will think that what it says is merely "a matter of opinion"; and some will think that, since it is a poem, it is not supposed to make sense anyway but only to suggest profound and beautiful things. What is needed is a procedure that will enable those readers in the first group to support their knowledge with convincing evidence; that will help those in the second group to discover the statements they have missed; that will define for those in the third group the limits within which "opinion" is permissible (and thus show them clearly why and where it is not); and that will convince those in the fourth group that a beautiful poem usually makes sense and that making sense does not detract from, but in fact enhances, the beauty.

The procedure we propose to satisfy these requirements is that of "reordering" † — converting the poem step by step into prose by re-

* l. 2 *Thrall to:* The original edition of the sonnets (1609), in apparent error, begins the second line by repeating "My sinfull earth"; "Thrall to" is one of a number of suggested emendations having no textual authority.

† "Reordering" differs from "paraphrase" in that it attempts to keep the structure and vocabulary of the original in so far as is consistent with normal prose usage; "paraphrase" is the rendering of the original into words and structures of the paraphraser.

It cannot be urged too strongly that these procedures are means to an end and not ends in themselves: their function is to help the reader clarify the prose statement of a poem so that he may understand it first in prose terms and thus may eventually see how far the poem transcends that sense. Used alone and erroneously, this chapter could be quite destructive to the right reading of poetry.

arranging its word order into that of normal modern discourse by
examining and clarifying its sentence structure and syntax — and
then defining those words that seem difficult or unusual. Somewhat
artificially isolating the problems of word order and syntax from
those of vocabulary, let us now see how the procedures can help us
understand at least the prose statement of a poem.

WORD ORDER AND SYNTAX

English is essentially a word-order language; we understand English statements largely through the order in which the words appear.
A noun is a subject or object, acts or is acted upon, because of its
position relative to the verb rather than because of any change in its
own form. When we read "Man eats fish," we know who did what to
whom; rearranging the order of the words changes the meaning considerably: "Fish eats man." In many languages the order can be
changed without affecting the meaning (or the meaning changed
without disturbing the order) because the noun is inflected, that is,
it has a slightly different form as subject or object. With the ending
-us indicating a subject, and *-um* an object, we could write our
sentence in a sort of pidgin-Latin thus: "Manus eats fishum." This
could be written "Fishum eats manus" without any change in meaning. Retaining the original order but changing the forms of the words,
"Manum eats fishus," results in a complete change in meaning.
Either of these three-word sentences can be written in any of six
permutations (*e.g.,* "Eats manum fishus," "Manum fishus eats")
without affecting its sense. But such flexibility of order is not possible
in English. We do inflect pronouns (I, me, my; he, him, his), and
nouns to show possession (the boy's dog), but, even so, we depend on
certain patterns in the order of the words and, even though it is
partially inflected, we lose the sense of so simple a sentence as "He
gave me the boy's dog" if it is reordered to "Gave dog me the boy's
he."

   Without resorting to a make-believe language we can see the same
principle at work in a word-for-word translation of the famous opening of Virgil's *Aeneid*:

> *Arma virumque cano, Troiae qui prima ab oris . . .*
> *Italiam . . . venit*

>   Arms man-and sing, Troy who first from shore . . .
>   Italy . . . came

It is difficult to see how anyone who did not already know what the
line said in Latin could understand this "translation"; at any rate it
is not yet "English." Even if we were to add those words which in
English replace the inflected endings, we would still have a somewhat
puzzling line:

>   Of arms of the man-and sing-I, Troy's who first from shore . . .
>   To Italy . . . came

Not until we change the word order are the relationships clear enough
to make us relatively certain of the meaning and to have the beginning of a sentence recognizably English:

>   Of arms and of the man I sing, who first from Troy's shore to
>   Italy . . . came

The line becomes clearer if we rearrange the words still further to
conform to the necessity in English of putting modifiers, including
modifying clauses, as close as possible to the word modified:

>   I sing of arms and of the man who first came to Italy from Troy's
>   shore . . .

Flexibility of word order in an inflected language such as Latin
obviously makes the writing of poetry in that language somewhat
easier. There is reason to believe, however, that it is the very difficulty
of manipulation which makes English the superb medium for poetry
that it is. It is likely that the very rigidity of word order, and thus of
the reader's expectations, makes it possible to gain impressive effects
through minor changes. Be that as it may, this brief discussion should
make it clear that word order determines prose sense in English, and
that English poetry therefore cannot entirely depart from the word
order of English prose.

There are of course few, if any, poems in English that, though extremely difficult to understand as they appear in verse, become mag-
ically simple once their words are reordered to conform to the patterns
of normal prose; a truly difficult poem is usually so from a number of
causes, not only word order, but syntax, vocabulary, and complexity
of suggestion, emotion, and idea. There are poems, however, which
are not perfectly and immediately clear to all readers and which are

considerably clearer to most once the words are put in a more usual order. Such a poem, perhaps, is this Wordsworth sonnet:

Composed upon Westminster Bridge, September 3, 1802

Earth has not anything to show more fair:
Dull would he be of soul who could pass by
A sight so touching in its majesty:
This City now doth, like a garment, wear
The beauty of the morning; silent, bare,   5
Ships, towers, domes, theatres, and temples lie
Open unto the fields, and to the sky;
All bright and glittering in the smokeless air.
Never did sun more beautifully steep
In his first splendour, valley, rock, or hill;   10
Ne'er saw I, never felt, a calm so deep!
The river glideth at his own sweet will:
Dear God! the very houses seem asleep;
And all that mighty heart is lying still!

Arranged in modern prose order and divided into syntactical units rather than poetic lines, that sonnet might read:

[The] earth has not anything more fair to show:
he who could pass by a sight so touching in its majesty would be
    dull of soul:
this City now (wears) the beauty of the morning like a garment;
silent [and] bare, ships, towers, domes, theatres, and temples lie
    open unto the fields and [un]to the sky;
all [of them lie] bright and glittering in the smokeless air.

[The] sun never (steeped) valley, rock, or hill more beautifully
    in his first splendour;
I ne[v]er saw, never felt, so deep a calm!

The river (glides) at his own sweet will:
Dear God!
the very houses seem asleep;
and all that mighty heart <the City> is lying still! *

* Additions are put in square brackets, changes in parentheses, and explanations in

He also would be rather dull of soul who could pass by this first example of reordering without troubled and searching questions. "If this is what Wordsworth really meant," goes the normal reaction, "then why didn't he say so in the first place?" If the answer to this question is merely that the poem is a more beautiful arrangement of the meaning of the prose statement, we are back to the sugar-coated-pill concept of poetry as a decorative covering of beautiful words around a hard core of meaning, a fallacy discussed and dismissed in the Introduction. However, this reordered version cannot be said to rob the original of images, or of the connotations of single words, since the prose retains virtually all the original words. Moreover, this particular poem does not appear to depend upon words or phrases which have more than one meaning and which lose such additional meaning when shifted to another position in the sentence. Yet there is a good deal lost, something that might be called "effectiveness" or "emphasis" but that might better be considered part of the actual *meaning* of the poem. Even without going into the intricacies of prosody and structure, it may be possible to show how some of this meaning is lost.

Two rhetorical devices that reinforce or modify the meanings of the statements in the original poem but are lost in reordering are periodic structure and parallelism. A periodic clause or sentence, like

---

pointed brackets. The reordering will not clarify the poem completely. Some may find the following notes helpful:

l. 1 Add to the end of the line, "than this sight"; see title.

l. 7 The ships, etc., are open to the sky, apparently, because there is no smoke hanging over them now, in the early morning, as there usually is in the middle of the day.

l. 8 Note that "smokeless," though a negative, actually brings the element of smoke into the poem (as suggested in the preceding note) — *i.e.,* the poem does not say "orchidless" though the air is just as free of orchids as it is of smoke. There is throughout this poem, of course, an implied contrast between the city as it now appears and the city as it usually appears, just as there is in much of the poem a contrast between this cityscape and a natural landscape.

l. 9 For "steep" read "soak" or "drench."

l. 10 For "his" read "its," but see the next note.

l. 12 For "his" read "its"; the line perhaps means free of water traffic and other daytime obstructions which divert and impede the flow of the river. But "his will" followed by "Dear God!" suggests the common phrase "God's will," and it is not out of harmony with the poem (or what we know of Wordsworth's philosophy) to think of the river flowing in accordance with God's will.

l. 13 For "the very houses" read "the houses themselves."

l. 14 "Still" must mean "quiet," not "yet."

this that you are now reading, is one which, until the very end, until the period or semicolon, withholds its sense. (The opposite and more "normal" structure is called "loose"; in it, modifying, but somewhat less than essential, words or phrases occur after the essential elements, such as subject, verb, object, and essential or "restrictive" modifiers.) Two such periodic clauses in the poem are loosened by reordering, in both cases by the shift of an adverbial modifier to the final position in the clause: in lines 4–5, "like a garment" appears in the middle of the clause which ends with its object, "the beauty," and its essential or restrictive modifier, "of the morning"; in the reordered version, the essential statement has already been made before the nonessential "like a garment" is tacked on. Similarly, in lines 9–10, the adverbial modifiers, "more beautifully" and "In his first splendour," occur before the verb and before the objects of the verb in the poem, but in the new version they appear only after the statement of the clause is essentially complete.

Parallelism is a device by which a repeated pattern of parts of speech forces a comparison of the phrases or clauses so paralleled; such structure is more forceful and apparent when the pattern is something other than the usual subject-verb-object sequence. Such is the case in the adverb-verb-subject patterns in lines 9 and 11 of the poem, a parallelism reinforced by the fact that the pattern begins each of the lines and by the repetition of the adverb "never" (though it is spelled "ne'er" in line 11 and though the verb in the pattern in line 9 is an auxiliary). The unusual word order in the poem suggests a comparison between the actions of the sun and the response of the poet or narrator (heightened by "more beautifully" and "so deep" and perhaps by the personification of the sun — in "*his* first splendour"). But this suggestion is obscured in the prose version by the normalcy of the subject-verb-object pattern.

The end of the first periodic clause (l. 5) is also the first instance — and one of only two such instances — of heavy punctuation within a poetic line. The second — "Dear God!" in line 13 — comes at what may be considered the emotional climax of the poem, and by its position gives added pressure to the exclamation. This stopping of the line not only heightens the impact but calls attention to the words: it suggests that the exclamation is not merely a stronger equivalent of "Dear me," but that the poet is at this point actually addressing God, a possibility easy to overlook in the prose.

The poem, then, expresses, emphasizes, and modifies the meanings of its words through such devices as periodic and parallel structures, available to prose, and through some devices, such as line-endings, rhyme, and meter (which we are not yet ready to discuss) peculiar to poetry. The reordered version, then, offers not so much the meaning that the poet has twisted into the form of the poem as the meaning that remains when the poem is reduced to the patterns of "normal" prose. In other words, the poem offers meaning that the prose version cannot express — that it can at best only approximate. We can never estimate the gap between normal prose and poetry, however, until we have put some poems into their prose denominators. Reordering, then, not only helps us understand the minimum statement of a poem but also helps us understand how inadequate the statement is to express the full meaning of the poem.

Reordering Wordsworth's "Composed upon Westminster Bridge" makes its prose sense somewhat more apparent. That poem is a rather simple one, however; few readers are likely to miss its elementary statement even upon first reading. Even if reordering did show up some of its subtleties ("hidden meanings" or "embellishments" certain readers might say), that somewhat unwieldy and unfamiliar exercise was not necessary to reveal the "central meaning" of the poem.

Let us, then, consider another poem, one by Robert Bridges, that is still relatively simple but is less likely than Wordsworth's to be immediately and entirely understood by all readers on first reading:

Nightingales

Beautiful must be the mountains whence ye come,
And bright in the fruitful valleys the streams wherefrom
      Ye learn your song:
Where are those starry woods? O might I wander there,
      Among the flowers, which in that heavenly air   5
      Bloom the year long!

Nay, barren are those mountains and spent the streams:
Our song is the voice of desire, that haunts our dreams,
      A throe of the heart,
Whose pining visions dim, forbidden hopes profound,   10

No dying cadence nor long sigh can sound,
        For all our art.

Alone, aloud in the raptured ear of men
We pour our dark nocturnal secret; and then,
        As night is withdrawn   15
From these sweet-springing meads and bursting boughs of May,
        Dream, while the innumerable choir of day
            Welcome the dawn.

This is how the poem might be reordered and arranged in syntactical units:

The mountains (from which) (you) come must be beautiful,
and in the fruitful valleys the streams (from which) (you) learn
        your song [must be] bright:
where are those starry woods?

O [that] I might wander there, among the flowers, which bloom
        [all] the year long in that heavenly air.

(No), those mountains are barren
and the streams [are] spent:
our song is the voice of desire, that haunts our dreams,
a throe of the heart whose dim, pining visions and profound, for-
        bidden hopes no dying cadence nor long sigh can sound,
for all our art.

Alone, we pour our dark nocturnal secret aloud in[to] the [en]rap-
        tured ear[s] of men (alone);
and then, as night is withdrawn from these sweet-springing
        mead[ow]s and bursting boughs of May,
[we] dream,
while the innumerable choir of day welcome the dawn.*

    * At this point definitions in the reordered version are being held to a minimum.
Supplementary definitions may be found in the following notes:
    l. 4 *starry woods:* presumably this suggests that stars are intermittently visible
through the leaves of the trees, giving the effect of the stars actually being in the woods
(see stanza four of Keats's "Ode to a Nightingale"), though the compression here also
gives the effect of etherializing the nightingales' woods ("starry woods," "heavenly
air").
    l. 7 *spent:* "depleted," "exhausted," or, here, "run dry"
    l. 9 *throe:* "pang"

The reordered version of "Nightingales" is somewhat more easily understood on first reading than is the poem itself because the word order in the reordered version conforms to the familiar pattern of subject-verb-object or subject-verb-complement. The rearrangement of "Nightingales" is perhaps more helpful than that of Wordsworth's sonnet because of the number and length of modifiers in the Bridges poem; it is sometimes difficult to hold in mind the unusually ordered elements of a sentence or clause while at the same time following out a long modifier or sequence of modifiers. Thus for some readers lines 2 and 3 of "Nightingales" may be more difficult to understand than is line 1, for in the second line not only does the subject of the clause, "streams," follow the implied verb but it is itself modified by a rather long clause that spills over onto the third line — "wherefrom / Ye learn your song." The reader must, in effect, hold in mind both "streams" and its long modifying clause while he relates this "displaced" subject to its proper verb. It is not surprising, then, that some readers by the time they get to the end of line 3, cannot remember whether the nightingales are said to learn their song from the valleys or from the streams.

---

l. 10 *pining:* "yearning"

l. 11 *cadence:* in music, "final notes or phrases of a composition or of part of a composition"

    sound: "utter" or "measure the depths of"; both meanings seem to apply here: "there is no cadence or sigh that can utter [or] express the hopes and visions and none that can measure the depths (of despair) of the hopes and visions."

l. 16 *sweet-springing:* "sweetly springing"; "springing with sweetness"; "sweetly beginning to appear"

The last meaning, though "spring" so used is rather archaic, seems to be the primary or basic sense of the phrase in this poem; the proximity of "bursting" suggests the possibility of "springing" here being another verb of violent motion. The proximity of "May" perhaps also suggests a seasonal association in "springing." Where there are several possible meanings and one applies and others do not, the one naturally is the "right" meaning; where there are several possible meanings and none applies, there is something wrong with the poem; where, as in this case, there are several possible meanings and several apply almost equally well, the poet has gained meanings and effects with an economy of words. Thus "springing" may be said to be the best word for this context precisely because it contains possibilities of action, season, and gradual appearance, all of which apply to meadow grasses in a May dawn and all of which are supported by the associations of surrounding words.

l. 17 *innumerable choir:* birds, specifically, those birds that, unlike the nightingale, sing at dawn and through the day. (Bridges presents the nightingale as singing only at night, a common misconception.)

Most readers, however, will understand the first few lines of "Night-ingales" and much of the rest of the poem merely by reading the poem over a few times; reordering, though perhaps helpful, will not for them be essential. But there is one passage in this poem — lines 10–12 — which a good many readers may not understand even after repeated readings. Because of the usual pattern of English syntax, it is tempting to render "dim" in line 10 as a verb, the force of which is expressed in the phrase "grow dim" — "Whose pining visions [grow] dim." Once on this tack, the reader may distort the rest of the clause in order to extract some sense from it, similarly inserting "grow" before "profound" perhaps, and inevitably making "sound" an in-transitive verb:

> whose pining visions [grow] dim [and] forbidden hopes
>   [grow] profound;
> no dying cadence nor long sigh can [make a] sound,

Such a reordering, whether it is written or merely an approximation in the mind of the reader, violates the probabilities of the language in its treatment of "profound" and "sound"; violates common sense in its version of line 11 (the cadence and sigh would make sounds, however inexpressive); and violates the progression of thought in the stanza (what the nightingales are trying to express and their inability to do so are left unrelated). A reader who understands these lines, it is true, gains little from reordering them other than the satisfaction of demonstrating his understanding. But one who is not sure or whose reading is roughly comparable to the faulty reordering given above, may, unless he writes out his reordered version, be content with a vague or erroneous impression. Writing it out may not immediately solve his difficulty, but he will be able to see more readily that his version of the poem's statement does not make sense.

Another result of reordering is apparent in line 13 — "Alone, aloud in the raptured ear of men / We pour . . ." — where there is no obvious difficulty. Reordering will force the reader to put "Alone" somewhere in the sentence other than its present position. He can put it before "We" — "Alone, we pour . . ." — or after "men" — "in the raptured ear of men alone." Are the nightingales saying, in effect, "Here we are all alone in the woods, the other birds having gone to sleep . . ."; or, "we tell our secrets only to men"? Though some may

argue that one of these alternatives is the better, they will not deny the
presence of a residue or suggestion of the other. They will see that the
position of "Alone" in the poem suggests both meanings and that
changing the position in reordering, though it may clarify one meaning, loses the suggestion of the other. The ordering of words in
a poem, then, does not merely adorn or "hide" an equivalent prose
meaning but achieves its own fuller and more precise meaning as explicitly and briefly as possible. Reordering, while it does help reveal
the minimal prose statement, also, by its own inadequacy, indicates
the range of meaning of the poem beyond its best possible paraphrase.

This loss of meaning through reordering may be further demonstrated by comparing the openings of the first two stanzas in the
poem and in the prose version. The parallelism of the first two lines
is retained in the reordering:

    mountains . . . must be beautiful
    streams . . . [must be] bright

So is the parellelism between these lines and the opening of the
second stanza:

    mountains are barren
    streams [are] spent

The original is somewhat more emphatic, of course, because not only
are the lines parallel but the word order is somewhat unusual, the
predicate adjectives preceding the verbs and subjects. In the poem the
parallelism is further emphasized by the identical use of ellipsis
(the omission of a word or words necessary for complete grammatical
construction but understood in the context). The missing element in
both stanzas is the verb whose subject is "streams" — "must be" in
the first stanza, "are" in the second.

The word that one uses to "fill in" elliptical clauses like these is
dictated by the earlier clause which the ellipsis parallels. Since the
verb in the first line is "must be," the "missing" verb in the second
line must be "must be" and similarly the "missing" verb in the second
clause of line 7 must be "are," because that is the verb in the first
clause in that line. But it is not just emphasis that the reordered
version loses; by shifting emphasis it very nearly distorts the meaning

of the poem. The prose rendering begins each of the first two stanzas with "mountains . . . streams," focusing attention on the comparison, similarity, or continuity of the stanzas and on the topographical features. In the poem these stanzas begin, "Beautiful . . . bright," "barren . . . spent," focusing attention on dissimilarity, contrast, and on the quality of or response to the landscape. These contrasting words summarize the main movement, if not meaning, of the stanzas: "Beautiful and bright?" "No, barren and spent."

There are other ways, of course, to discover and define the relationship between the first two stanzas. The pronouns indicate that the stanzas are spoken by different voices. In the first stanza the "I" addresses a plural audience ("ye," the plural of "thou," is less ambiguous than the "you" in the reordered version). In the second stanza the voice is plural ("*Our* dreams"), obviously those addressed as "ye" in stanza one, the nightingales of the title. Moreover, the "Nay" with which the second stanza begins indicates that what follows is a negative response to the conjectures of the first stanza. Finally, the verbs indicate that the first speaker is merely conjecturing ("must be") but that the answer of the nightingales is authoritative within the poem ("are").

In discussing a poem we must talk about one word, phrase, or element at a time, but this does not mean that these things exist separably in a poem, or that there is a pre-existing "thought" that they more or less effectively embody. The words and their order *are* the poem and are the meaning of the poem. The prose version is a rough approximation of the meaning of the poem, just as "blue" is a rough approximation of the color both of an October sky and of the field upon which the stars appear in the American flag. To change the "form" of a poem is to change its "content."

Though we are not yet ready to discuss "form" in any detail, let us consider one formal element in "Nightingales" to illustrate this last assertion. So far we have discussed portions of the first two stanzas only. The poem, however, is composed of three stanzas. One might assume, especially if he believed "form" has little relation to "content," that there is no significance to the fact that it takes the nightingales two stanzas to answer the speaker in the first stanza — maybe they are just long-winded or maybe Bridges was being paid by the line. Closer and more sympathetic attention to the third stanza reveals, however, that though it is a continuation of the nightingales' response it is not merely a continuation of their telling him he was wrong about the kind of place they came from and learned their song from; it tells him something about his world and perhaps about himself.

The poet or speaker has said in effect, "You nightingales sing so beautifully you must come from a place something like Paradise." The nightingales, in the second stanza, have answered, "No, the place we come from is bleak and what you hear in our song is not ecstatic pleasure but unfulfilled desire which we are trying to express but cannot." The third stanza does not merely elaborate this response; notice, for example, the nightingales' description of the day-world, the world of the speaker and of daytime birds: "sweet-springing," "bursting boughs of May." They are leaving this world to dream dreams that we know are haunted by inexpressible desire, while we are living our lives in a world that to them seems full of sweet grassy meadows, beautiful budding trees and flowers, and singing birds — a world, in fact, not too much different from that the speaker of the first stanza imagined to be the kind of place the nightingales came from. The third stanza, then, does more than continue to inform the speaker that he was wrong about the kind of place the nightingales come from; it tells him that they see in his world something like the beauty he imagined in theirs.

Any interpretation of the poem would have to take into account the third stanza as well as the second. Had the poem ended with line 12 its major statement would be, "The source of beauty (art?) is not pleasure but pain, yearning." This element is still in the poem, but the presence of the third stanza will not let us make it the central statement of the poem. At this point we might be tempted to say that the effect of the third stanza is to "adjust" the speaker to his world; the nightingales have told him that the world he lives in is a wonderful place and he should be happy with what he has instead of wanting to go wandering in "the heavenly air." But this is not a necessary conclusion. The yearning of the speaker at the beginning of the poem is no more or less accurate or justifiable than that of the nightingales. The presence of the third stanza does not erase the implied dissatisfaction of the first; the speaker knows that our world is not always full of sweet grasses and buds and Maytime. The nightingales and the speaker are both wrong about the imagined world of the other. It is from this point that a full reading of the poem must proceed.

It is now perhaps time to attack a really difficult poem, an Emily Dickinson poem usually identified by its first line — "After great pain a formal feeling comes" — and usually reprinted thus:

> After great pain a formal feeling comes —
> The Nerves sit ceremonious like tombs;
> The stiff Heart questions — was it He that bore?
> And yesterday — or centuries before?
>
> The feet mechanical   5
> Go round a wooden way
> Of ground or air or Ought, regardless grown,
> A quartz contentment like a stone.
>
> This is the hour of lead
> Remembered if outlived,   10
> As freezing persons recollect the snow —
> First chill, then stupor, then the letting go.

Most readers will grasp its general content even on first reading, but few, even after repeated readings, will feel confident they understand all its statements, much less its subtleties. Perhaps no one fully understands *Emily Dickinson's* poem; what is printed above, indeed, is not "her" poem but an edited — what one might call a "reordered" — version. In manuscript the first two stanzas of the poem appear thus:

> After great pain, a formal feeling comes —
> The Nerves sit ceremonious, like Tombs —
> The stiff Heart questions was it He, that bore,
> And yesterday, or Centuries before?
>
> 1   The Feet, mechanical, go round —
> 3   Of Ground, or Air, or Ought —
> 2   A Wooden way
> 4   Regardless grown,
>   A Quartz contentment, like a stone —

As you can see, Emily Dickinson had a highly personal system — if you can call it a system — of punctuation and capitalization. She did not publish this poem; perhaps she did not even "finish" it. Her manuscript obviously needs editing, but editing requires an understanding, a "reading" of the poem. The edited version printed first above, for example, normalizes stanzas, punctuation, and capitalization, thereby clarifying certain elements in the poem but at the cost of certain other possibilities, of distorting of the original, and of creating new difficulties. Eliminating a number of capitals but leaving those of "Heart" and "Ought," for example, puts special strain on the interpretation of those words; deleting the commas around "mechanical" raises the possibility that "mechanical" might be an adverb, although it is clearly an adjective in the manuscript.

In reordering the poem let us go back to the manuscript version, putting ourselves in the place of an editor trying to establish a text. Working thus with a poem that may not be finished, we might say, is merely an extreme example of a reader's helping to write the poem he is reading, for in reading any poem one participates to some extent in "completing" a communication that the poet has begun. The goal here, then, as in the reading of any poem, is to be as receptive, as thorough, and as faithful to the text as possible.

Since reordering this poem involves unusual complexities, it may be well to proceed a sentence, or even a clause or phrase, at a time as difficulty dictates.

The opening line of the poem offers little difficulty. Its sequence of clauses is chronological — "pain . . . formal feeling" — a frequent and logical if not syntactically "normal" order. You can — but need not — read it, "A formal feeling comes after great pain." The dash at the end of this line, of course, serves the function of a colon: what is to follow is an elaboration or definition of the formal feeling that follows a great pain. The word "formal" itself requires such explanation since it is not the kind of word usually associated with pain, but its meaning and relevance are made evident in some of the terms that follow: "ceremonious," "stiff," "mechanical."

The great pain is not defined as physical or mental, though the implication in the second stanza that the sufferer is walking around suggests that the pain is mental. While some of the images suggest that the pain is specifically grief and its occasion the death of someone dear, these images refer to the feelings of the speaker, not to the cause of his grief and we cannot say that the poem *states* any source of pain. Asserting that the poem is about grieving over the death of a loved one is inference and not a simple rendering of the prose statement of the poem.

Except for capitalization, which we will here ignore, there are no textual problems in the second line, though there seems to be a syntactical problem: does "ceremonious" modify "nerves" or "sit"? The answer to this question would help determine the reordering of the line, since there are several possibilities:

$$(1) \quad \begin{cases} \text{The nerves } [,] \text{ ceremonious } [,] \\ \text{The ceremonious nerves} \end{cases} \text{sit like tombs;}$$

$$\text{or} \quad (2) \quad \begin{cases} \text{The nerves sit ceremonious } [\text{ly}], \text{ like tombs;} \\ \text{The nerves sit like tombs, ceremonious } [\text{ly}]; \end{cases}$$

The question really involves a judgment as to whether the line makes two statements or one: to read "ceremonious" as an adjective results in a reading that might be paraphrased, "The nerves are quiet, formal, solemn, and polite, like people at a funeral or other ceremony, *and* they, like tombs, are associated with death, stillness, even chill"; to read "ceremonious" as an adverb implies a reading that might be paraphrased, "The nerves remain in a state that resembles or is related to a funeral ceremony just as tombs mark such a ceremony." The second, adverbial, one-statement reading requires changing the form of the word in the poem, though such a change may be justified by the general tendency in English to use adjectival forms as adverbs; it has the further disadvantage of forcing an image upon an image — "nerves sit like tombs" is a figure of speech; "tombs sit ceremoniously" implies a figure of speech, for though tombs (particularly in the sense of "tombstones") mark a ceremony they are not themselves "ceremonious." The first, adjectival reading has the disadvantage of separating "ceremonious" from "tombs," words that are obviously related, and putting them in separate statements. It seems clear in the rest of the poem, however, that this gradual shifting of statement is part of the procedure of development, with elements overlapping and the statement moving almost as much by association as by logic: "formal" leads to "ceremonious" which leads to "tombs" which leads to implications of crucifixion. This adjectival reading retains the part of speech in the poem and seems partly vindicated too by the similar use of "mechanical" in the next stanza. It is, we believe, closer to the prose statement of the poem. The other reading is not, however, "wrong"; it can be supported as a possible and reasonable reading of the denotation or statement of the line and the very ambiguity of the line makes it distinctly a part of the connotation or suggestion of the line — that is, "ceremonious" and "tombs" are connected in our minds even if we read them as part of different statements about the conditions of the nerves (just as we infer that the poem is about the grief that follows the loss of a loved one though the poem does not say so specifically).

One final note on this line: the edited version ends the line with a semicolon rather than with a dash, as in the manuscript. This seems a useful emendation since a dash here might suggest the end of the elaboration promised by the dash at the end of the first line, though it is clear from the rest of the stanza that the defining of the formal feeling is continuing.

Though the punctuation of the original is confusing, the dashes in the third and, particularly, fourth lines of the edited version offer little clarification. Since emendation seems necessary, a better form might be:

> The stiff heart questions, Was it he that bore?
> And, yesterday or centuries before?

or, while we are editing, we might clarify even further:

> The stiff heart questions, "Was it he that bore?"
> And, "Yesterday or centuries before?"

Further reordering, beyond the province of an editor, would require chiefly the "filling in" of elliptical constructions:

> The stiff heart questions, "Was it he [or I] that bore [such great pain]?"
> And, "[Was it] yesterday [that he or I bore it] or [was it] centuries (earlier)?"

The perplexity of the heart — it does not know if it really suffered the pain or if that pain were suffered recently or long ago — reflects its dislocation, the numb, almost incoherent unreality of the state of shock that follows intense pain. The effect of the questions, then, reinforced by the disrupted syntax, is both to magnify the intensity of the pain and to realize — *i.e.,* make real to the reader — the heart's present state. The questions, moreover, do not merely sug-

gest that the heart cannot decide whether it or "someone else" suffered
the pain, but whether it was it or a specific "he" — presumably Christ
("he" as Christ would, for many readers, justify retaining the capital
on that pronoun). This serves not just to compare the pain of the
speaker's heart to Christ's, but merges or identifies the pains, still
further magnifying and universalizing the "greatness" of the pain in
the poem.

The second stanza continues the definition of the formal feeling
but shifts the emphasis from the inner to the outer responses, from the
nerves and heart to the feet. It is the most difficult stanza in the poem
and the one that perhaps requires the most editing.

In both the revised manuscript and edited versions "a wooden way
of ground or air or ought" makes up a sense unit. Whether "way"
is defined as "path" or "manner" there is some difficulty in visualizing
a "way" that is simultaneously "wooden" and "of ground or air or
ought"; if the construction were "way of wood / Of ground or air or
ought," it would make more sense, but this seems quite a liberty to
take with the poem. In any case, the last line, if, as in either version,
it is left syntactically linked to "feet," compounds the confusion: we
would seem to have mechanical feet walking around in a wooden or
earthen or some such manner, inattentively ("regardless grown") in
a state of quartz, stone-like contentment (or quartz contentment, like
the contentment a stone has).

If we ignore Emily Dickinson's baffling punctuation, perhaps just-
ifying part of our editing by the assumption that when she renum-
bered the lines she neglected to alter the punctuation, we can, without
taking too many liberties, rationalize the lines:

> The feet, mechanical, go round
> A wooden way;
> Of ground or air or ought
> Regardless grown:
> A quartz contentment, like a stone.*

An editor, too, would wish to bring the stanza into line with the four-
line form of the first and last stanzas, despite the five lines indicated

---

* The precise punctuation is not important. What is important in this suggested
version is that ll. 3 and 4 be syntactically joined and 2 and 3 be separated, and that l.
5 be syntactically separated from the rest of the stanza — the "feet" — perhaps throwing attention forward to the "hour of lead" in the next stanza.

in the manuscript. Allowing for Emily Dickinson's characteristic "looseness" of rhyming, we see the stanzas made up of two pairs of rhyming lines (couplets): *comes–tombs, bore–before;* and *lead–out-lived, snow–go.* To conform to this pattern, we might print the second stanza thus:

> The feet, mechanical, go round
> A wooden way; of ground
> Or air or ought regardless grown:
> A quartz contentment, like a stone.

Reordered, this version might then read:

The mechanical feet go round $\left\{ \begin{matrix} [\text{in}] \text{ a wooden (manner)} \\ [\text{on}] \text{ a wooden (path)} \end{matrix} \right\}$;
[having] grown (inattentive to) ground or air or ought:
[this is] a [state of] quartz contentment, like [that of] a stone.*

There seem to be no serious textual problems in the last stanza, so that it may be reordered something like this:

This is the $\langle$time$\rangle$ of $\left\{ \begin{matrix} \text{lead(enness)} \\ \langle\text{heaviness}\rangle \end{matrix} \right\}$ [which will be] remembered
if [it is] $\left\{ \begin{matrix} \text{(survived)} \\ \text{lived (through)} \end{matrix} \right\}$,
[just] as freezing persons (remember) the snow(:)
first [there is] chill, then stupor, then (giving up).

Not all of the definitions and expansions of syntax in this reordering are necessary for most readers. Furthermore, this is about as far as you can go in reordering without involving yourself in interpretation, that is, going beyond the prose statement of the lines. Even here the reordering perhaps goes slightly beyond its proper bounds: the pointed brackets indicate that figures of speech have been reduced

---

* *ought:* "aught," *i.e.,* inattentive to anything at all; or "duty," that which one ought to do

quartz: usually, though not necessarily, related to crystal; the connotations here apparently involve stone-like, hard, heavy, colorless, and perhaps, common (*i.e.,* "diamond" has similar qualities but would suggest also precious and beautiful, associations not applicable to the context).

to their literal or paraphrasable denotations. Thus "lead" read as "heaviness" goes beyond definition: "lead" suggests but does not *denote* "heaviness." "Lead" is heavy, but it is also inert, lifeless, metallic, inorganic, gray, etc., so that reading it as "heavy" robs the poem of a good many appropriate connotations. Even in some of the more explicit definitions — the change of "letting go" to "giving up," for example — reordering reduces the implications of the poem: the original phrase applied to freezing persons no doubt does refer to "giving up," but related to the aftermath of great pain it may imply as well "losing control" or the shift from the "formal feeling" to emotional release. It may even suggest the blocking of memory, the "letting go" of the recollection of the snow or pain. Thus once again we see that reordering, definition, paraphrase get at the "meaning" or prose statement of a poem and are to this degree useful first steps toward the reading and understanding of the poem, but the gain in clarity is inevitably accompanied by a loss in potentiality: we get at one "meaning," perhaps a primary one, only to lose, in the reordered version, many of the other "meanings" which make the poem something more than its lowest common prose denominator. We must remember, then, while we are striving to specify the prose statement in a poem, that we should always go back to the poem to try to measure what we have lost. Reordering is at least as useful in revealing how far a poem transcends its statement as it is in helping us to understand that statement.

An experienced reader of poetry would have little or no difficulty in reordering or understanding the prose statement of the Wordsworth sonnet with which this chapter opened. He would no doubt soon overcome whatever initial difficulties or questions presented themselves in his reading of Bridges' "Nightingales." Though stymied perhaps by the Emily Dickinson poem, he could account for his trouble by noting that few readers are called upon to edit the manuscript of an unfinished poem. There are poems, however, finished and published by the poet, that offer not only initial difficulties but almost insoluble questions concerning their basic prose statement: some such poems, moreover — unlike, let us say, "Nightingales" — even when worked over and reordered, offer only alternative or probable readings rather than clearly "right" readings. Such a poem, perhaps, is the following by W. H. Auden:

Lay your sleeping head, my love,
Human on my faithless arm;
Time and fevers burn away
Individual beauty from
Thoughtful children, and the grave   5
Proves the child ephemeral:
But in my arms till break of day
Let the living creature lie,
Mortal, guilty, but to me
The entirely beautiful.   10

Soul and body have no bounds:
To lovers as they lie upon
Her tolerant enchanted slope
In their ordinary swoon,
Grave the vision Venus sends   15
Of supernatural sympathy,
Universal love and hope;
While an abstract insight wakes
Among the glaciers and the rocks
The hermit's sensual ecstasy.   20

Certainty, fidelity
On the stroke of midnight pass
Like vibrations of a bell,
And fashionable madmen raise
Their pedantic boring cry: 25
Every farthing of the cost,
All the dreaded cards foretell,
Shall be paid, but from this night
Not a whisper, not a thought,
Not a kiss nor look be lost.   30

Beauty, midnight, vision dies:
Let the winds of dawn that blow
Softly round your dreaming head
Such a day of sweetness show
Eye and knocking heart may bless,   35
Find the mortal world enough;
Noons of dryness see you fed
By the involuntary powers,

> Nights of insult let you pass
> Watched by every human love. 40

Since this poem is both more difficult and rather longer than the first three poems we have discussed, let us reorder it a stanza at a time:

> My love, lay your sleeping human head on my faithless arm;
> time and fevers burn individual beauty away from thoughtful children,
> and <death> proves the child [to be] ephemeral:
> but let the mortal, guilty, but to me entirely beautiful living creature lie in my arms till break of day.

The chief question of word-order concerns the placing of "human." It seems clearly to modify "head" and thus to belong, in normal prose order, next to the noun it modifies, as in the reordering. Its "displacement" in the poem, however, gives it a special emphasis, which, as we see later in the poem, it deserves. More immediately, its position in the poem places it about mid-way between "head" and "arm," both literally — two words from "head," three from "arm" — and formally — in syntax it "belongs" with "head," in the stanza it appears in the line of the poem which includes "arm" but not "head." Though grammar and syntax do not justify it, its position makes it affectively related to the "faithless arm." Both "head" and "arm" are "human," as is of course "my love," so that its meaning as well as its position ties the adjective, or permits it to be tied, to all three nouns. Finally, a displaced adjective like "human" has a tendency in English to have almost adverbial force, so that it has here a secondary suggestion of "humanly" or "in a human manner."

The question raised by the next clause is not, "What does it *say?*" but, "What does it *mean?*" The prose statement "time and fevers burn individual beauty away from thoughtful children" is perfectly clear. But why *individual* beauty? Why *thoughtful* children? Had the poem simply said, "time and fevers burn beauty away from children," both the statement and the meaning would have been clear; the passage would have been another in the long series of statements in prose and verse of the transience of beauty and the ravages of time.

The qualifications make the full meaning less certain. Does the statement here suggest that thoughtful children are more subject to "time and fevers," are more abused by "life," emotions and passions than are those children who are not thoughtful? Or does the statement imply that thoughtful children have a unique or individual beauty (beautiful individuality?) that other children do not have and so cannot lose? These questions clearly carry us beyond statement and thus beyond reordering, which may help establish only the statement, not the ultimate meaning of a poem.*

These questions, then, are not "insoluble questions concerning . . . basic prose statement," for the statement in these lines is clear even if the meaning is not. As we shall see later in this poem, however, statement and meaning, reordering and interpretation are not always so readily separable.

The second stanza might be reordered thus:

Soul and body have no bound [arie]s:
the vision of supernatural sympathy, universal love and hope
     [that] <Love> sends to lovers as they lie in their ordinary
     swoon upon her tolerant enchanted slope [is] grave;
while an abstract insight [a]wake[n]s the hermit's sensual ecstasy
     among the glaciers and the rocks.

The syntactical signpost here is the colon that ends the first line of the stanza. The two long clauses that follow and make up the rest of the stanza — the sentence — elaborate the statement in the first line that body and soul are not separate or unrelated entities (and surely not opposites). The experiences of the body raise moral or philosophical visions; the experiences of abstract thought raise passionate response.

* We shall discuss those areas beyond statement in later chapters. To serve as a basis for argument, rather than to silence argument, about the meaning of this stanza, we here offer a paraphrase (which differs from a reordering by inevitably involving interpretation and assertion about meaning):

Lay your sleeping head upon my arm, my love. Neither of us is faultless, the conditions of human life not permitting perfection. Nonetheless your human imperfection, subject to time and death and sin, is more entirely (fully or even perfectly) beautiful to me than is any ideal conception of beauty which, immortal and guiltless, would be thus inhuman.

There seem to be no difficulties in the statement here, though some of the words may need further definition.*

There are few if any difficulties of word order or syntax in the first half of the third stanza:

> Certainty [and] fidelity, like [the] vibrations of a bell, pass on the
>   stroke of midnight,
> and fashionable madmen raise their pedantic boring cry:

At this point we run right into a syntactical problem: what is the relationship between these first five lines and the remaining five lines of the stanza? The syntactical indicator here is again the punctuation, the colon at the end of line 25. Does this colon join or separate?

In modern usage the colon ordinarily joins, signifying either "as follows" or "that is." What follows then is either an example or an explanation of what has preceded the colon. This is the way the colon is used at the end of line 11; the rest of that stanza gives examples of the inseparability of body and soul.

There are, however, two other colons in the poem and neither of these is used in the ordinary modern way. The first appears in the sixth line of the first stanza and divides the two halves of an eight-line antithesis: the first two lines of the stanza make a statement (Lay your head on my arm) and the next eight lines more or less explain why, the first four describing the imperfection and transience of life and beauty and the next four saying, in effect, "nonetheless, lie here,

---

* There would seem to be, too, some question as to what this rather philosophical statement has to do with the particular lovers in the first stanza. The assertion of the inseparability of body and soul is the basis upon which the speaker can justify his considering that which is mortal and guilty "the entirely beautiful." "The entirely beautiful," like the immortal, perfect, and pure, usually assumes the existence of two worlds, the everyday world in which we humans live our physical, imperfect, and brief lives, and the spiritual world in which our immortal souls can experience perfection. To deny the separation of body and soul is to deny the existence of the two worlds, and, in this case, to assert that only the physical, imperfect, everyday world is real. It is here that we must know whatever we are to know of joy, beauty, life. It is this "human," "living" world that the speaker insists upon; it is in these terms that his beloved is "the entirely beautiful" and it is this world that he later hopes she finds "enough."

Again we must note that this "explanation" is not something *stated* by the poem and clarified by reordering; it is editorial or critical "interpretation." Moreover, this interpretation requires some knowledge of the history of ideas; alas, no "system" for reading poetry can free the reader from the need for other forms of knowledge.

for to me you are the entirely beautiful." * The colon here, then, acts almost as a weak semicolon: the semicolon divides the first two lines from the rest of the stanza and the colon makes a weaker separation between the first four and last four of the remaining eight lines. Indeed, the relationships here might have been clearer had the colon appeared at the end of line 2 and the semicolon at the end of line 6.

The last colon appears at the end of line 31 and is, also, somewhat unusual in modern usage; it has almost the force of "therefore," or, perhaps somewhat weaker, of "so now": "Beauty, midnight, vision dies $\left\{ \begin{matrix} [\text{therefore}] \\ [\text{so now}] \end{matrix} \right\}$ let the winds . . . ." However we read it, what follows is not an example or explanation of what precedes the colon.

In dealing with the first of these colons we are, as readers, almost in the same position as Emily Dickinson's editors: we edit the stanza in reading it, putting a colon at the end of line 2 and a semicolon at the end of line 6. If this is not the correct reading we would seem to be up against one of those "insoluble questions concerning . . . basic prose statement" which we warned about at the beginning of our discussion of this poem. Here, however, the difficulties do not seem insurmountable since the development of statement is reasonably clear, so that we can "edit" the punctuation with some confidence.

Indeed, Auden elsewhere warns us that he punctuates rhetorically — as a guide to dramatic pause or emphasis. Such punctuation courts danger unless the statement irrespective of punctuation is quite clear. A reader can reconstruct difficult statements from logical punctuation but in a poem punctuated rhetorically he either "gets it" or he does not, and if he does not there is no way he can retrace the logic of the statement through the logic of the punctuation. It is commonly assumed nowadays that the reader participates in re-creating the meaning of a poem; nevertheless, the meaning must first be created in order that it may be re-created.

What recourse to the other colons in this poem proves is merely that you cannot rely upon Auden's punctuation to establish relationships in a logical or conventional way; you cannot prove, then, how clauses relate by arguing in terms of the punctuation that divides (or joins) them. This idiosyncratic punctuation is acceptable so long as the meaning is established by other means, by the meanings of

* There is an antithesis within the antithesis, a "but" clause within the "but" clause, but that does not involve a colon.

words, repetitions, sign-words like conjunctions and prepositions, and so on. But when the relationship is not made wholly clear by these other means, the unconventional punctuation is an obstacle to understanding. So it is, we believe, in the third stanza.

The result is that there are at least two quite different ways of reading this stanza; it is ambiguous. We call *ambiguous* — or speak of the *ambiguity* of — any passage which can justifiably be reordered in two (or more) ways resulting in disparate prose statements, neither of which is fully confirmed or wholly denied by the syntax or the context. Reordering such a passage does not lead to solutions or "right answers" to questions raised by the phrasing of the poem, but rather to alternative possibilities. When each of the alternative possibilities adds something of value to understanding the poem, we may say that the ambiguity is an enrichment of the meaning,* but when the alternatives are such as to require the reader to choose one *or* the other while the poem does not make one alternative clearly "right," we may consider the ambiguity a flaw in the poem, slight or serious depending upon the divergence of the alternative meanings. The problems in the third stanza, since they cannot be resolved other than arbitrarily, leave us with several possible reorderings. To choose among the alternatives, directly involves interpretation, so that reordering ceases to be merely an intermediate step. Given alternative possible statements, there are naturally alternative possible meanings — for the lines, for the stanza, and thus, ultimately, for the whole poem. Since these meanings contradict or exclude each other, we must consider the multiplicity a confusion rather than an enrichment.

If the colon in line 25 signifies "as follows," it can only mean that what follows is the indirectly stated cry of the fashionable madmen. Few readers will have difficulty accepting the first three lines of what follows as an indirect quotation of that cry: the madmen say we shall have to pay the price for this night. But what of the next two lines? Is the statement that nothing shall be lost from this night or the exhortation to lose nothing from this night † also part of the madmen's

---

* This enriching form of ambiguity is sometimes called *ambivalence*.

† There would seem to be a second ambiguity in these lines. Is the "be" in line 30 a finite, subjunctive verb: "[Let] not a whisper . . . be lost"? Or is there an elliptical "shall": "Not a whisper . . . [shall] be lost"? The latter would be somewhat unusual: if the verb were to be suppressed by ellipsis, it would seem normal to suppress it entirely, so that lines 26–30 would read, " . . . all the dreaded cards foretell shall be paid, but from this night not a whisper, not a thought, not a kiss nor look lost."

cry? There is nothing in the way of punctuation and nothing certain in the syntax to justify our ending the cry with "paid." The result of not doing so is to derive a most unconventional statement from the second half of the stanza: fashionable madmen cry out that all that the cards prophesy will be paid but that nothing will (or should — see preceding note) be lost from this night. Since these are madmen, the poem is implicitly rejecting their cry and affirming that this night too will be lost. The wishfulness of the last stanza — may you find the mortal world enough, etc. — then becomes even more tentative and muted, even more forlorn and hopeless, than in the more conventional reading of this portion of the poem.

This conventional reading — and "conventional" is here a descriptive term and does not imply either "superficial" or "commonsensical" — can be justified by either of two arguments. If the colon does join and what follows it is to be read as the cry of the fashionable madmen, the "but" in line 28 and the subjunctive "be" which shifts the grammatical mood may be considered forceful enough to signal the end of the cry (so that the madmen cry only that everything must be paid for). If the colon here, as in line 6, should operate as a semicolon, separating parts of the stanza, nothing that follows the colon has anything to do with the madmen's cry (note, for example, that the cards and not the madmen foretell the cost): certainty and fidelity pass and madmen raise a cry; we must pay for it, but let us not forget this night.

It may seem rather overscrupulous to base so much of the statement of a poem on the nice distinction between a colon and semicolon or on the presence of a comma (in l. 28) rather than a semicolon. Indeed, if all other indications of statement and meaning were clear this would be a rather far-fetched exercise in reading meaning by punctuation alone. But who are the madmen? Why are they called "fashionable"? What is their cry and why is it pedantic? Some may argue that these are men who preach conventional (fashionable) morality which is so restrictive of human potential, so unrelated to reality as to be "mad." Others may argue that the fashionable is not the conventional at all, but the "modern" or "advanced" thinkers who

---

But once doubt is raised about the colon — and unresolved by clarity of statement and meaning — the entire logic of the stanza becomes doubtful and the strong suggestion of parallelism in "Shall be paid . . . be lost" offers the possibility of an unusual ellipsis.

reject traditional morality and try to justify their rejection on the ground of pragmatic results while at the same time romanticizing the values of sexual love. The poet does not stay for an answer. The punctuation is symptomatic of "almost insoluble questions concerning . . . basic prose statement" which we find in this stanza.

The reader of a poem always has a certain degree of latitude, of course, but here he must almost write his own stanza, and within surprisingly wide limits. The stanza he writes for himself will naturally determine his final understanding of the poem, though the real danger is that his presuppositions about the poem may too easily determine his reading of the stanza, which will then merely strengthen his presuppositions. If, for example, he has taken the even-the-affirmation-is-mad view, the first line of the fourth stanza — "Beauty, midnight, vision dies" — will strike him as an immediate confirmation: the conventional affirmation cannot stand up against the fact in this flat statement, and the poet is left with only a hope for his beloved of the best that the human lot allows. If, however, he has taken the wishful-affirmative view, that line will strike him as repeating "Certainty, fidelity . . . pass," in order to prepare for a repeated or a further wish-affirmation.

A number of syntactical difficulties occur in this fourth stanza also, though none of them is as far-reaching as are those in the third stanza. There is, to begin with, the singular verb following the apparently multiple subject in this opening line. One way to account for it would be to understand an implied collective pronoun: "Beauty, midnight, vision [, each] dies." Another would be to understand "midnight" and "vision" as appositives for — and therefore synonyms defining — the singular subject "Beauty." Although there is no contradiction in the two possibilities, their meanings are different. The second is probably the stronger and is closer to the effect of that unexpected singular verb which tends to force the three nouns into a single concept. The three nouns tend also to unite the preceding stanzas: "beauty" (stanza 1), "midnight" (stanza 3), "vision" (stanza 2) — with the disruption of order a slight further encouragement for seeing the elements as interchangeable and, as in this statement, three aspects of the one experience.

We might notice that here also, as in the third stanza, either reading could be justified as correct; either is syntactically possible and fits the full context of the poem. There is a divergence of meaning, but it is slight: the implied collective pronoun merely provides a possible but less effective way of understanding the lines than does the recognition of appositives. Auden's syntax throughout the final stanza is so elliptical, however, and therefore at times so ambiguous, that we continue to be forced to guess at his details. Though we make our selection from justifiable possibilities, we cannot be certain that we are not simply fitting the stanza to our preconceptions and our determination of the third stanza. Let us give a reordered version of this final stanza, and then discuss some of the problems with which we have had to deal:

> Beauty, midnight, vision[,] dies:
> [therefore] let the winds of dawn that blow softly [a]round your
>   dreaming head show such a day of sweetness [that] eye and
>   knocking heart may bless [the mortal world], [and may] find
>   the mortal world [to be] enough;
> [let] noons of dryness see you fed by the involuntary powers [;]
> [let] nights of insult let you pass watched [over] by every human
>   love.

We would take the full implication of the colon at the end of line 31 to be: "As a result of this statement, the next statement follows." "Therefore" would appear to be the conjunctive adverb closest to the implied logic — "This being true, the best I can ask for you is . . ." — though it perhaps lacks some of the temporal ("afterwards") suggestion of the original.

"Show," in line 34, might well be held to imply a specific indirect object — "show [you] such a day" — but the word may also be understood in the sense of "display," which will not require that indirect object. We think the latter is consistent with the immediate singular "eye" rather than "eyes." Both the omission of the pronoun and the use of the singular noun tend to move away from the personal "show [you] such a day of sweetness [that your] eye[s] and knocking heart may bless . . ." to the more general "(display) such a day of sweetness [that any human] eye and knocking heart may bless. . . ." However, either is possible and both meanings enrich the poem.

"Bless" causes problems because it is transitive, requiring an object. One is tempted at first to try the apparently simple solution of letting the "such" imply an "as" and thus using the common elliptical construction in which the object would be an implied repetition of "day":

> . . . show such a day of sweetness [as] eye and knocking heart
> may bless, . . .

Unfortunately, this way of reordering the passage runs into immediate
trouble in the next line. How can "Find the mortal world enough"
be understood to follow upon the "such . . . as" construction? This
would require some such ellipsis as:

> . . . show such a day of sweetness [as] eye and knocking heart
> may bless, [and such as may lead eye and knocking heart to]
> find the mortal world [to be] enough; . . .

This, though possible, would seem excessively awkward, especially
since the adjacent verbs "bless, / Find" appear in the poem to be more
directly parallel. Perhaps, hanging on to "day" as the object, one
could exhibit this parallelism with a "such . . . that" construction:

> . . . show such a day of sweetness [that] eye and knocking heart
> may bless [it], [and may] find the mortal world [to be]
> enough; . . .

That is less awkward, and requires fewer interpolations. It is therefore probably preferable to the more awkward "such . . . as" reordering, which nevertheless remains a *possible* way of understanding
the lines. As for the difference between this second version and the one
which we finally accepted, we can only say that either version supplies an acceptable object for "bless." But we find it also to be a confusion rather than an enriching ambiguity, and we prefer one version
to the other primarily because of the emphasis which it puts upon
"the mortal world," a central concept in the poem; once again, interpretation has stepped in to resolve questions concerning basic prose
statement that seem insoluble within the limits of statement and reordering. The poet has not given much assistance in making this
choice, however; he has left the reader to flounder among undifferentiated possibilities, and to that degree the syntactical structure is
weak — fuzzily, not meaningfully, ambiguous.

The last four lines are clear enough, with the parallelism of "Noons
of dryness" and "Nights of insult" helping to enforce the syntactical
parallelism with the much earlier "Let the winds of dawn." Again,
however, one has to admit that the poet might have given more assistance, and this time by the simple expedient of a semicolon after

line 38 to enforce further the parallelism of the three clauses. The absence of that semicolon makes relating these final two clauses awkward, and one could make a case for reading them thus:

[let] noons of dryness see you fed by the involuntary powers,
[and] let you pass nights of insult watched [over] by every human love.

The difference would be that in this reordering you "pass nights" while in the other the nights "let you pass." One might argue that "pass" in the latter instance is vague, while the phrase "pass nights" is clear, a more normal syntactical pattern, and therefore preferable. "Pass" may be intransitive as well as transitive, however — it was so used in line 22 — and the structure enforced by the parallelism of the clauses (in spite of the missing semicolon) takes precedence over a reordering which reverses the two halves of the line for the sake of an unnecessary direct object. Nor is the awkward duplication of the reordered version — "[let] nights of insult let you pass" — any argument against it, for that repetition is an accident of the expansion of reordering and was in fact avoided by the poet.

Other difficulties within the stanza are matters of definition or interpretation rather than of grammar, syntax, or relationship. We have already discussed the effect of "eye" (for "eyes"). In a full understanding of the poem, "knocking" would also require attention, as would the key noun phrases of the last four lines.

Normally, after all the difficulties in the poem have been isolated and most of them resolved, the final and more significant question remains: What is the total meaning of the poem and how is each of the parts (or stanzas) related to that meaning? The answer to this question is beyond syntax, reordering, and conclusive or definitive demonstration. It is in the area of paraphrase, interpretation, "reading between the lines," in which the reader's cherished "personal opinion" has some scope. There are limits beyond which the individual reader cannot go, however, limits set by the poem and even the reordered statement of the poem, and it is to these that one, in interpreting, must constantly refer. Though the poem with which we have been dealing also sets limits, too often, as we have amply seen, those limits allow alternative and contradictory meanings. Reordering cannot solve the problems of meaning in this poem; it can help us, however, to understand the precise nature of those problems.

Now that we have reordered simple and not so simple poems, a
poem whose text needs editing as well as reordering, and one that
cannot be conclusively reordered, let us return to the Shakespeare
sonnet introduced earlier, and, this time, reorder without defining
words to see how far toward understanding, or clearer definition of
our understanding, the process of reordering will take us. Here, first,
is the text again, and then the reordered version:

> Poore soule, the center of my sinfull earth,
> Thrall to these rebbell powres that thee array,
> Why dost thou pine within and suffer dearth,
> Painting thy outward walls so costlie gay?
> Why so large cost, having so short a lease,   5
> Dost thou upon thy fading mansion spend?
> Shall wormes, inheritors of this excesse,
> Eate up thy charge? is this thy bodie's end?
> Then, soule, live thou upon thy servant's losse,
> And let that pine to aggravat thy store;   10
> Buy tearms divine in selling hours of drosse,
> Within be fed, without be rich no more:
>> So shalt thou feed on Death, that feeds on men,
>> And Death once dead, ther's no more dying then.

Poore soule, the center of my sinfull earth, [and] thrall to these
    rebbell powres that array thee,
why dost thou pine within and suffer dearth,
[while] painting thy outward walls so costlie gay?

Having so short a lease, why dost thou spend so large [a] cost upon
    thy fading mansion?

Shall wormes, [the] inheritors of this excesse, eate up thy charge?

Is this thy bodie's end?

Then, soule, live thou upon thy servant's losse, and let that pine to
    aggravat thy store;
buy divine tearms in selling hours of drosse[;]
be fed within, be rich no more without:
so shalt thou feed on Death, that feeds on men,
and once Death [is] dead, then ther's no more dying.

A few difficulties are resolved; our reading of certain passages is made clearer: the second line, with the interpolation of "and," becomes more distinctly the appositive of "Poore soule"; the temptation to make "thee" the subject of "array" is avoided ("thee" is the accusative case of "thou" and thus cannot be a subject); the sentence and clause divisions are made more apparent by the arrangement on the page. But, for those who initially found the poem difficult, reordering alone is of only limited help. It is true that reordering has here been held to a minimum, restricted to its narrowest operation — the changing of word-order and expansion of the abbreviated constructions — but it would be difficult to go beyond this small step toward clarification without defining some of the less familiar words in the poem. Such definition is an inseparable part of coming to an understanding of the primary prose sense of a poem. Definition, then, is the subject of the next chapter, at the end of which we shall return to this sonnet.

II
Definition

prose, — words in their best order;
poetry, — the best words in their best order.
COLERIDGE

Poetry uses language most precisely and exploits all of the resources of language most fully. The previous chapter sought to demonstrate that the frequently "difficult" word order and syntax of poetry are not arbitrary distortions seeking to impress the reader by their obscurity, originality, or "mysterious beauty"; rather, they are used to explore, create, and express precise meanings, utilizing all the resources of order and relationship in the language. To "normalize" the word order or sentence structure is thus to "clarify" the meaning at the cost of blunting it by generalizing. Normalizing or reordering can be useful, however, not only to reveal the general or basic meaning but also to help gauge the precision of the statement of the poem by measuring it against the rough approximation of its meaning in the reordered version.

What is true of the word order and syntax of poetry is also true of its individual words: they are at times, in themselves or in their use, out of the ordinary and therefore "difficult"; the difficulty is the result not of striving for obscurity, originality, or mysterious and vague beauty but of seeking precision of meaning through the fullest exploitation of the resources of language; to clarify by normalizing — in this case, defining — may at times be useful and necessary but the defined version will be only a rough approximation of the exact statement of the poem.

It is a common misconception that most difficult words are those that are highly abstract or general; in fact, they are usually those that are most concrete and specific. If a friend of ours were to say, "I saw a dog," we would all "know what he means," even though each of us, perhaps, would have a somewhat different mental image or concept of the dog. In many cases, there would be no need for him to be more precise and the differences in our images or concepts would be unimportant. If, on the other hand, our friend were to say, "I saw a schnauzer," those of us who know what a schnauzer is would have a much more precise image of what it was our friend saw. Those who did not know the word but looked it up in a dictionary would have images of varying degrees of precision, depending upon their experience or lack of experience with regard to dogs in general and schnauzers in particular. Those who did not know the breed itself but knew that the schnauzer is a breed of dog and did not look up the word would have perhaps only as imprecise an image as they would have had had our friend simply said "dog." If his precision of statement were important to his meaning, therefore, they would not really understand him. If, on the other hand, he were being more precise than necessary for his meaning, his particularizing the breed would be poor judgment, for fewer people in his audience would understand him. Someone might even think a schnauzer is a blunt-nosed German revolver.

Let us give our friend a few more lines. Suppose he said, "I saw a schnauzer this morning sniffing at a brioche. A sign of the times, I guess." He laughs and so do two or three others. Some look around, see laughing faces, and snicker uncomfortably. One young lady gazes in misty-eyed admiration.

Those who know vaguely that a schnauzer is some kind of dog and a brioche some kind of bun or roll "understand" the first statement but do not see what a dog sniffing a roll has to do with "the times." Those who, even if they do not know the meaning of the two nouns, recognize *schnauzer* as a German word and *brioche* as a French word may get the reference to recent Franco-German co-operation within the framework of the Common Market (notice that knowledge of historical context is sometimes as important as knowledge of the meanings of words in understanding what one reads or hears), but they will miss the mildly humorous tone by failing to see the image of the dog and the roll. The young lady, who fancies herself a great admirer of poetry, sees in the statements a criminal (with a snub-nosed German revolver) holding up a dowager (with a brooch pinned to her dress) as the symbol of our amoral and violent times ("sniff-ing" is the "poetic" way of saying "pointing at").

To understand our friend fully, then, we need to know the general meaning of the words ("dog," "roll"), a specific portion of their meaning or origin ("German dog," "French roll"), and even the historical context. And, it might be pointed out, had our friend not known these things he not only could not have "expressed himself" but he could not have had the experience itself — that is, he might have seen the dog sniffing the roll but he could not have made the connection with the Common Market.

Moving from this rather ridiculous make-believe to a real poem, we can see these same principles operating in our reading of this stanza from Tennyson's "The Lotos-Eaters":

> But propt on beds of amaranth and moly
> How sweet, (while warm airs lull us, blowing lowly)
> With half-dropt eyelid still,
> Beneath a heaven dark and holy,
> To watch the long bright river drawing slowly   5
> His waters from the purple hill —
> To hear the dewy echoes calling
> From cave to cave thro' the thick-twined vine —
> To watch the emerald-colour'd water falling
> Thro' many a wov'n acanthus-wreath divine;   10
> Only to hear and see the far-off sparkling brine,
> Only to hear were sweet, stretch'd out beneath the pine.

How important is it to know the precise nature of "amaranth," "moly," and "acanthus"? Is it enough to know that they refer to plants or flowers? We would then read the relevant lines thus: "But propt on beds of (two different kinds of flowers), / How sweet . . . To watch the . . . water falling / Thro' many a wov'n (flower)-wreath divine." Some, like our young lady of the revolver, would rightly protest that "flower" is too common a synonym, that the lines lose their exotic, mysterious, Romantic nature if we so reduce them. They might even protest — wrongly, this time — that it is indeed better not to know precisely what kind of plants or flowers are being referred to: what if these lovely names turned out to mean "dandelion," "crabgrass," and "poison ivy"? But Tennyson has chosen to use these particular, if somewhat uncommon, names, and if we respect his art at all, we ought at least to assume that he has chosen the names with precision. As it turns out, of course, knowing something about these flowers and plants does not detract from the exotic nature of the passage but serves to define the scene and thus our response more precisely. "Amaranth" (though also the name of an actual family of plants) is an imaginary flower, thought to be showy and unfading; surely this sharpens and heightens the Eden-like nature of the scene. "Moly" is a mythical plant with a milk-white flower and black roots which, according to Homer, Hermes gave Odysseus (Ulysses) to protect him against the blandishments of Circe (who turned men into swine); thus the Homeric nature of the passage ("The Lotos-Eaters" is based on the *Odyssey*) is reinforced, the beauty of the scene is made more specific, and the deadening of desire is implied — all of which further tends to sharpen the precise nature and meaning of the scene. Finally, "acanthus," in Greek (and notice that all three names, like the myth upon which the poem is based, are Greek) literally means "thorn-tree"; the luxuriances and irresponsibility of the lotos-eaters is thus heightened by our knowledge that the wreath through which they watch the water falling is a wreath of thorns. Furthermore, the acanthus leaf was the design on the capitol of the Corinthian column, used on many of the public buildings and temples of Greece; thus there is a faint suggestion of disloyalty, of national or religious betrayal, in the passage. The scene, mood, and meaning evoked are quite definite, and we owe the poem at least the effort to discover the precise meaning of its words rather than resting content with an erroneous or unnecessarily vague and general impression.

DENOTATION AND CONNOTATION

You will notice in the discussion of the three plant-words in the Tennyson passage that two more or less distinct kinds of meaning were involved: One kind of meaning was essentially a description of the plant — *acanthus*, "thorn-tree"; *moly*, "mythical plant with white flower and black roots." The other meaning has to do with an association that the word brings with it — *acanthus,* Corinthian columns, perhaps temples; *moly,* Homer, Circe, therefore the deadening of sensual desire. The first kind of meaning, roughly defined as what the word points to, is called "denotation"; the second kind of meaning, roughly defined as what the word suggests, is called "connotation." *

Different words, then, are said to have the same denotations but rather different connotations: *dog, pooch, cur, hound; fat, obese, plump, hefty, heavy, overweight, chubby.* Even the same word can, depending on context, have different connotations. The word *dog,* for example, in its various forms (*dogged, doggedly,* etc.), can in various contexts suggest such disparate qualities as loyalty, tenacity, obsequiousness, liveliness, brutishness, etc.

Awareness of the connotation as well as the denotation of words can be extremely important in reading poetry. If Robert Herrick, in the famous opening lines of "To the Virgins, to Make Much of Time" —

> Gather ye Rose-buds while ye may,
> Old Time is still a-flying:
> And this same flower that smiles today,
> To-morrow will be dying

— had substituted for "Rose-buds" the word "flowers" or "daisies" or "violets," the change in denotation would have been relatively unimportant. The change in connotation, and thus in total meaning, would have been great, however; for centuries the rose, in relevant contexts, has suggested beauty, romantic love, the transience of youth — and all these associations are part of the meaning of the lines. (Indeed, so insistent had the connotations of "rose" become that many twentieth-century readers of poetry have felt Gertrude Stein's "Rose is a rose is a rose is a rose" to be an appropriate and necessary antidote.)

The "meaning" of a word in prose as well as poetry, but especially in poetry, is not just its denotation, but its denotation and connotation. It is largely for this reason that substitution of a synonym or defining phrase for a word in a poem, while it may clarify for those

---

* Using these terms in this way, widespread in discussions of literature and language, is an extension, and something of a distortion, of their meanings in logic in which a term *denotes* all the members of its class, so that "dog" denotes "Lassie," "Rin Tin Tin," "Fido," etc.; it *connotes* all the qualities or attributes of the class, "dog" thus connoting four-leggedness, carnivorousness, etc.

readers unfamiliar with the original word, usually involves considerable loss of exactness of meaning. (Though, again, it is sometimes possible to gauge the precision of the word in the poem only by substituting the best possible synonym and measuring its meaning against that of the original.)

Usually it is the precision both of denotation and of connotation that determines "the best word" in a given context.* Indeed, it is often difficult and sometimes impossible — as well as for the most part unnecessary — to distinguish denotation and connotation with certainty. Is the German element in *schnauzer* or the French element in *brioche*, for example, part of the denotation or connotation of these words? Let us look at the word "steep" in the first poem discussed in the first chapter:

> Never did sun more beautifully steep
> In his first splendour, valley, rock, or hill;

Several possible synonyms suggest themselves: "soak," "drench," "saturate." "Steep" denotes an action slightly different from those of the other words since in steeping one of the elements is more or less transformed; thus when water drenches (or soaks or saturates) a sponge you still have water and sponge, but when tea leaves are steeped in water you no longer have water but tea. The landscape here, then, does not have the sunlight "added to" it but is transformed by it. On the other hand, there are several connotative differences. First of all, "drench" and "soak" and perhaps "saturate" are all vaguely unpleasant in their associations, while "steep" is not. (It is difficult, indeed, to dissociate "steep" from tea and for English readers, perhaps, this would make the association specifically pleasant, as well as bringing with it the proper liquid-gold suffusing color association). It may well seem far-fetched at first, but it is likely that the other, indeed more common meaning of "steep" — "precipitous" — offers appropriate secondary connotations here, despite the fact that the syntax makes no connection between "steep" and the landscape. Would the word seem as effective if, for example, the landscape details were "meadow, field, or plain" rather than "valley, rock, or hill"? Both the exact denotation and the wide spectrum of connotations make "steep" the

* We are here leaving out such considerations as length and sound of words, which, though sometimes allied to connotation, are best discussed in relation to meter, rhyme, and other patterns.

"best word" for the most precise and fullest expression of meaning in this passage.

Similarly, in Bridges' "Nightingales," we defined the word "spent" — "Nay, barren are those mountains and spent the streams" — as "depleted" or "exhausted." But "spent," like "exhausted" but unlike "depleted," suggests both "tired" and "having consumed or wasted something essential." Moreover, "spent," unlike both other words, also suggests the loss of reproductive powers — both literally and figuratively — and this connotation relates to "barren" in the same line and even to "voice of desire" in the next. "Spent," then, to use Coleridge's phrase that heads this chapter, is "the best word" for the context, and to understand it, not only in its general meaning, which relates it to "exhausted" and "depleted," but in its specific and precise meaning, which differentiates it from its alleged "synonyms," is to understand the line and the poem more precisely and effectively.

MULTIPLE MEANINGS

Often a poet will choose a particular word not only because its connotations or associations are appropriate to his purposes, or even because, like "spent" in the example above, its full meaning is more pertinent to his context, but because it has *two* meanings, or more, that he wants.

The most obvious instance of such multiple meaning is perhaps the overtly humorous pun. Puns are often the basis of obvious jokes, with the result that they have been deprecated as "the lowest form of wit." In fact, however, any attempt to exploit the full potentialities of language must inevitably involve puns, and "the lowest form of wit" is frequently the vehicle for the highest concentration of poetic force. Many of the finest literary artists have been the most incorrigible punsters. Shakespeare frequently transfers his own delight in the pun to a character, like Mercutio in *Romeo and Juliet,* who, punning throughout, cannot resist a pun even when he is upon the point of death: "Ask for me tomorrow and you shall find me a grave man" (III, i).

Words with multiple meanings can function in a variety of ways. One of the meanings can be clearly primary and another, though appropriate, clearly secondary, often figurative. Both meanings may be literal and of equal importance. Mercutio is clearly saying that he will be dead tomorrow, but it would be difficult to decide whether his "primary" meaning is that he will be in his grave, or that he will at last be serious.

Nor need a pun be humorous. A few lines later in the same scene, for example, Romeo says:

> O sweet Juliet,
> Thy beauty hath made me effeminate,
> And in my temper softened valor's steel!

The word "temper" both is the technical term for the process of hardening metal and was, in Shakespeare's time, synonymous with "character" (compare our word "temperament"). These lines can thus be paraphrased: Juliet's beauty has weakened the element of bravery in Romeo's character. The paraphrase, however, leaves out the metaphorical element of the last line — not Romeo's valor but his "valor's steel" has been "softened," and this at the very time, or in the very process by which, it should have been hardened. The metaphor, reinforcing the general statement of the line, also involves a slight adjustment and enrichment of meaning: it defines the role valor should play in character and even defines to a degree Romeo's conception of character itself. Bravery or valor, through the metaphor, is identified as that element which gives firmness to character. (You can see, incidentally, how inadequate "firmness" is as a paraphrase of "steel"; it is difficult to "translate" the precise quality of "steel" into suitable, literal abstractions — it is hard, firm, resilient, and, in fact, the very instrument of valor, for it is by using his sword against Juliet's family, revenging the death of his friend, that Romeo's valor should be manifest.) But it is the double meaning of "temper" that lends concreteness and precision to the general statement of the line and indeed generates the entire metaphorical element. "Character," then, is metaphorically the quality or degree of one's firmness, and valor is that element in the alloy of character, which, like steel, lends hardness. The metaphor thus reinforces, enriches, and serves to define the statement, and the metaphor springs from the two meanings inherent in the word "temper."

There are instances of multiple meanings in which, even though one meaning may be more specifically literal and the other clearly metaphorical, both are essential to the general statement itself, the metaphorical meaning being in no sense "secondary." In Andrew Marvell's "On a Drop of Dew," the dew seems to be the literal subject, though the poem is in fact an extended comparison between a drop of dew and the human soul, running through a whole catalogue of similarities and ending with the lines,

> Such did the Manna's sacred Dew distill;
> White, and intire, though congeal'd and chill.
> Congeal'd on Earth: but does, dissolving, run
> Into the Glories of th' Almighty Sun.

Even ignoring capitalization (which was far from regularized in the seventeenth century when Marvell wrote his poem but has been retained here to avoid editorial interpretation or "interference"), it is impossible to read these lines attentively without being aware that the "Almighty Sun" refers both to the natural sun that evaporates the dew, drawing it back to itself, and the Divine Sun (Son?) who calls the soul back to Himself. The natural sun may be the literal referent, just as the drop of dew is the literal subject, but the entire poem is based on the identification of dew and soul — the subject of the poem being, in fact, the comparison rather than the dew itself — so that the "other" meaning of "Sun" is not secondary, not an embellishment or even a reinforcement of the meaning, but is essential, is indeed the culmination of the extended comparison.

Multiple meanings do not necessarily involve a figurative meaning. Indeed, it is when several meanings are both appropriate and literal that the distinction between primary and secondary meaning most often disappears. Such is the case, perhaps, with "sweet-springing" — "and then, / As night is withdrawn / From these sweet-springing meads and bursting boughs of May . . ." — in Bridges' "Nightingales," which we discussed earlier. In our notes to this line we suggested that this phrase could be read "sweetly springing" or "springing with sweetness," as well as the somewhat archaic but perhaps most appropriate "sweetly beginning to appear." Here defining the phrase is not a matter of settling upon the one primary meaning, nor is its multiple meaning effective because the poet thereby "speaks" to more readers who will understand one or the other of the meanings or choose the meaning he "likes best." The alert reader will be aware of all the possibilities and the poet will, in effect, have "said" three things at once. As we said in the note, " 'springing' may be said to be the best word for this context precisely because it contains possibilities of action, season, and gradual appearance, all of which apply to meadow grasses in a May dawn and all of which are supported by the associations of surrounding words."

OLD WORDS AND OLD MEANINGS

We usually think of words as fixed, natural, almost supernatural signs. Intellectually, we know that a Frenchman has a right to call a dog *"chien,"* though we feel that if he thought about it he would admit that "dog" is really the right word and *"chien"* one of those endearing eccentricities common to foreigners. It is difficult, then, really to *feel* that words are only arbitrary signs, and it is sometimes a shaking experience to realize that even within our own language words have changed and are changing meanings. Some words have disappeared or almost disappeared from the language. Somewhat paradoxically, these are easier to deal with than those which have remained in use but have changed meaning. When we run across "caitiff" for the first time we know at least that we do not know what it means, and it thus gives us no more difficulty than a word still in general use but unfamiliar to us. But a great many words have changed meaning over the years, sometimes drastically. Consider the word "nice." Very often we use it as an almost meaningless sound of approval, which the dictionary expands to "pleasing" or "agreeable." More sophisticated readers, or those with old-fashioned teachers, know that the word *really* means, "minute, fine, subtle," as in such expressions as "a nice discrimination." But if one reads a dictionary entry right to the end, including the definitions marked *"Obsolete,"* or if he refers to the historical dictionary (the *Oxford* or *New English Dictionary* — referred to as *OED* or *NED*), he finds such meanings as "coy" or "shy," others such as "wanton," and even "foolish." He discovers, perhaps to his amazement, that the word comes into English through the Latin *nescius* meaning "not knowing." You are not now likely to get slapped in the face by a young lady if you call her "nice," but you might be somewhat puzzled by the actions of "nice young ladies" as they are described in older texts.

Words, then, have histories and have changed with time, though not all of them so dramatically as "nice." It is thus important in reading a poem to have some idea of the century or even decade in which it was written. In the Shakespeare sonnet we reordered at the end of the last chapter, for example, one line reads, "And let that pine to aggravat thy store." "That" refers to the body. The line thus may be read, "And let [the body] (grieve) to aggravat your (supply)." The word "aggravate," which for us means little more than "annoy," meant in the sixteenth and seventeenth centuries "increase," "add to," or "add weight to" (notice the root -grav- as in "gravity"). In reading poems a century or more old, then, one must at times refer to a good historical dictionary.

The little poem by Charles Sackville, Earl of Dorset, that follows, for example, is all but incomprehensible if we do not know the seventeenth- or eighteenth-century meaning of the word "link," and, even if we can make a vague or general guess at the word from context, we miss a good deal of the precise statement and effect of the poem if we do not have a rather specific definition of the word:

Dorinda

Dorinda's sparkling wit, and eyes,
    United cast too fierce a light,
Which blazes high, but quickly dies,
    Pains not the heart, but hurts the sight.

Love is a calmer, gentler joy,
    Smooth are his looks and soft his pace,
Her Cupid is a blackguard boy
    That runs his link full in your face.

A "link" is, or was, a torch, usually made of pitch. Dorinda's "too fierce a light" is most appropriately climaxed in the image of the "blackguard" Cupid shoving a black torch, burning brightly, into the speaker's face, defining that which underlies Dorinda's brilliance.

Recovering the historical meaning of a word is not a special exercise in the reading of poetry but merely one aspect of our alertness to the fullest possible ramifications of words. It is related also to the assumption that poetry makes sense: we cannot be content either to skip over words we do not know, as in the case of old words which have more or less disappeared from the language, or make do with meanings which are not wholly appropriate to their context, as in the case of words that are still in the language but have changed meaning. This requires eternal vigilance. "Annoy your store" in the context of the Shakespeare sonnet does not make sense and ought to drive us back to the *OED*. Cupid shoving a piece of chain (the most common modern meaning of "link") in Dorinda's face might do on first reading of the Sackville poem but sooner or later we ought to wonder what "chain" has to do with the rest of the poem and our dissatisfaction with the sense of the "link" as we understand it ought to force us to investigate the history of the word. In Milton's well-known sonnet usually called "On His Blindness" there is also at least one familiar word which, in its modern meaning, makes a statement in its context but a statement that somehow seems strangely inappropriate; that word is "fondly" in line 8:

> When I consider how my light is spent,
>> Ere half my days, in this dark world and wide,
>> And that one Talent which is death to hide,
>> Lodg'd with me useless, though my soul more bent
> To serve therewith my Maker, and present   5
>> My true account, lest he returning chide,
>> Doth God exact day-labour, light deny'd,
>> I fondly ask; But Patience, to prevent
> That murmur, soon replies, God doth not need
>> Either man's work, or his own gifts: who best   10
>> Bear his milde yoak, they serve him best: his State
> Is Kingly. Thousands at his bidding speed
>> And post o're Land and Ocean without rest:
>> They also serve who only stand and waite.

The first seven-plus lines of the sonnet may be reordered thus:

When I consider how my <sight> is (gone) (before) half my days in this dark and wide world [are gone],
and [how] that one talent which [it] is (fatal) to hide [is] lodged with[in] me useless, though my soul [is] more (determined) [than before] to serve my Maker (with that talent), and [to] present my true account, lest He (my Maker) [,] returning [,] chide [me], —

I fondly ask, ["](Does) God (require) day-labour [of me, hav-
ing] denied [me] light[?"]

Why should the poet ask that rather accusing question of God
"fondly"? We might read the poem a number of times without asking ourselves this question; but sooner or later, if we read carefully,
demanding that the poem "make sense," the adverb will give us
pause. It is immediately tempting to try merely to explain it away:
Milton is asking God, in effect, if He is unjust, but because the poet
is a religious man, he asks his question not in an accusing manner
but "lovingly," one might say "prayerfully." Surely, however, "fondly"
is a rather weak, even patronizing, form of "lovingly"; no one
says, "I'm rather fond of God, you know." We might suspect, then,
that "fondly" was a stronger expression of affection three hundred
years ago than it is today. Suspicion is not enough; there is a way of
being certain — we go to the *OED*. The problem then disappears.
Though our suspicion proved wrong — "fondly" was not so intense
as "lovingly" — we find that in the seventeenth century the word
meant "foolishly." The poet says that he asked this potentially blas-
phemous question "foolishly," for of course God is just and could not
be guilty of making unjust demands.

We cannot, perhaps, entirely avoid putting a modern construction
on a word which has in fact changed its meaning. Close study of a
period and intensive study of its language, browsing through the
OED, looking up as many words as we have time for, will help to
prevent such errors, but few of us can become expert in the entire
history of our language and equally few can look up every word we
read in texts from periods not our own. What we can do, however,
is insist that each statement in each poem we read make at least
literal prose sense in its context; if we come across a passage that does
not do so, within our limits of the knowledge of the language, we can
isolate the key word or words and check them in a historical dictionary of the language. Much of the time, we will discover that a
changing word is at the root of our difficulty.

Indeed, this awareness of the historical change in language will
help us read new poems as well as old, for many poets are themselves
deeply aware of the histories of words and this is another area in
which they exploit the full resources of language. We have already

seen that Bridges, writing in our own century, seems to have drawn upon the historical meaning of "spring" ("begin to appear") for one of the meanings of his most appropriately described "sweet-springing meads and bursting boughs of May."

NEW WORDS

The poet is not merely a receptive and sensitive repository of language, one who knows words and their histories thoroughly, uses them precisely, and exploits their potential richness and multiplicity of meaning fully; he is also a creator of language. When necessary, he invents words or new uses for words. Sometimes he will take one part of speech and use it as another. This is quite common in Shakespeare, and not uncommon in the works of other poets. Keats, for example, in "To Autumn," uses the adjective "plump" as a verb: "To swell the gourd, and plump the hazel shells." In "Ode to a Nightingale" he uses the verb "drain" as a noun, not in the ordinary sense of a system of pipes or tubes to carry away liquids, but in the sense of "the very last drop drained," almost as a synonym of "dregs," but with a greater insistence on the very limits of emptiness:

> My heart aches, and a drowsy numbness pains
> My sense, as though of hemlock I had drunk,
> Or emptied some dull opiate to the drains
> One minute past, and Lethe-wards had sunk:

Few readers will have difficulty understanding "plump." They will recognize it as a verb — aided by the parallel "swell" — and, knowing its meaning as an adjective, will be able with the poet to create the new meaning. With "drains" there may be a slightly greater margin for error, since there is already an identical noun which the reader must dismiss, going back to the verb, as it were, and creating the new noun from it. If he is not reading carefully and demanding that the poem "make sense," he may slip over this new word that looks like an old one and miss both the full sense and the full force of the lines.

Another form of word-invention involves combining words or elements of words into new entities. Gerard Manley Hopkins, though at times perhaps inordinately fond of creating his own language, compounds a number of new words effectively. In one particularly rich and moving poem, he twice coins two words in single lines:

Spring and Fall:
to a young child

Márgarét, are you griéving
Over Goldengrove unleaving?
Léaves, líke the things of man, you
With your fresh thoughts care for, can you?
Áh! ás the heart grows older   5
It will come to such sights colder
By and by, nor spare a sigh
Though worlds of wanwood leafmeal lie;
And yet you wíll weep and know why.
Now no matter child, the name: 10
Sórrow's spríngs áre the same.
Nor mouth had, no nor mind, expressed
What heart heard of, ghost guessed:
It ís the blight man was born for,
It is Margaret you mourn for.   15

The poem at first reading perhaps gives the impression of considerable syntactical difficulty, but there are only two passages that seem to require reordering for clarity, at the cost of effectiveness and richness of meaning — lines 3 and 4: "Can you, with your fresh thoughts, care for leaves like (*or,* as you do care for) the things of man?"; and line 12: "(Neither) mouth, no nor mind, had expressed." (Perhaps the end of line 7 might be expanded to "nor [will it] spare a sigh," the "it" referring, of course, to "the heart"; we will discuss the possible syntactical confusion of line 8 below.) The real difficulty lies in understanding individual words, particularly the four coined by compounding: "Goldengrove," "unleaving," "wanwood," "leafmeal."

"Goldengrove," indeed, may seem at first a rather simple and almost gratuitous invention. The capital makes it look, to a modern eye, like a name for a suburban development. It consists of two ordinary words merely printed as one. Its immediate meaning seems scarcely to justify the typographical coinage; it appears to be merely a description of a

NEW WORDS

grove of trees the leaves of which have turned red and yellow, or
"gold." The unleaving of the Goldengrove, however, gains wider
implications as the poem develops. The speaker begins by questioning
whether the child can really be grieving over the mere falling of leaves
and warning her that as she grows older she will have other things to
weep about than an unleaving Goldengrove; but he immediately reverses or nearly reverses his own argument: the leaves now, to Margaret, *are* "like the things of man," for "Sorrow's springs are the
same," and, in mourning for the leaves, the child is really mourning
for herself. Why leaves are "like the things of man" ("things" both as
possessions and as everything pertaining to the human being), why
Margaret is here in fact grieving for herself, is not spelled out in the
body of the poem (even "it," in the line "it is the blight man was born
for," has as antecedent only the equally unspecific pronoun "what"
in the phrase "What heart heard of . . ."). The "Spring" in the title
provides a possible answer, however, for it has no literal relevance to
the poem and can only refer to Margaret's youth — the springtime of
life — and so connects this poem with the traditional analogy between the seasons of the year and the chronological stages of a human's
life. Within these terms, what Margaret weeps for is the inevitable
process of her aging, declining, dying. And within these terms, the
Goldengrove is the "golden days of youth" as well as the autumnal
woods. Hopkins needs a new word here because by confronting a child
with the sad meaning of autumn he is not drawing fully upon the
common parallel of seasons of the year and the ages of man and so
needs a term that is equally appropriate to youth and autumn. Such
a word is "Goldengrove." The combination of two separate word
elements into a single, new word is thus justified: it is the precise word
that can express the full and complex range of meaning required by
the context.

Though the rich and complex implications of "Goldengrove" justify
its coinage, they do not clearly indicate the reason it is capitalized.
The capitalization itself, however, alerts us to other suggestions in the
poem: the phrasing of "*worlds* of wanwood," "*ghost* guessed," "the
blight man was born for"; the open invitation to expand the relevance
of the poem in the line "Sorrow's springs are the same"; the possible
double meaning of "Fall" in the title by the equating of leaves and
man in the argument of the poem. In this context, "Goldengrove"
takes on implications of the Garden of Eden, so that given its multiple

functions it is more than ever the one right word. The "Goldengrove," which at first appeared so ordinary a term for autumn, elevated to novelty by typography, now reverberates with suggestions of youth and Eden. For so complex and rich a system of references there was no single word. Hopkins invented one.

The origin and meaning of the second coined word in the line, "unleaving," seems clear enough: it is composed of the noun "leaf" used as a verb with the negative prefix *un-*, to mean "losing leaves." There is, however, a source for possible misunderstanding: "unleaving" might appear to be the compound of *un-* and the verb "leave." Such a reading of "unleaving" would have the line state the opposite of its apparently intended meaning, for surely in context the leaves *are* leaving not *un*-leaving ("remaining"). It is tempting, particularly in the light of the complexity of "Goldengrove," to justify this alternative derivation and thus the ambiguity of the coined word. To suggest that though the Goldengrove is "un-leaf-ing," it is at the same time — by virtue of its cyclical re-enactment of autumn, of man's inevitable decline toward death, and of man's Fall — a permanent-temporary or changelessly changing condition ("unleaveing") seems at first rather too ingenious and far-fetched. Since, as we shall see, "wanwood" is similarly capable of ambiguity, such ingenious complexity becomes a disturbing possibility within the tactics of the poem. Such over-interpretation, if indeed this is over-interpretation, is a risk the inventive poet runs. Whether we rest content with the apparent meaning of "unleaving" ("un-leaf-ing") and blame either the poet or the too ingenious critic for the ambiguity, or insist upon and attempt to justify the ambiguity, is a matter of interpretation and thus critical judgment supported by critical argument. In this instance, in fact, it is a matter of editorial judgment, for the editor of Hopkins' poems points out that in most manuscripts the word appears as "unleafing," though to choose the form that "corrects" the rhyme is not necessarily to defend the ambiguity.

It may have been inaccurate to omit line 8, the other line in this poem that contains two invented words, when we rather briefly discussed the syntactical difficulties in "Spring and Fall," for some readers have been uncertain as to the parts of speech of these words. Both the rhythm of the line and the alliterative pairing of "wanwood" with "worlds" and "leafmeal" with "lie" strongly suggest that "wanwood" is a noun and "leafmeal" an adverb; "though worlds of wanwood lie leafmeal" might be the clearer, reordered version. The alternative reading — "wanwood" as an adjective and "leafmeal" as a noun — not only violates the structure of the line but is difficult to reduce to sense. There is no denying, however, that this line has given many readers initial difficulty, though primarily, we feel, because of the words themselves not the syntax. "Wood" is apparently used in the sense of "forest" or "grove" (in the United States we usually use the plural, "woods"); "wan" usually means "pale." The woods are literally pale because the trees have shed their leaves and the leaves lost their color. This scene is not the exact equivalent of the Goldengrove unleaving but a later one, since here the leaves have already fallen, the branches of the trees are apparently bare, and the brilliance of autumn colors has faded. "Wan" is appropriate, too, to the analogy of seasons and the ages of man since it suggests the pallor of sickness or death. The clarity of the new word is somewhat reduced, however, because Hopkins has so alerted us to multiple possibilities that when we discover that "wan" is one of those words that has reversed its meaning in its history — in its Old English form, *wann* meant "dark" — we find ourselves again faced with a word that points in opposite directions. It seems most sensible to be content with the apparent meanings — "pale wood," "un-leaf-ing" — though the coincidence of two such words in a brief poem and a poem that centers on the paradoxical fusion of spring and fall could justify our keeping the more remote possibilities in mind.

"Leafmeal" is not as immediately meaningful a coinage as the three we have already discussed in the poem, for one of the elements of the compound (-*meal*) is rarely used any longer as a compounding element. The analogy is, it seems clear, with "piecemeal," which means "piece by piece," the new word thus meaning "leaf by leaf." As in the instance of "Goldengrove," however, here alternative possibilities enrich the term: the leaves have not only fallen one by one but have now decayed into a "mealy" substance. Hopkins has achieved implications both of the passage of time and of death and decay in his invented word. The line, much expanded, may be read: "though huge areas of dark, colorless groves have dropped their leaves on the ground, one by one to decay, becoming a mass of mealy matter."

Both Keats and Hopkins have used the common resources of language and invented new words by extending the common processes of its development and growth (shifting parts of speech, compounding new words from old elements). Invention can be irresponsible and its results incomprehensible. We can arbitrarily make up a word — "phlar," let us say — with no roots in English, and assign it a wholly arbitrary meaning — "to empty slowly, *as,* 'to phlar a tub.'" Even working within the language itself, we may combine too many existing aberrations or real but exceptional elements, so that no reader could re-create its meaning — just as George Bernard Shaw's invented spelling "ghoti," based on actual sounds of its letters in some English words, is almost undecipherable. (It is made up of the *gh* from "enough," the *o* from "women," the *ti* from "nation," and so spells "fish.")

Lewis Carroll is not, in this well-known poem from *Through the Looking Glass*, concerned with spelling, but he too has fun in inventing words:

Jabberwocky

'Twas brillig, and the slithy toves
    Did gyre and gimble in the wabe:
All mimsy were the borogroves,
    And the mome raths outgrabe.

"Beware the Jabberwock, my son!   5
    The jaws that bite, the claws that catch!
Beware the Jubjub bird, and shun
    The frumious Bandersnatch!"

He took his vorpal sword in hand:
    Long time the manxome foe he sought —   10
So rested he by the Tumtum tree,
    And stood awhile in thought.

And as in uffish thought he stood,
    The Jabberwock, with eyes of flame,
Came whiffling through the tulgey wood,   15
    And burbled as it came!

One, two! One, two! And through and through
    The vorpal blade went snicker-snack!
He left it dead, and with its head
    He went galumphing back.   20

"And hast thou slain the Jabberwock?
   Come to my arms, my beamish boy!
O frabjous day! Callooh! Callay!"
   He chortled in his joy.

'Twas brillig, and the slithy toves   25
   Did gyre and gimble in the wabe:
All mimsy were the borogroves,
   And the mome raths outgrabe.

The skeleton of meaning in this nonsense poem is carried by the real words: we may not know what a "Jabberwock" is but we know that it is fearful, with "jaws that bite," "claws that catch" and "eyes of flame." We know that the father warns his son about it, that the son kills it with a sword, brings its head back to his father, and is congratulated. This skeletal meaning is filled out somewhat by the ballad form — in meter, spoken passages, and even subject matter. The coined words are often recognizable as specific parts of speech by their endings (-y, -ious, -ish, -ing, -ed), by grammatical indicators such as "the," or by their order in the sentence. Some of them at least are "portmanteau" words, made up of parts of existing words (like "leaf-meal"): "chortled," which was invented by Lewis Carroll but has now become part of the language, is made up of "chuckled" and "snorted"; many of the words have identifiable parts: "snatch" in "Bander-snatch," "gallop" in "galumphing," "slither" in "slithy," "beam" in "beamish," "brilliant" in "brillig," "gambol" in "gimble." A good deal remains (intentionally, of course) more or less incomprehensible: what is a "vorpal" sword, an "uffish" thought, a "Jubjub" bird, or a "Bandersnatch"? What, precisely, is a "Jabberwock"? What does the first stanza — repeated at the end of the poem — mean? It is indicative of Lewis Carroll's genius that we can — if, perhaps, with ludicrous solemnity — talk about the meaning of his nonsense verse: he has given enough meaning, stayed just close enough to (and far enough away from) the structure and order of the language, and thrown in just enough teasing hints at further meaning in using existing roots of words, to give the illusion of meaning, which makes his nonsense the parody of rather than the antithesis of sense. His poem is a useful example of the tremendous resources and the dangers of inventing words.

For the poet, inventiveness in language is an important, though not inevitably necessary, tool of his art; it is one, but only one, of the ways in which he explores the resources of his medium, language, in order to create and express his vision most fully and precisely. When it is indulged for its own sake, like the pun it degenerates and defeats its own purposes. Like any word well used in poetry, the invented word functions best when it is the most precise word, the one wholly right word, for the occasion.

NAMES AND ALLUSIONS

The necessity for becoming informed about an unfamiliar term and the method of getting the required information and applying it to the poem in which it appears are the same whether the term is a proper name or any other unfamiliar word, though names sometimes require recourse to historical, classical, mythological, or other specialized dictionaries or reference works. A simple instance of the necessity for identifying names occurs in the Wordsworth sonnet referred to earlier, "The world is too much with us . . . ." The speaker complains that, because we devote so much time to "getting and spending," nowadays "little we see in Nature that is ours" and that for everything, even standing by the sea, "we are out of tune." He concludes, shockingly for those more religious times:

> Great God! I'd rather be
> A Pagan suckled in a creed outworn,
> So might I, standing on this pleasant lea,
> Have glimpses that would make me less forlorn;
> Have sight of Proteus rising from the sea;
> Or hear old Triton blow his wreathèd horn.

If the names "Proteus" and "Triton" were totally unfamiliar to us, the statement of the last two lines and their relationship to the rest of the poem would completely escape us. Knowing or discovering that in Greek mythology (a pagan creed outworn) Proteus was a sea-god and Triton a demi-god of the sea, opens the way to understanding.

In the preceding instance, a very little additional information would also explain the mention of Triton's "wreathèd horn," and we would then, perhaps, have all the information necessary to understand the reference. It is not always easy, however, to know what constitutes adequate information in identifying a name. Most readers of Andrew Marvell's "An Horation Ode upon Cromwell's Return from Ireland," for example, recognize the name "Cromwell," but, remembering him only as the dictatorial leader of the Commonwealth, would find the last part of the poem — "How fit he is to sway / That can so well obey," etc. — a rather oddly blind defense of a totalitarian ruler. Men, like words, have histories, and when Cromwell was returning from Ireland and Marvell wrote this ode, the military hero had not yet set himself above Parliament. Marvell may have been unduly optimistic in this poem, but he was not denying existing political realities. Recognizing the name "Cromwell," then, is not enough; we must often go far beyond mere recognition to understand the precise relevance of a name.

Names, even when they are not those of the subjects of poems but are allusions or references to literary or historical persons, places, or things, at times require more than simple recognition. Like other words, they are most often used with some precision. Few readers have difficulty in recognizing the reference to Shakespeare's tragic hero in this line from T. S. Eliot's "The Love Song of J. Alfred Prufrock": "No! I am not Prince Hamlet, nor was meant to be." But why specifically Hamlet? If Prufrock were merely saying, "No! I am not a tragic hero, nor was meant to be," other names — Oedipus, Lear — would do equally well. There is a superficial resemblance between Prufrock and Hamlet (at least in one of the traditional readings of the tragedy), however, that makes the denial more meaningful and pointed: both men hesitate before taking (or not taking) important actions. To understand the allusion, then, we must know enough of *Hamlet* to read the lines, roughly, "No! despite the fact that we both hesitate before taking important actions, I am not a tragic hero like Prince Hamlet, nor was meant to be." And we may even infer, "I am rather more like Polonius than Hamlet."

Allusion may seem to border on metaphor since both involve comparison, but, as we shall see in the chapter on imagery, comparison alone is not enough to constitute metaphor: the comparison must be figurative, the things being compared must be essentially different; two men, even when one is fictional, are not "essentially" different; and the comparison is literal, not figurative. A good many allusions-by-name are of this kind, comparisons but not metaphors.

If proper nouns, like other words, must be understood fully and precisely, like other words too, they are capable of multiple meanings. We see such an instance in this satiric portrait from Pope's "Epistle II: Of the Characters of Women" from *Moral Essays:*

> But what are these to great Atossa's mind?
> Scarce once herself, by turns all Womankind!
> Who, with herself, or others, from her birth
> Finds all her life one warfare upon earth:
> Shines in exposing Knaves, and painting Fools,   5
> Yet is, whate'er she hates and ridicules.
> No Thought advances, but her Eddy Brain
> Whisks it about, and down it goes again.
> Full sixty years the World has been her Trade,
> The wisest Fool much Time has ever made.   10
> From loveless youth to unrespected age,
> No Passion gratify'd except her Rage.
> So much the Fury still out-ran the Wit,
> The Pleasure miss'd her, and the Scandal hit.
> Who breaks with her, provokes Revenge from Hell,   15
> But he's a bolder man who dares be well:
> Her ev'ry turn with Violence pursu'd,
> Nor more a storm her Hate than Gratitude.
> To that each Passion turns, or soon or late;
> Love, if it makes her yield, must make her hate: 20
> Superiors? death! and Equals? what a curse!
> But an Inferior not dependant? worse.
> Offend her, and she knows not to forgive;
> Oblige her, and she'll hate you while you live:
> But die, and she'll adore you — Then the Bust   25
> And Temple rise — then fall again to dust.
> Last night, her Lord was all that's good and great,
> A Knave this morning, and his Will a Cheat.
> Strange! by the Means defeated of the Ends,
> By Spirit robb'd of Pow'r, by Warmth of Friends,   30
> By Wealth of Followers! without one distress
> Sick of herself thro' very selfishness!
> Atossa, curs'd with ev'ry granted pray'r,
> Childless with all her Children, wants an Heir.

> To Heirs unknown descends th'unguarded store,   35
> Or wanders, Heav'n-directed, to the Poor.

The description is too specific and detailed to be a mere type-portrait, but we can with pleasure and understanding read it as a fictional characterization, the name "Atossa" understood simply as an arbitrary name, like Jenny Jones, assigned to that fictional character. But the name is scarcely arbitrary: the Persian princess of that name was famous, or infamous, for her temper, and so the modern woman of temper is appropriately called by the same name. This knowledge adds little, perhaps, to the portrait, but in its antiquity suggests a recurrence if not a type of such a woman, lifting it above the particular to a wider relevance (as does our recognition of some of these traits in our own acquaintances — if we are perceptive and unlucky enough to see them). The Atossa of history was rather well connected: her father was Cyrus, conqueror of Croesus; her husband, Darius, conqueror of Babylon. There would seem to be little relevance of this relationship to the portrait as fiction, but the satire is aimed at another lady of violent temper and wife of a conqueror, the Duchess of Marlborough, so that the name is appropriate in itself for the character portrayed and even more relevant to the actual target of the satire. Indeed, Atossa is not so much a source of multiple meaning as a path through one allusion to another. Recognizing the name, and through the name the object of the satire, enhances without limiting the implications of the description. Without following up the allusion, we can understand the statement but not its implications. (We will have more to say about implication in the next chapter.)

Not all names are allusions, nor are all allusions made by naming. "Cromwell," in Marvell's poem, is the subject of the poem, not an allusion to someone with whom the subject is to be compared. The passage that follows, from T. S. Eliot's "The Burial of the Dead," the first section of *The Waste Land,* is full of names that are not allusions and allusions that are not names:

> Unreal City,
> Under the brown fog of a winter dawn,
> A crowd flowed over London Bridge, so many,
> I had not thought death had undone so many.
> Sighs, short and infrequent, were exhaled,   5
> And each man fixed his eyes before his feet.

Flowed up the hill and down King William Street,
To where Saint Mary Woolnoth kept the hours
With a dead sound on the final stroke of nine.
There I saw one I knew, and stopped him, crying: "Stetson!   10
"You who were with me in the ships at Mylae!
"That corpse you planted last year in your garden,
"Has it begun to sprout? Will it bloom this year?
"Or has the sudden frost disturbed its bed?
"Oh keep the Dog far hence, that's friend to men,   15
"Or with his nails he'll dig it up again!
"You! hypocrite lecteur! — mon semblable, — mon frère!"

The scene is the City, the central, commercial section of London. The passage specifies the location: London Bridge, King William Street (that leads from the Bridge into the City proper), the church of Saint Mary Woolnoth. These are no more allusions than the description of the fog, the crowd hurrying to work, the clock striking nine; they are part of the setting. Nor does the name "Stetson" appear to be an allusion: he is one of the men in the hurrying crowd, a friend of the speaker's. "Mylae," however, appears to be an allusion by name, for though it would seem to refer to a real past encounter of the speaker and Stetson, apparently during a war (not "with me in the ship" but "ships"), probably World War I (*The Waste Land* was first published in 1922), Mylae is most famous as the scene of a Roman naval victory over Carthage during the first Punic War, thousands of years earlier. If, as it seems, the intent of the allusion is to compare — indeed, to fuse — the modern and the ancient war, it is just as necessary to understand that the expected reference is to the recent war as it is to recognize the reference to the ancient one: to recognize the allusion but not to relate it to the subject matter of the poem is worse than not understanding the reference at all.

Most of the allusions in the passage are not in the form of names. This raises the difficulty of knowing when a passage *is* an allusion, much less what the allusion is. Let us first, however, read as much of the passage as we can without concerning ourselves with references or echoes of other works, people, places, or things. We see the crowd of City employees hurrying to work on a foggy winter morning just as the clock strikes nine. An unidentified speaker (the rest of the poem from which this passage is excerpted does not make the identity of the speaker much more specific) thinks of these people as dead (l. 4) and the crowd becomes a rather ghostly one, an image helped a bit in our imaginations by the fog. Here we are, of course, handicapped by having only an excerpt. The earlier portions of this first section of *The Waste Land* gradually suggest that "living" in modern urban society is a kind of spiritual death. The living people in this conformist, commercial crowd are thus spiritually dead as well as ghostly in appearance because of the fog.

The speaker recognizes one of the crowd, and here our real difficulties begin. He is apparently a wartime friend, but "Mylae," makes us a bit uncertain in what war they have fought; or, if we can assume that it is World War I, we are alerted by the allusion to the possibility that a mythical frame of reference is being imposed upon the historic. The question the speaker asks — whether the corpse in Stetson's garden has begun to sprout — seems to rip apart the otherwise plausible surface of the passage. If, however, we can temporarily accept the planting of a corpse (perhaps only by reading it as a figurative term for seed of some sort), the questions — "Has it begun to sprout? Will it bloom this year? / Or has the sudden frost disturbed its bed?" — and the warning to keep the Dog away (ignoring the capital for the moment) so he won't dig it up, make sense. The last line, however, even assuming we can translate the French ("hypocritical reader! — you who resemble me [*or,* my double] — my brother!") disorients us somewhat. We expect the "You" to be Stetson, until "reader" comes in, and then we think it might be ourselves being referred to. Perhaps we adjust to the line by assuming we have been identified with Stetson. The rest of the line, then, once we have made the shift in identification, becomes a bit easier — we are Stetson and, if not the speaker himself, at least his near-twin. Speaker, reader, and Stetson are, by the end of the passage, one, or very alike.

Undoubtedly the passage is still strange and disconcerting. It makes sense, but a rather extraordinary and troublesome kind of sense, like that of a dream — or nightmare. Except for the place names, including the dubious allusion in "Mylae," we have read it without recourse to any allusions whatsover. Yet the passage, like the rest of the poem, is full of allusions, so much so that the poet was prevailed upon to append notes. The notes pertaining to this passage point out that the reader should compare the Unreal City with Baudelaire's "Fourmillante cité, cité pleine de rêves, / Où le spectre en plein jour raccroche le passant" ("Swarming city, city full of dreams,/ Where the specter accosts the passer-by in broad daylight"); should compare, "I had not thought death had undone so many" with Dante's *Inferno*, III, 55–7; should compare, "Sighs, short and infrequent, were exhaled," with *Inferno*, IV, 25–7; and should compare "Oh keep . . . dig it up again" with the Dirge in Webster's *The White Devil* (V, iv). Eliot also indicates that the "dead sound on the final stroke of nine" is "A phenomenon which I have often noticed," and that for the last line we should see (but he does not suggest compare) the Preface to Baudelaire's *Les Fleurs du Mal*.

What do these notes contribute to our understanding of the *statement* of the poem? Relatively little. The allusions do, however, confirm our confusion, as it were, and do enrich the total *sense* or *meaning* of the poem. In Baudelaire the dead accosts the living; in Dante, the living accost the dead. This contributes to the ambivalence of the scene and even the poem, in which we who live in *The Waste Land* — modern materialist, Godless, and valueless society — are spiritually dead. Nor do we want to become spiritually alive, for this will mean physical death at least to the extent of "denying the flesh," the pursuit of comfort and pleasure, that we have mistakenly come to call life. Spirits or specters are physically dead but spiritually alive; we in the crowd in the Unreal City are physically alive, but spiritually dead. The unidentified and rather disembodied speaker is one of us, yet in his awareness that The Waste Land is a waste land he is perhaps on the verge of spiritual life. All of this — which depends in part on the whole poem rather than merely on this excerpt — confirms the ambivalence of life and death in the passage and perhaps makes it acceptable and meaningful, but the ambivalence itself is evident even in this short passage, even without the notes.

The relevant lines in Webster's Dirge (the situation in the play seems to have little relation to that in *The Waste Land* except that it concerns the burying of a corpse) are these:

> But keepe the wolfe far thence, that's foe to men,
> For with his nailes hee'll dig them up agen.

This does little to clarify the issue of the planted corpse in Stetson's garden, though it does, by the changes Eliot has made, call special attention to the Dog (otherwise emphasized by the capitalization). Without resorting to other possible allusions here (we shall come back to Dog allusions) we can perhaps now tie the passage in to the over-all ambivalence of the life-death theme: the Dog, by digging up the corpse, will presumably keep it from sprouting (or being reborn?). Does Stetson want the corpse to sprout, or is it only the speaker, who, wishing for spiritual rebirth of The Waste Land, wants the corpse to sprout? If the sprouting is real or spiritual rebirth, and if the inhabitants of The Waste Land do not wish for such fertility and rebirth, the Dog will be a friend in preventing what they do not wish, and the speaker is warning Stetson for the sake of his soul. If, on the other hand, the sprouting is merely material growth, Stetson would wish to prevent the Dog from digging up the corpse, and the Dog "[usually] friend to man" here must be restrained for the sake of Stetson's material comfort. Once more, within the terms of these notes alone, the allusions only serve to emphasize the ambivalence rather than to yield a simple solution.

In his general note to the whole poem, Eliot suggests that Jesse Weston's *From Ritual to Romance* and Frazer's *The Golden Bough* offer a good many general glosses to his poem. This is not the place to give a complete reading of the poem, but we might note Frazer's account of the ancient Egyptian practice of burying an effigy of the corn-god ("corn" in the British sense of "cereal") with a few seeds embedded in it, digging up the effigy later, finding the seeds had sprouted, and thus divining that the gods had assured a crop for the coming year. Our previous "hunch" (based on the context of "planted," "sprouted," "bloom") that the corpse may be considered figuratively as a plant of some kind is thus to a degree confirmed but considerably extended in meaning: the corpse is vegetative in a sense, but also more specifically a corpse, and the strange passage is related to the mythological fertility-rite motif that runs through the poem.

Frazer also discusses two mythological Egyptian dogs involved in fertility or resurrection ceremonies: Sirius, who heralded the rise of the waters of the Nile and thus augured the fertility of the land, and Anubis, the guardian of the dead, who helped preserve Osiris, the fertility god who was to be resurrected. Both are thus "friend to man," if man wants rebirth; if he does not, he must keep these dogs from the corpse. Neither mythological dog, however, digs up the corpse, and it is perhaps this that has led other commentators on the poem to seek other allusions, among which are Psalms 22:20 — "Deliver my soul from the sword; my darling from the power of the dog" — and

Eliot's own poem "Marina" — "Those who sharpen the tooth of the dog, meaning / Death." If the Dog is Death, or some such sinister power, he would seem to threaten the possible rebirth of the corpse, so that the ordinary "friend to man" would here be doing a disservice — unless we did not really want a rebirth. After all this digging into allusion then, we are left with the same ambivalence: the Dog may either aid or threaten rebirth; Stetson may be warned to prevent rebirth or to assist it in keeping the Dog away from the corpse. We are perhaps wiser in our awareness of the depths of the ambivalence, but no nearer to resolving it into a simple, straightforward statement.

At this point there are two possible erroneous impressions which must be dispelled: either that this discussion demonstrates that it is unnecessary to understand allusions; or that Eliot's poem, or at least this passage, is a failure because it depends upon a network of allusions to rather abstruse items outside itself and so is largely meaningless as an independent work of art.

As we saw from our rather uninformed reading of the passage before considering allusions, the passage makes statements we can understand even before we understand the allusions. Because of the whole concept of the passage and the poem, however, these statements are difficult to comprehend fully: that the living can be spiritually dead, the modern world more materially fertile and more spiritually sterile than other ages, that we must die to be reborn, inevitably makes for complexity and even confusion in understanding the sense of all terms having to do with life and death, fertility and sterility, in the poem. This complexity or ambivalence can make a poem or a passage "difficult to understand" without rendering it meaningless, and this, we believe, is the nature of *The Waste Land*. This complexity is to a large degree available in the poem to the understanding of the reader who does not and, unaided, cannot know or discover the relevance or even the presence of the network of allusion. To this extent, the poem does not depend upon the allusions.

Knowing, or having found, all or most of the allusions, the basic difficulties remain, for the basic statement, with such concepts as life-is-death and death-leads-to-life, remains as complex as before. There is even some question as to how allusions when discovered (for example, the Dog) are to be applied or whether they are applicable in several or even opposite ways. Nonetheless, the allusions — for example, those to Baudelaire and Dante — confirm the complexities of the uninformed reading, in some cases do clarify the statement to a degree, and almost always widen and deepen the scope, the significance, and even the emotional impact of the poem. To treat the corpse as a figuratively described seed is adequate for the extracting of a natural statement, but to know the allusion to the planting of seed in the corpse or effigy of a fertility god is to verify the figure, deepen the significance, connect it with traditional meanings, and reveal its relationship to the rest of the poem.

The passage, the whole poem perhaps, can be read meaningfully and effectively without awareness of the network of allusion; to apprehend the allusions makes the experience of the poem richer and deeper. (It must be added that to read the poem merely as an intellectual parlor game or crossword puzzle without the immediate felt experience and created statement is not to read the poem as poem at all; but it should not be necessary to choose between this and reading it as an unallusive poem.)

We must admit, however, that a poet who uses, though he does not wholly depend on, so complex a network of allusions creates for himself difficulties comparable to those of the poet who invents a good deal of his language. Having invited the reader to be alert for allusions, how can he control the search? Are we to assume that what Eliot does not annotate in his specific or general notes is not an allusion? If so, the Dog can only allude to something in Frazer, and the line from the Psalms or the passage from "Marina" is inappropriate. This would resolve one difficulty. But does the "final stroke of nine" not refer to Luke 23:44, to the ninth hour of the Crucifixion? Where do we stop the search? How does the poet control the accidental (not to mention the overly-ingenious) association of his words and phrases with those from contexts outside his own? Of course he must rely on the critical intelligence and common sense of his readers, but he must be held to some degree responsible for tempting them to "over-read" his poem.

Let us now return once again to the Shakespeare sonnet we reordered at the end of Chapter I. The text is, you will remember:

> Poore soule, the center of my sinfull earth,
> Thrall to these rebbell powres that thee array,
> Why dost thou pine within and suffer dearth,

Painting thy outward walls so costlie gay?
Why so large cost, having so short a lease,   5
Dost thou upon thy fading mansion spend?
Shall wormes, inheritors of this excesse,
Eate up thy charge? is this thy bodie's end?
Then, soule, live thou upon thy servant's losse,
And let that pine to aggravat thy store;   10
Buy tearms divine in selling hours of drosse,
Within be fed, without be rich no more:
    So shalt thou feed on Death, that feeds on men,
    And Death once dead, ther's no more dying then.

We can now modernize the spelling, define the less familiar words, keeping in mind the changes in language since Shakespeare's day and the multiple possibilities of words, and, in parentheses, insert the definitions into the reordered version that appears at the end of the previous chapter, indicating multiple possibilities by brackets:

Poor soul, $\left\{ \begin{array}{l} \text{[at] the center} \\ \text{the (most important part)} \end{array} \right\}$ of my sinful $\left\{ \begin{array}{l} \text{(world)} \\ \text{(dust)} \end{array} \right\}$,

[who are now] $\left\{ \begin{array}{l} \text{(enchanted by)} \\ \text{(enslaved by)} \end{array} \right\}$ those rebel(lious) powers that

$\left\{ \begin{array}{l} \text{(clothe)} \\ \text{(surround)} \\ \text{(afflict)} \end{array} \right\}$ (you),

why (do) (you) (grieve and waste away) (inside) and suffer (privation),

[while] painting (your) outward walls so $\left\{ \begin{array}{l} \text{(damningly)} \\ \text{(expensively)} \end{array} \right\}$ gay?

Having so short a lease, why (do) (you) spend (that much) upon (your) fading mansion?

Shall worms, [the] (heirs) of this $\left\{ \begin{array}{l} \text{(excessive spending)} \\ \text{(non-essential thing)} \end{array} \right\}$, eat up (that which is left in your) charge?

Is this $\left\{ \begin{array}{l} \text{[to be the] end} \\ \text{(the purpose)} \end{array} \right\}$ of your body?

(In that case), soul, (you) live upon (your) <body's> loss
and let (your body) (grieve and waste away) to (add to) (your)
    [soul's] (wealth);
buy divine $\left\{ \begin{matrix} \text{(long periods of time)} \\ \text{(contractual conditions)} \end{matrix} \right\}$ (by) selling hours of (worth-
    lessness);
be fed (inwardly), be rich (outwardly) no (longer): ——
so (you) (shall) feed on death, that feeds on men,
and once death [is] dead, then there's no more dying.

    Not all difficulties or all responsibilities of alert reading have been magically made to disappear by this reordering-with-definition, but the statement of the poem is largely clarified and at least the direction in which solutions may be found — the identification of the "rebbell powres" as the senses or powers of the body, the identification of the "servant" as the body, etc. — has been made more apparent. Reordering and defining reveal, even where simple reading or repeated reading may not have done so, that the speaker is addressing his soul and telling it that it should not let the body continue to indulge itself and thereby deprive the soul (of immortal life), for the body will inevitably die soon anyway; the soul must instead deprive the body in order to ensure its own immortality.

    On the other hand, the reordering and defining has perhaps revealed richness in the poem that even those who understood its statement upon first reading may have missed: that "earth" is a uniquely appropriate word because it means both the whole world or the self and at the same time signifies that the body is mere "dust"; that "excess" is similarly appropriate because while the lavish spending on the body is "excessive," in religious terms the body itself is "excessive"; and so forth.

    This prose version of the poem, clarifying the statement and revealing some of the richness of the poem as it does, is not, or should not be, the end of our reading and re-reading of the poem. There is a good deal more both within and beyond the statement of the poem that may be revealed. Certain areas of meaning which lie beyond even the richest statement of a poem are the concern of the next chapter, at the end of which the reader might well return once more to this sonnet.

III

Beyond Statement

To this point we have been discussing primarily what the words, phrases, and sentences of a poem *state,* what can be said to be "on the page." In dealing with words we considered such aspects of meaning as connotation, multiple meaning, and allusion which may have seemed to some to go beyond statement, but, no matter how complex the meanings we derived from a word, we did have the word itself "on the page" and its meanings in the language and so could claim that we were dealing with *statement* even if in a somewhat broad sense. In dealing with such constructions as ellipsis we supplied in our reorderings words and phrases that were not in fact "on the page," but we could claim that the completed constructions are inherent in the structure and conventions of the language and so they, too, are elements of statement. In this chapter we shall take short and perhaps dangerous steps beyond verbal and structural meaning, beyond what may be considered as stated in the poem; we shall discuss the contributions to the meaning of the poem of such elements as implication, tone, and form.

IMPLICATION

A good deal of human discourse is less direct than most of us are normally aware. A young man whose requests for a date are rejected time after time by a certain young lady soon "gets the point," though each time she seems to have a legitimate reason for turning him down. A university admissions officer who receives a letter of recommendation stressing an applicant's agreeable personality, pleasant manner, and co-operative spirit, "reads between the lines" that he may not be a very good student. "Getting the point" and "reading between the lines" are acts of *inference*, that is, drawing conclusions from indirect hints or suggestions of meaning, sometimes from what is *not* said that might have been expected; the indirect suggestions are *implications*.

Inference, you will notice, may be mistaken in two ways: it can treat a detail as an implication which is in fact not an implication, or it can draw the wrong conclusions from an implication. Thus the young lady in the first instance may have wanted to go out with the persistent young man but have been prevented by a series of co-incidences; her excuses may have been truthful and valid, and without implication. The writer of the letter of recommendation may have assumed that a student's academic record speaks for itself and that the university admissions officer would be more interested in such matters as character and personality which do not show up in records. On the other hand, it is possible that the young lady may have been playing hard to get and overplaying her role, or that the young man may have called often but always at the last minute; that the letter-writer thought the university in question a "country club," interested more in a student's social than in his intellectual attainments. There were, in these last instances, implications, but the wrong inferences were drawn from them.

A poem, like other discourse, is frequently indirect: it often implies a good deal more than it states. The reader, then, must go beyond its *statement,* or explicit meaning, to its *sense,* or implicit meaning. While taking this necessary step beyond the page toward understanding, he must remember the possibilities of error to which inference is prone. Equally important and equally difficult, *he must constantly be aware of the difference between what the poem states and what he infers.*

Let us take as our first example this poem by John Donne:

The Flea

Marke but this flea, and marke in this,
How little that which thou deny'st me is;

It suck'd me first, and now sucks thee,
And in this flea, our two bloods mingled bee;
Thou know'st that this cannot be said   5
A sinne, nor shame, nor losse of maidenhead,
    Yet this enjoyes before it wooe,
    And pamper'd swells with one blood made of two,
    And this, alas, is more than wee would doe.

Oh stay, three lives in one flea spare,   10
Where wee almost, yea more than maryed are,
This flea is you and I, and this
Our mariage bed, and mariage temple is;
Though parents grudge, and you, w'are met,
And cloysterd in these living walls of Jet.   15
    Though use make you apt to kill me,
    Let not to that, selfe murder added bee,
    And sacrilege, three sinnes in killing three.

Cruell and sodaine, hast thou since
Purpled thy naile, in blood of innocence?   20
Wherein could this flea guilty bee,
Except in that drop which it suckt from thee?
Yet thou triumph'st, and saist that thou
Find'st not thy selfe, nor me the weaker now;
    'Tis true, then learne how false, feares bee;   25
    Just so much honor, when thou yeeld'st to mee,
    Will wast, as this flea's death took life from thee.

The poem opens abruptly with an imperative: "(Just notice) this flea, and (notice) in this [that I am about to say], how $\begin{cases} \text{little} \\ \text{(unimportant)} \end{cases}$ is that which (you) (are denying) me . . . ." We know from the imperative that someone is speaking; from "thou" that he is speaking to one person, whom we have not yet identified but who, we know, is denying the speaker something; and we know that the speaker is pointing to or pointing out a flea. We know from the third line that the flea has bitten the speaker and the person spoken to, so that at this point we can tentatively eliminate certain possible references of "thou": it is unlikely to be the speaker's soul or other self or God or the reader. We infer, for the moment at least, that it is another person, someone present to the speaker. We are thus searching for a contextual antecedent for the pronoun; we are on the borderline of statement and implication. We are also searching for the reference of "that which" in line 2. We discover both together. From the details of the rest of the stanza — "sinne . . . shame . . . losse of maidenhead . . . wooe . . . more than wee would doe" — we conclude that the speaker is a man who is trying to seduce the woman to whom he addresses the argument of the poem. All of this is so obvious that the only question likely to be raised is whether we are dealing with indirect suggestion (implication) or direct statement. In fact, however, without setting the stage, describing the situation, or identifying the characters, the poem has forced us to construct our own little drama in which to set this bit of monologue.

The "play" continues, and though we still hear only the one speaker we infer action and response. The action we literally "read between the lines" — or between stanzas. The opening line of the second stanza implies that the woman addressed has caught the flea and is preparing to kill it. (Fleas must be pinched, not swatted, so that the executioner should properly be seen either holding the flea between her fingertips or nails or pinning it down with one nail, not holding her arm up prepared to swat — see "naile," line 20, to confirm this.) The opening two lines of the third stanza imply she has completed her task. In lines 23–4 the speaker repeats her triumphant rebuttal. (Since the form in which the response appears is known as *"indirect* quotation," we are perhaps justified in considering her side of the argument implied rather than stated.) Moreover, we infer from her response that her killing the flea was not merely a "natural" or unconscious act but part of her side of the argument.

All of these implications (with the possible exception of the last) are perfectly clear even upon a first reading of the poem. We have thus far deliberately belabored the obvious precisely to show how much we understand immediately in a poem, or in prose, that is not stated directly but implied, and how shadowy is the line between statement and implication (or between the *statement* and what we may call the *sense* of a poem). It is essential that we be aware of the distinction between "reading what is there on the page" and inferring, however, for not all implications are so obvious as these.

Even in this poem it is possible to wander into erroneous or dubious paths of inference. Is it proper to infer, for example, that these are rather "low" characters — after all, what "decent" people have fleas? This could be argued on moral or experiential grounds, but it would probably be safer to base one's argument on history: three hundred and fifty years ago or more, when this poem was written, fleas were not uncommon even in the best of families. It remains possible to argue that these cannot be very "respectable" people (though historical awareness of differing mores might still pertain), but such an argument would depend largely on one's own ethical and moral outlook and not on implications within the poem; the attitudes, while legitimately held by the reader, must not be attributed to the poet or the poem.

Is it proper to infer that this is a mock argument, that the speaker is merely offering the lady an excuse for yielding as she intended all along? Such an inference seems based not on history or on the attitudes of the reader to the subject matter (though it may be influenced by such attitudes) but on a reading of a single passage in the poem. To what does "this," the last word in line 12, refer? Is the speaker pointing to a bed he and his lady are occupying? If so, it would weigh heavily in favor of the inference that this is indeed a mock argument (though still one's attitudes toward human nature and conduct would be involved). The context, however, seems more fully to support the conclusion that it is the flea to which "this" refers: "This flea is you and I, and this [flea] [is] our mar[r]iage bed, and mar[r]iage temple." The specific passage in the context supporting this reading is line 15: "And [we are] clo(i)ster[e]d in these living walls of Jet." To read "this" as referring to the bed and the room in which the lovers are speaking would make the continuity of statement here rather ridiculous: "This flea is you and I, and this [bed we are in] [is] our mar[r]iage bed, and mar[r]iage temple . . . (we have come together) and [are] clo(i)ster[e]d in <the body of the flea>." It would, as it were, take the bed inside the flea.

Thus, though inference is undeniably influenced by the reader's own attitudes and beliefs, before claiming his right to an opinion about the attitudes and beliefs within the poem, he should take into account historical or geographical differences in mores and, first and most important, the full context of the poem.

The implications in the next poem, by Robert Browning, though even more fundamental to the story, are less obvious on first reading and go further beyond story than do those in the Donne poem.

My Last Duchess
Ferrara

That's my last Duchess painted on the wall
Looking as if she were alive. I call
That piece a wonder, now: Frà Pandolf's hands
Worked busily a day, and there she stands.
Will 't please you sit and look at her? I said   5
"Frà Pandolf" by design, for never read
Strangers like you that pictured countenance,
The depth and passion of its earnest glance,
But to myself they turned (since none puts by
The curtain I have drawn for you, but I)   10
And seemed as they would ask me, if they durst,
How such a glance came there; so, not the first
Are you to turn and ask thus. Sir, 'twas not
Her husband's presence only, called that spot
Of joy into the Duchess' cheek: perhaps   15
Frà Pandolf chanced to say "Her mantle laps
"Over my lady's wrist too much," or "Paint
"Must never hope to reproduce the faint
"Half-flush that dies along her throat": such stuff
Was courtesy, she thought, and cause enough   20
For calling up that spot of joy. She had
A heart — how shall I say? — too soon made glad,
Too easily impressed; she liked whate'er
She looked on, and her looks went everywhere.
Sir, 'twas all one! My favour at her breast,   25
The dropping of the daylight in the West,
The bough of cherries some officious fool
Broke in the orchard for her, the white mule
She rode with round the terrace — all and each
Would draw from her alike the approving speech,   30

Or blush, at least. She thanked men, — good! but thanked
Somehow — I know not how — as if she ranked
My gift of a nine-hundred-years-old name
With anybody's gift. Who'd stoop to blame
This sort of trifling? Even had you skill   35
In speech — (which I have not) — to make your will
Quite clear to such an one, and say, "Just this
"Or that in you disgusts me; here you miss
"Or there exceed the mark" — and if she let
Herself be lessoned so, nor plainly set   40
Her wits to yours, forsooth, and made excuse,
— E'en then would be some stooping; and I choose
Never to stoop. Oh sir, she smiled, no doubt,
Whene'er I passed her; but who passed without
Much the same smile? This grew; I gave commands;   45
Then all smiles stopped together. There she stands
As if alive. Will 't please you rise? We'll meet
The company below, then. I repeat,
The Count your master's known munificence
Is ample warrant that no just pretence   50
Of mine for dowry will be disallowed;
Though his fair daughter's self, as I avowed
At starting, is my object. Nay, we'll go
Together down, sir. Notice Neptune, though,
Taming a sea-horse, thought a rarity,   55
Which Claus of Innsbruck cast in bronze for me!

    The implied story is as follows: The speaker is a duke, probably
the Duke of Ferrara — the name at the head of the poem may identify
the setting (a city in Italy), or the speaker, or both; it seems logical,
if not wholly necessary, to infer that the speaker is the Duke of Ferrara. The person to whom he is speaking is a stranger (l. 7), and as
we learn much later (l. 49) the minion of a count; he has come to
Ferrara to arrange a wedding between the Duke and the Count's
daughter (ll. 49–53). The Duke and his companion are about to go
downstairs to meet with others. Before going down, the Duke draws
aside a curtain and shows his companion a portrait of the former
Duchess (does "last" — rather than "late" — imply that there were
duchesses before her whose portrait is shown?) and tells the stranger

something about her. He then brings up the subject of dowry but makes no specific arrangements with the Count's ambassador. Throughout, the Duke implies a good deal more than he states, though precisely what and for what purpose, if any, we must infer.

The Duke is critical of his late wife. The Duchess did not fail to appreciate him — "she smiled, no doubt, / Whene'er I passed her" — but she appreciated everyone equally, almost as if she made no distinction between "others" and her husband — "She had / A heart — how shall I say? — too soon made glad, . . . she liked whate'er / She looked on, and her looks went everywhere"; "She thanked men, — good! but thanked / Somehow — I know not how — as if she ranked / My gift of a nine-hundred-years-old name / With anybody's gift." But what does the Duke's jealousy, if it may be called jealousy, imply? Is he consciously but delicately suggesting that his wife was unfaithful to him, bestowing her favors too generally? If so, he is not offering much evidence — Frà Pandolf's courtesy, cherry blossoms "some officious fool" brought her, unnamed gifts. Perhaps he is too proud to produce more scandalous details. But what of her appreciation of "The dropping of the daylight in the West" and the white mule? Surely these suggest that the source of his irritation was not necessarily suspicion of his wife's conduct but her failure to attend only him. What he is demanding is not merely marital fidelity but the total submission of his wife, total possession of her, even of her attention. If this demand is rather excessive — almost admittedly so in the Duke's apparent inability to express her faults ("how shall I say"; "I know not how") does it follow that he is therefore inadvertently telling the Count's representative more than he means to reveal? May he not be quite conscious of the implications of his story, even of its reflection on himself? What, indeed, is his motive in telling the minion anything at all of the former Duchess? To answer these and similar questions, we cannot merely conjecture on the basis of our attitudes toward and opinions of "human nature"; we must instead return to the details of the poem.

What happened to the Duchess? The Duke says that to have "lessoned" her about her too ready and general pleasure would have meant either arguments or apologies, and in either instance would have meant "stooping." And, he says, "I choose / Never to stoop." Is this merely pride compulsively asserting itself, or is he trying to tell the representative of the Count something?

Whether or not the Duke is trying to hide the flimsiness of his reasons for having been displeased with his last Duchess, he surely is not trying to hide his having caused her death: "I gave commands; / Then all smiles stopped together. There she stands / As if alive." There are those who would maintain that this does not necessarily imply that he had her murdered; certainly it does not *say* so. Others may maintain that it does not matter whether the Duchess was murdered or not: the Duke is implying a cause-and-effect relationship between his commands, the end of her smiling, and her no longer being alive. The implication is so bald the Duke can scarcely be unaware of it. Whether she was murdered or died of a broken heart (from lack of smiling), he effectively eliminated what displeased him without "stooping."

Though the chief disagreement as to what can safely be inferred from the Duke's story is likely at first to center on whether he in fact murdered her, this is not so important to the final reading of the poem as inference of his motive in telling the story of his last Duchess. Regardless of the exact nature of his responsibility for her death, why is he telling the ambassador of his future father-in-law such a story in the very act of arranging his next marriage? Many readers would claim that the Duke has no motive. He is so proud he is blind to — or contemptuous of — his listener's ability to infer the facts and to interpret those facts in a way unfavorable to the Duke from the Duke's own version of the story. Some might even claim that, since "murder will out," the evil man is inevitably tripped up by his own guilt or his compulsion to brag about his evil. In either case the poem is held to be an unconscious self-portrait by this intensely proud and possessive Italian Renaissance nobleman (who is, perhaps, an example of that era of Michelangelo, Machiavelli, and the Medici, when intense appreciation of art and learning went hand in hand with manipulation and murder).

That this is the nature of the poem is sometimes "demonstrated" by the final — and thus emphatic — detail of the Duke's calling his companion's attention to the fine bronze statue of Neptune. The juxtaposition of the story of the Duchess and the statue, both revealing the Duke's appreciation of beauty, his pride, and greedy possessiveness (note also the final word of the poem), may be held to confirm the central emphasis of the poem upon the Duke's unconscious self-revelation.

Granting the degree of self-revelation (and its possible relation to a reading of the Renaissance character), does it necessarily follow that the Duke is too contemptuously proud to be aware of these implications? We must look even more closely at the details.

The story of the Duchess and the pointing out of the bronze Neptune are not actually juxtaposed: there intervene the lines about the Count's daughter and the dowry. This juxtaposition of the Duchess and the arrangements for the new marriage suggests the possibility that the Duke is not merely engaging in proud and blind boastfulness but is making his marriage terms clear. From the story of the last Duchess the Count will now know what is expected: substantial dowry and complete submission of his daughter. This is consistent with the Duke's refusal to specify the dowry: not only does he refuse to discuss such a "sordid" detail, especially with a mere representative of the Count, but his story of the last Duchess clearly indicates how highly he values himself, his name, his rights. The Count will not now dare make a paltry offer of dowry. If it may be objected that no father would marry off his daughter on such terms, it must be remembered that the Duke is higher up the ladder of nobility than the Count: the Count cannot expect to climb without cost; the Duke is in a position to demand terms. To read the poem in this way seems on the whole more satisfying than to read it as merely an unconscious self-revelation: it is more consistent with the precise details and sequences of the poem (story-*dowry*-statue) and with the character, intelligence, and subtlety of the Duke. It explains, too, the poet's strategy in withholding the identity of the person spoken to for fifty lines: the Duke's apparently blind self-revelation becomes almost grotesque when we discover, so late in the poem, that he is speaking to a representative of the father of the girl he now plans to marry; as we gradually apprehend his motive in the revelation, we are both shocked by and convinced of his cold shrewdness — he is, as it were, magnified in evil. (To maintain that the self-revelation is unconscious not only diminishes the Duke but also the Count's minion: we must assume either that we are more perceptive than he or that he will recommend to the Count that he not give his daughter to the Duke.) None of the essential elements of the previous reading need be lost: the Duke's character remains but is, if anything, heightened; his function as a typical Italian Renaissance nobleman remains and is similarly heightened; the last lines not only remain consistent with his proud pos-

sessiveness but reveal also that he considers the discussion closed —
and his point clear.

Let us turn to a poem by Keats which is not quite so dependent
upon implication for scene, setting, or story as the Donne and Browning poems just discussed, but the full sense of which, like that of "My
Last Duchess," depends upon our inferences:

Ode to a Nightingale

My heart aches, and a drowsy numbness pains
    My sense, as though of hemlock I had drunk,
Or emptied some dull opiate to the drains
    One minute past, and Lethe-wards had sunk:
'Tis not through envy of thy happy lot,   5
    But being too happy in thine happiness, —
        That thou, light-wingèd Dryad of the trees,
           On some melodious plot
Of beechen green, and shadows numberless,
    Singest of summer in full-throated ease.   10

O for a draught of vintage! that hath been
    Cool'd a long age in the deep-delvèd earth,
Tasting of Flora and the country green,
    Dance, and Provençal song, and sunburnt mirth!
O for a beaker full of the warm South,   15
    Full of the true, the blushful Hippocrene,
        With beaded bubbles winking at the brim,
           And purple-stainèd mouth;
That I might drink, and leave the world unseen,
    And with thee fade away into the forest dim: 20

Fade far away, dissolve, and quite forget
    What thou among the leaves hast never known,
The weariness, the fever, and the fret
    Here, where men sit and hear each other groan;
Where palsy shakes a few, sad, last grey hairs,   25
    Where youth grows pale, and spectre-thin, and dies;
        Where but to think is to be full of sorrow

And leaden-eyed despairs;
   Where Beauty cannot keep her lustrous eyes,
      Or new Love pine at them beyond to-morrow.   30

Away! away! for I will fly to thee,
   Not charioted by Bacchus and his pards,
But on the viewless wings of Poesy,
   Though the dull brain perplexes and retards:
Already with thee! tender is the night,   35
   And haply the Queen-Moon is on her throne,
      Cluster'd around by all her starry Fays;
        But here there is no light,
   Save what from heaven is with the breezes blown
      Through verdurous glooms and winding mossy ways. 40

I cannot see what flowers are at my feet,
   Nor what soft incense hangs upon the boughs,
But, in embalmèd darkness, guess each sweet
   Wherewith the seasonable month endows
The grass, the thicket, and the fruit-tree wild;   45
   White hawthorn, and the pastoral eglantine;
      Fast-fading violets cover'd up in leaves;
        And mid-May's eldest child,
   The coming musk-rose, full of dewy wine,
      The murmurous haunt of flies on summer eves.   50

Darkling I listen; and, for many a time
   I have been half in love with easeful Death,
Call'd him soft names in many a musèd rhyme,
   To take into the air my quiet breath;
Now more than ever seems it rich to die,   55
   To cease upon the midnight with no pain,
      While thou art pouring forth thy soul abroad
        In such an ecstasy!
   Still wouldst thou sing, and I have ears in vain —
      To thy high requiem become a sod.   60

Thou wast not born for death, immortal Bird!
   No hungry generations tread thee down;
The voice I hear this passing night was heard
   In ancient days by emperor and clown:

Perhaps the self-same song that found a path   65
   Through the sad heart of Ruth, when, sick for home,
     She stood in tears amid the alien corn;
      The same that oft-times hath
   Charm'd magic casements, opening on the foam
     Of perilous seas, in faery lands forlorn.   70

Forlorn! the very word is like a bell
   To toll me back from thee to my sole self!
Adieu! the fancy cannot cheat so well
   As she is famed to do, deceiving elf.
Adieu! adieu! thy plaintive anthem fades   75
   Past the near meadows, over the still stream,
     Up the hill-side; and now 'tis buried deep
      In the next valley-glades:
   Was it a vision, or a waking dream?
     Fled is that music: — Do I wake or sleep?   80

The implied situation of the speaker is quite evident from the long-ing in the second stanza; the bleak description of "The weariness, the fever, and the fret / Here . . ." and the other details of the third stanza; the confession by the speaker in lines 51–2 that "many a time / I have been half in love with easeful Death, . . ."; and the fact that it is the word "forlorn" that calls him back to his everyday self. He is, to put it mildly, unhappy. The details are so numerous and specific that generalization seems scarcely inference.

    A little less obvious perhaps is the implied action in the poem. There are two means by which the speaker feels he can "fade away into the forest dim" with the nightingale: wine ("a draught of vintage"; "Bacchus") and imagination ("Poesy" in l. 33; "fancy" in l. 73). The speaker chooses the way of "Poesy," and the implication is that between lines 34 and 35 he successfully "fades" — or imagines himself as fading — into the forest ("Already with thee"). There are those who will say that this is not implication but statement, an elliptical sentence without the obvious subject and verb "I am." If so, it is an ellipsis not governed by the usual rules of the construction — there is no parallel sentence containing this subject and verb that controls the "filling in" of the structure. It is thus perhaps more accurate to consider it an implication rather than part of the statement of the poem. Whether statement or implication, "Already with thee" must indicate the speaker's presence in the "forest dim." Understanding this is essential for the reading of at least the next fifteen lines, which describe the speaker's imagined physical experience in the forest. In the sixth and seventh stanzas, until the word "forlorn" brings him back to his "sole self," the speaker is still in the forest with the nightingale; though, because these stanzas merely describe the thoughts and impressions the song of the nightingale gives rise to, their substance can be understood — if somewhat less correctly — independent of the "fading" into the forest implied in lines 34–5.

The implied situation is quite apparent. The implied action is somewhat less obvious. (It has been our experience that a number of readers, even those quite familiar with the poem, do not "see" that the speaker has imaginatively faded into the forest.) It can, however, be demonstrated conclusively in the poem. The experience described in the poem through statement and implication is thus clear, but what does it *mean*?

Interpretation of the meaning of the experience seems to hinge on how we read the two questions with which the poem ends: "Was it a vision, or a waking dream? . . . Do I wake or sleep?"

Many readers first infer that these questions are rhetorical. Ignoring the comma and failing to see any important distinction between "vision" and "waking dream," they answer "Yes": "Was it a vision-or-waking-dream?" "Yes, of course." Reading the second question as even more rhetorical (of course he is awake now), the answer is *wake*. Changing tense (the "real" question the speaker "means to ask" is, "*Did* I wake or sleep?" — in other words, did I have a waking dream or a sleeping dream?), the answer is *sleep*. In either case the answer is clear. Many readers are nonetheless disturbed, not only by the apparent contradiction of the two answers, neither of which seems conclusive, but also by the violence done to the poem in making "vision" and "waking dream" merely redundant or in "correcting" the tense without textual justification.

Some, after further readings of this poem or even of other poems of Keats, insist that both questions are real not rhetorical. They see that "vision" and "waking dream" are not synonymous: "vision," particularly in mystic experience, does not signify seeing something that is not real but seeing into the inner reality of experience, phenomena, life, or the universe. The speaker's question is, then, did I see into the inner reality or was I merely daydreaming? It then follows that the second question is also real and its present tense justified: Am I awake, apprehending the true reality now, or have I fallen from the mystical, imaginative experience of the true reality, back into that sleep we call "everyday reality" or "life"?

The latter reading is clearly the more adequate since it accounts for Keats's use of both "vision" and "waking dream" and for the present tense in the second question, but it brings with it its own dangers. Since the "common sense" notion of reality is questioned, some readers — particularly after partial readings of other Keats poems and generalizations about Romanticism — will assume that this "everyday reality" is denied outright. They will read the poem to *mean* that the imagined, mystically apprehended reality is the true reality, and everyday reality is merely superficial. But the poem is more cautious, more ambivalent than that. The speaker admits, for example, that he has been "*half* in love with easeful Death" and that now it *seems* more "rich to die"; he is brought back to his "sole *self*" (does "sole" mean "alone" or "only" or both?); he finds that "the fancy cannot cheat so well / As she is famed to do" (but note that this is almost turned into a conundrum by "deceiving elf"). The poem ends, after all, with a question, not with an affirmation of the meaning of the experience. In other words, the interpretation of the experience as a dream, a wish-fulfilling escape from reality, is left open as a possibility. It is not denied, it is merely balanced by an alternative possibility. The meaning of the poem exists in its description of a particular, but potentially universal, human experience and its questions as to the meaning of that experience. The first interpretation is not "wrong" but partial. It can be corrected but not contradicted by a fuller reading of the details, their contexts, the whole poem.

The following poem, by Thomas Hardy, is rather strikingly similar to that of Keats both in subject matter and resolution, and the very similarities, while reinforcing some of the principles and procedures of inference already discussed, force comparison and thus raise new issues.

The Darkling Thrush

I leant upon a coppice gate
When Frost was spectre-gray,

And Winter's dregs made desolate
    The weakening eye of day.
The tangled bine-stems scored the sky   5
    Like strings of broken lyres,
And all mankind that haunted nigh
    Had sought their household fires.

The land's sharp features seemed to be
    The Century's corpse outleant,   10
His crypt the cloudy canopy,
    The wind his death-lament.
The ancient pulse of germ and birth
    Was shrunken hard and dry,
And every spirit upon earth   15
    Seemed fervourless as I.

At once a voice arose among
    The bleak twigs overhead
In a full-hearted evensong
    Of joy illimited;   20
An aged thrush, frail, gaunt, and small,
    In blast-beruffled plume,
Had chosen thus to fling his soul
    Upon the growing gloom.

So little cause for carolings   25
    Of such ecstatic sound
Was written on terrestrial things
    Afar or nigh around,
That I could think there trembled through
    His happy good-night air   30
Some blessed Hope, whereof he knew
    And I was unaware.

December 1900.

* l. 1 *coppice gate:* a gate leading to a coppice, or small grove of trees
l. 5 *bine-stems:* the stems of creeping plants or vines
    scored: "scratched" or "made lines across" and, perhaps, given the many references to music in the poem, "arranged as a musical composition"
l. 10 *outleant:* "outleaned," "outlined" (?); "stretched out"; these are possible literal meanings, but there would seem to be additional connotations in this unusual word. See note on the date.

The similarity of this poem and the Keats ode is evident: the world to both speakers is gloomy; the joyous song of a bird seems to offer some promise of possible relief from that gloom. Not quite so apparent is the similar irresolution with which the poems close. Keats left us with questions; Hardy leaves us with doubt.

Many readers find the Hardy poem optimistic; to them the song of the thrush overcomes the gloom of the environment, revealing to the speaker that no matter how bad things look there is reason for hope. A closer look at the last sentence of the poem reveals, however, that the speaker says merely that he "*could* think" the thrush knew of some reason for hope of which he was unaware; not, be it noted, that he *did* think so, much less that now he *knew* there was reason for hope. Other readers find the poem crushingly pessimistic, almost a grim joke on the silly bird. The bleak detail of "terrestrial things," including the thrush's own bedraggled physical appearance, so overwhelms the unsubstantial song and the unsubstantiated hope that it seems to these readers that the thrush is, as it were, whistling in the dark. In fact, this poem, like "Ode to a Nightingale," exists in the balance of these forces. All the material evidence points to gloom; the song holds out hope. Hardy remains, with the final word of his poem, "unaware," but he does not deny the experience of the song. Indeed, the poem almost defines hope: the spiritual or emotional belief that all will be well *despite* appearances. Like Keats, Hardy defines the alternatives; in neither poem (whatever may be true in other works by the same authors) is the final choice made as to which alternative is "right." Intellectually, Hardy's poem is weighted toward the lack of evidence of any basis for hope; emotionally, it is weighted toward the beauty and persistence of hope. Keats also balances his brief emotional experience against a background of continuing awareness of human suffering, and then ends with the dazed aftermath of the experience, questioning which is reality.

These similarities may serve to blur certain real differences in the

---

l. 13 *germ:* "germination," "seed"; the line may be paraphrased, "The age-old cycle of the sprouting of plants and the birth of animals . . ."

l. 19 *evensong:* "evening song," but specifically, in the Church of England, "Evening Prayer"

the date: this is the end of the nineteenth century (the twentieth century begins not with 1900 but 1901, there being no year 0). This should clarify the reference to the Century's corpse in l. 10 and intensify the "deadness" of the scene — winter, the end of the year, the end of the century.

two poems. This is a danger inherent in all comparison, especially when such comparison involves abstraction or generalization that moves away from the specific details being compared. Since any paraphrase or summary of the sense of a poem almost inevitably involves abstracting, it is particularly susceptible to such distortion. Here, for example, one might read both poems as questioning the nature of reality and opposing to everyday reality spiritual (or imaginative) truth. But let us look at some of the dissimilarities between the two poems.

The world that confronts the speaker in the Hardy poem seems even darker than the fever and fret of human life described by Keats, for here, at the end of a century, the whole cycle of life-death-birth seems to have ended. Though Hardy's view is more sweepingly pessimistic, it is in many ways less formidable. Keats, though describing only the trials and defects of human life, treats them as particularized, inevitable, and real evils. Hardy deals not with actual human evils but with a barren scene being looked at in a listless mood; the speaker and the scene are only figurative and hypothetical comments on life. Keats deals with experience, Hardy with mood. Keats's view is tragic, Hardy's pessimistic. Hardy's speaker may change mood when the sun comes out; Keats's speaker may be gay tomorrow but life will still be full of fever and fret, the old will weaken, the young grow old or sicken, beauty will fade, and all will die.

Hardy's concentration upon mood rather than upon experiential fact also weakens the role of the bird. The nightingale is literally out of this world in the Keats poem; its song offers an alternative to the world of fever and fret — a region of immortality, beauty and joy — the realm of the imagination. The thrush offers the possibility of vague hope — either of better days on earth (spring will come again), suggested by singing joyously despite the wintry scene; or of a better other world (heaven, suggested by the quasi-religious imagery surrounding the bird — evensong, carolings, the capitalization of "Hope"). The nightingale offers or seems to offer a *reality* different from ours while the thrush offers or seems to offer a *mood* different from ours.

Noteworthy, too, is the difference in emphasis in the two poems. The Keats ode from beginning to end concentrates upon the experience of the song of the nightingale, giving the speaker's view of everyday reality within his description of the experience. Hardy divides his poem more or less in half, the thrush, despite his prominent place in the title, entering the poem only after the first two stanzas. Keats concentrates upon the occasion, nature, and limitations of the imaginative experience — almost as if he could take the tragic view of human life for granted; Hardy concentrates upon the dark view of all life (even after the thrush appears a good deal of space is devoted to describing its bedraggled appearance) — almost as if he needed to convince his audience of the legitimacy of pessimism but could take the particulars of hope for granted.

Finally, and perhaps most important, the poems ask different questions. "The Darkling Thrush," in effect, asks, "Is there any reason for hope?" "Ode to a Nightingale" asks, "What is the nature of reality?" It may be argued that ultimately Hardy too is questioning the nature of reality, and in terms quite similar to those of Keats. The quasi-religious imagery set against the "terrestrial things" suggests an opposition of spiritual and material "truth" comparable to the opposition of imaginative and physical reality in Keats. But the nature of reality is at the center of the Keats poem and is only an extrapolation of the Hardy poem. If Hope is described in immaterial terms, so too is the gloomy opening scene — the "Frost" (why capitalized if not in opposition to "Hope") is "*spectre*-gray"; the men have gone home who "*haunted* nigh"; every "*spirit* upon earth" seems as lacking in enthusiasm as the speaker. The expression of spirit, song, also appears in the opening stanzas (despite the "broken lyres") in the "death lament" of the wind. "Ode to a Nightingale" is about the nature of things. Imagination in that poem is either a faculty that permits man to see into the inner or higher reality, or it is an escapist dream. The Hardy poem centers on the immaterial on both sides of the fence: the disconsolate, pessimistic spirit as opposed to the joyous, optimistic spirit. It is about how we should think or feel about things.

The area beyond the page on which a poem appears is a shadowy but real realm. Given the inherent indirectness of human discourse, it is at times impossible to find the *sense* beyond the *statement* without going beyond the words themselves. Nevertheless, the words and context are there as a check against irresponsible wandering from the statement. Even the mere recognition of dealing with implication rather than statement is a useful safeguard against senseless argument or wild speculation. When the reader goes beyond that first cautious step off the edge of the page and attempts, as he eventually must, to abstract and paraphrase the generalized import, or *meaning,* of a poem, he must be even more cautious. The safeguard, once again, is knowing what he is doing, knowing that he is in fact departing from the statement and the page, and, in putting the particulars of the poem into a generalized statement in his own words, that he is inevitably distorting. Even in this rarified atmosphere of interpretation, he must keep in constant touch with the details of the poem. He must take into account the full statement, the clear implications, the sequences, and the context. And he must recognize that this "interpretation" is not the poem itself, for the final meaning of the poem exists in itself, its unique selection and arrangement of words and details. Interpretation, then, no matter how necessary, is several steps beyond the poem: there is the poem; the reordered version (including definitions) which renders its statement, or lowest-common-denominator of meaning, into prose; the paraphrase, or the rendering into the words of the reader the statements and implications of the poem; and the interpretation, or the summary of the paraphrase in relatively abstract and general terms. The interpretive statement is no more the poem (or even "the point" of the poem) than a map is a photograph — but, like a map, it can be a useful and even necessary aid to understanding.

VOICE

Reading "The Flea" or "My Last Duchess," we had to construct by inference what amounted to a little play, complete with speaker, person spoken to, setting, and even action. Precisely because of their resemblance to miniature plays, in which the story or events are taking place in the "now" of the poem, such poems are called *dramatic.* They imply a speaking voice of one involved in the present action of the poem. The seduction or argument of "The Flea" is taking place in the present of the poem — indeed, as we mentioned, between the very lines; though the actions of the Duchess and her death took place in the past of the poem, the conversation or monologue of the Duke takes place in the present of the poem and he is speaking, pointing out a picture and a statue "now." It is through the voices of the lover and the Duke that we receive the two poems.

When a poem tells a story by describing the characters and actions rather than by having the people and events act themselves out, it is called *narrative*. The voice of the poem is that of the narrator or story-teller and the action is in the past of the poem, as can be seen, for example, in these opening lines from Matthew Arnold's "Sohrab and Rustum":

> And the first grey of morning fill'd the east,
> And the fog rose out of the Oxus stream.
> But all the Tartar camp along the stream
> Was hush'd, and still the men were plunged in sleep;
> Sohrab alone, he slept not; all night long   5
> He had lain wakeful, tossing on his bed;
> But when the grey dawn stole into his tent,
> He rose, and clad himself, and girt his sword,
> And took his horseman's cloak, and left his tent,
> And went abroad into the cold wet fog,   10
> Through the dim camp to Peran-Wisa's tent.

The story-teller need not use the third person but the action he describes, even if described in the first person, has taken place in the past. The narrator in prose fiction is generally presented as a writer; in poetry he is most frequently a speaker or even singer. There are speakers or tale-tellers in prose, like Marlowe who tells the whole of *The Heart of Darkness* and appears in others of Conrad's tales, and Henry James's Douglas who "reads aloud" *The Turn of the Screw*, but most prose narrative assumes the written word and therefore a reader: Samuel Richardson's Pamela writes quantities of long letters; we were addressed for more than a century as "gentle reader"; and even when a character seems to be addressing us from the page of a novel, he often assumes the written word. Dowell, for example, in Ford Madox Ford's *The Good Soldier,* despite the conversational tone of the prose and structure of the story, is aware of himself as a writer-narrator: "From here, at this moment, I am actually writing. You may well ask why I write. . . ." There are poetic as well as prose epistles, but even they, like other poetic narratives, seem to assume the spoken word, as does Pope's "Epistle to Dr. Arbuthnot," for example: it begins thus, "*P.* Shut, shut the door, good John! fatigu'd, I said," and proceeds in dialogue form. There are many narrative poems that do not specifically imply a mode of discourse, written or spoken, and there are no doubt a few that state or imply the written word, but the vast majority assume a story-teller or speaker.

Indeed, the convention persists that poems are songs and poets are singers. Narrowly defined, songs intended literally or conventionally to be sung are called *lyric,* but the line between these and the dramatic and narrative is shadowy indeed. Not only are there story-songs like the ballad but even long narratives like the epic assume the conventional pose of song. The most famous epic in the language, for example, begins:

> Of Mans First Disobedience, and the Fruit
> Of that Forbidd'n Tree, whose mortal tast
> Brought Death into the World, and all our woe,
> With loss of *Eden,* till one greater Man
> Restore us, and regain the blissful Seat,
> Sing Heav'nly Muse . . .

> . . . I . . .
> Invoke thy aid to my adventrous Song,

No one seriously imagines Milton singing the thousands and thousands of blank verse lines of *Paradise Lost* to even the most patient of audiences, but the convention is ancient and persistent. It begins no doubt with the assumption that the Homeric epics were sung. The Latin poets, imitating the Greek, pretended they too were writing songs (see, for example, the opening of the *Aeneid* quoted in the first chapter). Poets in the emerging modern European languages imitated the classics; most English epics begin with pleas to the muse to "sing" or with announcements of the subject which, the poet says, "I sing." From Virgil to Pope in his mock-epic *The Dunciad,* the convention wavers or incorporates "singing" with "telling" or "saying"; thus Pope begins:

> The Mighty Mother, and her Son who brings
> The Smithfield Muses to the ear of Kings,
> I sing. Say you, her instruments the Great!
> Call'd to this work by Dulness, Jove, and Fate;
> You by whose care, in vain decry'd and curst,
> Still Dunce the second reigns like Dunce the first;

> Say, how the Goddess bade Britannia sleep,
> And pour'd her Spirit o'er the land and deep.*

The epic is perhaps as far as one can get from poetry as song; that the convention of song persists even in that genre is indicative of the strength of the lyric tradition. A good many lyric poems are literally songs, having been written for or set to music: Ben Jonson's "Song to Celia" ("Drink to me only with thine eyes"), for example, or Robert Burns's "Auld Lang Syne." The words to most songs are poems — often bad ones — and almost any poem in regular meters can be set to music, but relatively few songs nowadays are written as serious poems as well, and, though less uncommon, few poems are written to be set to music. Perhaps the most accomplished poet-musician in English is Thomas Campion. His books of "airs" are more literally songs than many poems called songs. One of his loveliest, which uses music as its subject matter as well as in its form, is the following:

> Rose-cheekt Laura, come,
> Sing thou smoothly with thy beautie's
> Silent musick, either other
>   Sweetly gracing.
>
> Lovely formes do flowe   5
> From concent divinely framèd;
> Heav'n is musick, and thy beautie's
>   Birth is heavenly.
>
> These dull notes we sing
> Discords need for helps to grace them;   10
> Only beauty purely loving
>   Knows no discord,
>
> But still moves delight
> Like cleare springs renu'd by flowing,

---

*l. 1 . . . *Mother* . . . *Son:* The Goddess of Dulness, whose son, Pope says, is Colley Cibber (1671–1757), Poet Laureate after 1730 and substitute for the original Prince of Dulness, Lewis Theobald (1688–1744) in the 1728 version of *The Dunciad.*

l. 2 *Smithfield:* Pope's own note reads, in part: "the place where Bartholomew Fair was kept, whose shows, machines, and dramatical entertainments, formerly agreeable only to the taste of the Rabble, were, by the Hero of this poem and others of equal genius, brought to the Theatres of Covent-garden, Lincolns-inn-fields, and the Haymarket, to be the reigning pleasures of the Court and Town."

> Ever perfet, ever in them-   15
> selves eternall. *

Such titles as "song," "hymn," "ballad," and "ode" indicate the musical origins and enduring convention in lyric poetry, but, as we have
seen, these far from exhaust the traditional mask of the poet as singer.

The convention of poem as song may be seen as implication in reverse: here the poem may *state* that the poet is singing but we know,
especially in such cases as *Paradise Lost,* that he does not "really mean
it"; we read "sing" and "song," then, to imply less than they state.
On the other hand, the image of the speaker or singer as a character
or presence is frequently implied by the slightest of indications, at
times indeed only assumed.

Speaker or singer, that which transmits the poem to us is almost
always an implied *voice.* In a novel, even without textual indications,
we infer a writer and see ourselves reading; so strong is the oral convention in poetry that, in the absence of contrary indications, we infer
a voice and, though we know we are reading words on a page, create
for and of ourselves an imaginary listener. In effect, we *read* a novel
but *hear* a poem. The greater role of sounds of words and meter in
poetry is obvious confirmation of this oral convention.

We might at this point, however, recognize that interesting if
eccentric tradition of poems written for the eye. In the poem that follows, for example, from Francis Quarles's *Hieroglyphics of the Life
of Man,* not only is the stanza form reinforced by the pyramidal appearance of the stanza on the page, but the italicized first lines of each
stanza themselves compose a shorter poem on the theme of the longer:

> *He cometh forth like a flower, and is cut down*
> *Job xiv. 2*
> *Behold*
> How short a span
> Was long enough, of old,
> To measure out the life of Man!
> In those wel-temper'd days his time was then   5
> Survey'd, cast up, and found but threescore years and ten.

---

* l. 6 *concent:* harmony

l. 10 *Discords* and *grace:* here used in the musical as well as the more general sense;
the sense is that irregular or disharmonic or imperfect notes are needed in music to
break up the perfect harmony to prevent monotony and add beauty. (Laura's) Beauty

Alas,
And what is that?
They come and slide and pass
Before my Pen can tell thee what.   10
The Posts of Time are swift, which having run
Their sev'n short stages o're, their short-liv'd task is don.

Our daies
Begun, wee lend
To sleepe, to antick plaies   15
And Toyes, until the first stage end:
12 waining Moons, twice 5 times told, we give
To unrecover'd loss: Wee rather breathe than live.

Wee spend
A ten years' breath   20
Before wee apprehend
What is to live, or feare a death:
Our childish dreams are fil'd with painted joys,
Which please our sense a while, and waking, prove but Toies.

How vaine,   25
How wretched is
Poore man, that doth remain
A slave to such a State as this!
His daies are short, at longest; few, at most;
They are but bad, at best; yet lavisht out, or lost.   30

They bee
The secret Springs
That make our minits flee
On wheels more swift than Eagles' wings;
Our life's a Clocke, and every gaspe of breath   35
Breathes forth a warning grief, til Time shall strike a death.

How soone
Our new-born Light
Attaines to full-ag'd noone!
And this, how soon to gray-hayr'd night!   40
Wee spring, we bud, we blossome, and we blast
Ere we can count our daies; Our daies they flee so fast.

needs no such imperfections to grace it and is therefore the more perfect, more nearly
divine, and thus eternal.

> *They end*
> When scarce begun;
> And ere wee apprehend 45
> That we begin to live, our life is don!
> Man, Count thy daies; and if they flee too fast
> For thy dull thoughts to count, count ev'rie day thy last.

The ear can hear the rhythm and rhyme and might thereby get some indication of stanza form even without the shape on the page, but it seems most unlikely that one could hear the poem-within-a-poem created by the short first lines.

The seventeenth century was relatively rich in such visual experimentation. George Herbert, for example, wrote a number of poems in which the shape echoed the subject. The following can be heard no doubt as rhyming pairs of varying length but only visually can the form reflect the subject:

The Altar

A broken *Altar,* Lord, thy servant reares,
Made of a heart, and cemented with teares;
Whose parts are as thy hand did frame;
No workman's tool hath touch'd the same.
A *Heart* alone 5
Is such a stone,
As nothing but
Thy pow'r doth cut.
Wherefore each part
Of my hard heart 10
Meets in this frame,
To praise thy name.
That if I chance to hold my peace,
These stones to praise thee may not cease.
O let thy blessed *Sacrifice* be mine, 15
And sanctifie this *Altar* to be thine.

A more common and somewhat less elaborate form of "eye-poem" is the *acrostic* which bears some relation to the poem-within-a-poem device in the Quarles "hieroglyphic." In the basic form of the acrostic the initial letters of the lines form a word that relates to, amplifies, or otherwise adds to the lines themselves. Thus the name of the famous British composer Purcell is spelled out by the initial letters of these seven musical lines from Robert Bridges' *Eros and Psyche:*

P athetic strains and passionate they wove,
U rgent in ecstasies of heavenly sense;
R esponsive rivalries, that, while they strove
C ombined in full harmonious suspense,
E ntrancing wild desire, then fell at last
L ull'd in soft closes, and with gay contrast
L aunch'd forth their fresh unwearied excellence.

There are other forms of acrostic in which last letters, middle letters, letters on a diagonal through the lines, or some combination of these designs, spell names or words. There are other visual designs and forms, from those found in the illustrated manuscripts of monks to those in modern children's verse. Visual poetry predates printing; its origin lies well back in antiquity. Nevertheless, it forms only a very small portion of the total body of poetry and certainly lies far from the center of the main tradition, which is the largely auditory tradition of Western poetry.

Even these poems, written for the page and the eye, assume, if not actual reading aloud, at least a sounding on the inner ear; they are metrical, rhymed, and full of such sound devices as alliteration. Typical perhaps of the virtually unconscious insistence of the oral-aural tradition is the line in the Quarles poem which is most self-consciously written but into which the notion of voice metaphorically intrudes: "Before my *Pen* can *tell* thee what."

For most poems, then, even though we are reading rather than listening, we can assume a voice. We must try to infer as accurately and as fully as possible the nature and identity of this voice, for, as we shall see, it is one of the chief elements of context that can help qualify or augment the meanings of the individual words and structures of the poem. It is well to register how explicitly the voice is incorporated into the poem, whether the voice is that of speaker or singer, where he is in relation to the poem and to the reader, whether he is an identifiable character or person, and indeed anything else that might prove of value in the fuller understanding and visualizing of the poem.

We might here examine the most common and troublesome of identities, the "I" who appears in so many poems. It seems quite natural initially to assume that the "I" of a poem is the poet. Often, especially in dramatic poems, however, it soon becomes clear that the "I" is not the poet but a character who is assumed to be speaking the lines, like the Duke in "My Last Duchess." Most such poems offer enough evidence for the proper identification of the speaker so that we are not likely to confuse the character with the poet for very long. It has become common in recent years to suggest that all poetry is dramatic and that the "I" in a poem should never be identified as the poet. Though such an assumption is at times a useful antidote and may prevent some misuse of skimpy biographical materials and avoid the naïve treatment of poems as if they were primarily biographical documents, it can lead to abuses of its own. Surely the Milton sonnet which is traditionally entitled "On His Blindness" (but not so called by Milton) is at least initially about a blind poet who bears a striking resemblance to John Milton. Indeed, there is nothing in the sonnet itself that explicitly names the affliction as blindness — "my light is spent," "dark world," "Talent . . . Lodg'd with me useless," "light deny'd," can, ignoring what we know of Milton, be read with more or less ingenuity as imprisonment, ignorance, excommunication, or some other deprivation. It would, of course, be ridiculous to do so; not only is there no need to deny ourselves this knowledge but it is as culpable a restriction as our ignoring of any other allusion. Little is to be gained by ignoring the factual references to Oldham, his poetry, and his relation to Dryden in the following elegy:

To the Memory of Mr. Oldham

> Farewel, too little and too lately known,
> Whom I began to think and call my own;
> For sure our Souls were near ally'd; and thine
> Cast in the same Poetick mould with mine.
> One common Note on either Lyre did strike,   5
> And Knaves and Fools we both abhorr'd alike:

To the same Goal did both our Studies drive,
The last set out the soonest did arrive.
Thus *Nisus* fell upon the slippery place,
Whilst his young Friend perform'd and won the Race.   10
O early ripe! to thy abundant store
What could advancing Age have added more?
It might (what Nature never gives the young)
Have taught the numbers of thy native Tongue.
But Satyr needs not those, and Wit will shine   15
Through the harsh Cadence of a rugged line.
A noble Error, and but seldom made,
When Poets are by too much force betray'd.
Thy generous fruits, though gather'd ere their prime
Still shew'd a quickness; and maturing time   20
But mellows what we write to the dull Sweets of Rime.
Once more, hail and farewel; farewel thou young,
But ah too short, *Marcellus* of our Tongue;
Thy Brows with Ivy, and with Laurels bound;
But Fate and gloomy Night encompass thee around.*   25

The name "Oldham" is certainly no less relevant to the full understanding of the poems than are those of "Nisus" and "Marcellus."
His early success, harsh cadence, satiric wit, and relation to Dryden
are certainly no less relevant than the stories of Nisus and Marcellus
in the *Aeneid*. Perhaps, indeed, it is best to describe the relevance of
biographical detail to such a poem precisely as a form of allusion: like
historical or literary allusion it is ignored at our peril but it is capable of overemphasis, distortion, and misuse.

* *Oldham:* John Oldham, 1653–83, was 22 years younger than Dryden, but became well known early, in 1679, with *Satyrs Upon the Jesuits*.
   ll. 9–10: See Virgil's *Aeneid*, v:328. In a race before Aeneas, Nisus slips in ox blood
but helps his young friend Euryalus win by tripping another opponent. In Dryden's
translation the relevant portion of the story appears in ll. 426–43. See also v:295f
(Dryden translation, v:386–8): "*Eurylus* a Boy of blooming years; / With sprightly
Grace, and equal Beauty crown'd: / *Nisus*, for friendship to the Youth, renown'd."
   ll. 22–5: See *Aeneid*, vi:854–86 (Dryden, vi:1190–1225). The younger Marcellus
gives promise of outstripping the elder but dies at an early age — Virgil himself is told
by Anchises, "Ah, cou'dst thou break through Fates severe Decree, / A new *Marcellus*
shall arise in thee!"

Most poems with first-person voices are neither clearly dramatic nor incontrovertibly autobiographical. Often, as in "Poore soule," "Stopping by Woods on a Snowy Evening," or even in poems dealing with love or desire such as "The Flea," the first-person voice is not so much an individual as "man" or "a man." Without considerable evidence to go on and clearly established relevancy to the poem it may be better not to call the "I" the poet or Shakespeare, Frost, or Donne. These may or may not be "real" experiences or even "real" — especially in the sense of "permanent" — attitudes. It seems best to be alert for those cases in which the poem is demonstrably a dramatic utterance or a bit of autobiography but, until either is shown to be the case, to consider the voice to be that of a *persona,* a surrogate of the poet but neither himself in the full literal sense nor someone else.

Most of the poems quoted to this point have been first-person utterances. So predominant is this tradition, as part of the general oral tradition of poetry, that many poems imply a first-person speaker though neither "I" nor any of the other forms of that pronoun appear in the poem. Such is the case in Hopkins' "Spring and Fall," and such is the case in the Matthew Arnold poem that follows:

Philomela

Hark! ah, the nightingale —
The tawny-throated!
Hark, from the moonlit cedar what a burst!
What triumph! hark! — what pain!

O wanderer from a Grecian shore,   5
Still, after many years, in distant lands,
Still nourishing in thy bewilder'd brain
That wild, unquench'd, deep-sunken, old-world pain —
Say, will it never heal?
And can this fragrant lawn   10
With its cool trees, and night,
And the sweet, tranquil Thames,
And moonshine, and the dew,
To thy rack'd heart and brain
Afford no balm?   15

Dost thou to-night behold,
Here, through the moonlight on this English grass,
The unfriendly palace in the Thracian wild?
Dost thou again peruse
With hot cheeks and seared eyes   20
The too clear web, and thy dumb sister's shame?
Dost thou once more assay
Thy flight, and feel come over thee,
Poor fugitive, the feathery change
Once more, and once more seem to make resound   25
With love and hate, triumph and agony,
Lone Daulis, and the high Cephissian vale?
Listen, Eugenia —
How thick the bursts come crowding through the leaves!
Again — thou hearest?   30
Eternal passion!
Eternal pain! *

Nowhere in the poem does the voice refer to itself or to speaking or
singing rather than writing this poem. Nonetheless, from the very
first word, the imperative "Hark!," a first-person voice is implied.
This is further emphasized by the exclamations, and, beginning in
the second verse-paragraph, the questions. The poem is dramatic, one
side as it were of a conversation, exactly like "The Flea" in this
regard except for the absence of "I." Here, indeed, the conversational
or spoken nature of the poem is heightened by the irregular length of
line, the frequent run-on lines (lines in which the end-pause is held
to a minimum by the fact that the sense is incomplete) and the absence of regular rhyme.

The speaker in this poem first addresses a person, then the nightingale, then the person once again; we must properly infer these auditors

* *Philomela:* the nightingale. There are several versions of this myth. In the one
Arnold apparently used, Philomela's husband, Tereus, king of Thrace, raped Philomela's sister, Procne, then cut out her tongue to prevent her revealing the fact. She
wove the story into a piece of embroidery and gave it to Philomela, who revenged
herself by serving Tereus a dish in which one of the ingredients was his own son. When
he discovered the horrible truth, he chased and nearly caught the fleeing Procne and
Philomela. A pitying god changed them into birds. Philomela, according to this version,
became the nightingale, and Procne the swallow.

l. 27 *Daulis, Cephissian vale:* Thracian place names

to understand the statements of the poem, and we may be surprised how much of the sense of the whole poem depends upon our inferences concerning these auditors. In Bridges' "Nightingales," the shift from "I" in the first stanza to "our" in the second indicated a change in speakers for the two stanzas, from the persona of the poet to the dramatic character of the nightingales; in "The Flea" part of the inference necessary to construct the drama involved the identification of "thou"; in "My Last Duchess" the delayed identification of the person addressed heightens the enormity of the Duke's revelations. In "Philomela" the "thou" of lines 5–27 is clearly the nightingale, "wanderer from a Grecian shore," but it is just as clearly not the nightingale who is addressed in the first four lines and urged to listen. This person, also addressed as "thou" (l. 30), is rather abruptly and mysteriously called "Eugenia" in line 28. To our knowledge, Eugenia has never been identified nor her presence by name explained. A name at this point is, of course, convenient since it makes the shift from the address to the nightingale back to the auditor of the first four lines apparent. But why are the last five lines not, like the first four, set off in a verse-paragraph of their own? And why "Eugenia"? When the poem was first published Eugenie had very recently become Empress of France, but this would seem to have little relevance. The name is of Greek derivation, as the nightingale itself is here said to be, but nothing is made of this in the poem. The name means "well born," which is perhaps another connection with the royal Philomela, though again nothing is made of this in the poem. Indeed, all but the first of these purposes could have been served as well by the use of another name, "Eugene"! Why not? Would not a male friend be equally impressed by the beauty of the song of the nightingale expressing eternal passion and eternal pain? (For some reason, no matter how we deny that the speaker can be identified with the poet, we assume he is a man; try to imagine a woman speaking these lines.) There is not one word in the poem that *states* the obvious, that this is to some degree a love poem. (Why can Eugenia not be the speaker's aunt or the neighbor's little girl?) It is in part the subject matter, the use of the second-person singular "thou" (though this does not, historically, eliminate the aunt or the little girl), the frequent exclamations, the setting (moonlight in the garden), the rather poetic or lofty diction (despite the loose, almost conversational nature of the verse form) — all of which together, though none separately, strongly imply that this is essentially a love poem. We have come quite a way "off the page"; that "Philomela" is more or less a love poem is not a "fact," not a close reading of its *statement,* but an inference about its *sense.*

VANTAGE POINT

In considering voice much of our concern has been to identify the speaker (writer or singer) as fully as possible: Is he identifiable as a dramatic character? as the poet? as a persona of the poet? Despite our concentration on the speaker, we had to inquire as well about the auditor and the possible effect of the identity of the auditor on the matter and manner of the speaker. Now we turn our attention to another aspect of voice, the position of the speaker with relation to the events or details of the poem. This position we shall call the *vantage point.**

Specifying vantage point can make a description comprehensible or credible. If someone were to tell you he saw the top of a card table as a parallelogram with pairs of angles of sixty and one hundred and twenty degress, you might not know whether to doubt him or your own understanding of the nature of card tables. If he told you the position from which he was viewing the table you might then understand that the distortion of the square was a matter of perspective and would then believe he was correctly reporting what he saw (and, perhaps, realize he was seeing more accurately and less conventionally than you were). So it is with the clarifying and convincing qualities of the vantage point in a poem.

Let us take, for example, two very similar poems, both written in the same period (early nineteenth century), both describing an admirable woman and describing her in terms of a balance of elements, and both moving from the physical to the moral beauty of the woman described. The first, by Lord Byron, is a lyric written for a Hebrew melody:

* We use this term rather than the more common *point of view* because it is narrower. Point of view involves the nature and identity of the speaker, his knowledge and opinions, and other matters that we find it more meaningful to discuss separately. We try to limit *vantage point* to the position of the speaker in relation to the material and the consequent implications thereof.

I

She walks in beauty, like the night
    Of cloudless climes and starry skies;
And all that's best of dark and bright
    Meet in her aspect and her eyes:
Thus mellow'd to that tender light   5
    Which heaven to gaudy day denies.

II

One shade the more, one ray the less,
    Had half impair'd the nameless grace
Which waves in every raven tress,
    Or softly lightens o'er her face;   10
Where thoughts serenely sweet express
    How pure, how dear their dwelling-place.

III

And on that cheek, and o'er that brow,
    So soft, so calm, yet eloquent,
The smiles that win, the tints that glow,   15
    But tell of days in goodness spent,
A mind at peace with all below,
    A heart whose love is innocent.

The second is one of William Wordsworth's "Poems of the Imagination":

She was a Phantom of delight
When first she gleamed upon my sight;
A lovely Apparition, sent
To be a moment's ornament;
Her eyes as stars of Twilight fair;   5
Like Twilight's too, her dusky hair;
But all things else about her drawn
From May-time and the cheerful Dawn;
A dancing Shape, an Image gay,
To haunt, to startle, and way-lay.   10

I saw her upon nearer view,
A spirit, yet a Woman too;

Her household motions light and free,
And steps of virgin-liberty;
A countenance in which did meet   15
Sweet records, promises as sweet;
A Creature not too bright or good
For human nature's daily food;
For transient sorrows, simple wiles,
Praise, blame, love, kisses, tears, and smiles.   20

And now I see with eye serene
The very pulse of the machine;
A Being breathing thoughtful breath,
A Traveller between life and death;
The reason firm, the temperate will,   25
Endurance, foresight, strength, and skill;
A perfect Woman, nobly planned,
To warn, to comfort, and command;
And yet a Spirit still, and bright
With something of angelic light.*   30

No speaker (or singer) is identified in the Byron poem. The description, as a result, appears objective, authoritative: her beauty is not just "one man's opinion." Though no speaker is identified, a location of sorts is implied — we see the lady only from the outside, and indeed from a distance. Though we are close enough to her to see her physical features, and even the light in her eyes, we are not close enough to touch her nor are we presented with her thoughts or feelings. There is no sense of closeness or intimacy or even of any long acquaintance. When, therefore, with line 11, the poem describes the lady's inner qualities, this close-but-not-intimate vantage point leads to difficulties. We are not told, dogmatically and authoritatively, that she is pure, good, innocent, as we are told that in every tress waves "nameless grace"; this would be to violate the external vantage point. We are told instead that her character can be ascertained from her appearance, a rather naïve and dubious proposition that may well run counter to our experience. It is as if we were told that the parallelogram of the card table had pairs of angles of fifty and one hundred

---

* l. 22 *machine:* here used in the archaic sense of "body," especially human body

degrees: the evidence does not add up to what we know or think we know axiomatically or experientially (about the number of degrees in the angles of a quadrangle; about telling wine by the barrel it is in, a book by its cover, etc.). Thus what the physical description gained in objectivity by the impersonal external vantage point, the moral description loses in authority by the limitations of that vantage point.

Wordsworth, on the other hand, sacrifices the immediate authority of the objectified view by using a first-person speaker. Since the implied relationship in the first stanza is as distant and brief as that in the Byron poem, his description has, if anything, even less authority. But the second stanza offers a "nearer view" and implies somewhat longer acquaintance ("household motions"); still, at least to line 16, and perhaps a few lines beyond, the moral qualities are described externally and in physical terms. In the third stanza, the dramatic "now" of the poem, she seems to be known very well indeed and her moral or spiritual qualities judged at close range over a protracted period of time. Though there is always possibility of error in one person's judgment of another, and we have no absolute authority for the lady's spiritual qualities, the speaker has gained authority and conviction by the intimate if limited vantage point.

Vantage point helps to define the limits of the material and the mode of its presentation. It can lend clarity or substance or conviction. It is one of the many conditioning factors of context within which implications contribute to the sense of the poem.

TONE

Voice and vantage point are elements in the definition of a larger and more elusive aspect of the whole poem, *tone,* a metaphor appropriately enough drawn from the area of music and sound, to express certain qualities of context.

In face-to-face conversation we have many devices other than words with which to indicate feelings or attitudes, to qualify statements, and even to create meanings. A look or movement can at times do away with the need for words; think, for example, of the range of nonverbal but expressive responses you might make to the question, "What kind of a time did you have last night?" Moreover, tone of voice, with or without gestures or facial expressions, can emphasize, limit, or even reverse the meanings of your words; think, for example, of the many ways you might say, "What do you think?"

Poets do not normally attach to their poems stage directions for reading, with illustrated facial expressions and gestures or with directions for tone of voice. In most poems, as in most written prose, the words and their meanings (including connotation), the syntactical structures, the selection of detail, and, especially in poetry, the rhythm establish within limits the proper delivery, reading, or *tone*. In most discourse, tone is virtually inseparable from these other elements. Even conversation, so subject to expression and gesture, necessarily depends upon these verbal elements for its full tone.

In the following pair of religious poems — the first by Ben Jonson, the second by Gerard Manley Hopkins — for example, tone is a *function* or by-product of sense.

To Heaven

Good, and great God, can I not thinke of thee,
   But it must, straight, my melancholy bee?
Is it interpreted in me disease,
   That, laden with my sinnes, I seeke for ease?
O, be thou witnesse, that the reynes dost know,   5
   And hearts of all, if I be sad for show,
And judge me after: if I dare pretend
   To ought but grace, or ayme at other end.
As thou art all, so be thou all to mee,
   First, midst, and last, converted one, and three;   10
My faith, my hope, my love: and in this state,
   My judge, my witnesse, and my advocate.
Where have I beene, this while exil'd from thee?
   And whither rap'd, now thou but stoup'st to mee?
Dwell, dwell here still: O, being every-where,   15
   How can I doubt to finde thee ever, here?
I know my state, both full of shame, and scorne,
   Conceiv'd in sinne, and unto labour borne,
Standing with feare, and must with horror fall,
   And destin'd unto judgement, after all.   20
I feele my griefes too, and there scarce is ground,

Upon my flesh t'inflict another wound.
Yet dare I not complaine, or wish for death
With holy *Paul,* lest it be thought the breath
Of discontent; or that these prayers bee 25
For wearinesse of life, not love of thee.*

This poem begins almost as if the speaker is frustrated by the complexity of the motivations or appearance of motivations for prayer. He swears to his sincerity (ll. 5–8 can virtually be paraphrased, "I'll be damned if I don't mean it"). Self-doubt borders on the doubt of God's presence (ll. 9–15), and humility, contrition itself, becomes a trap leading to self-destruction and back to the original question of motivation. The whole poem seems a deeply felt self-examination, attempting to define the proper spiritual balance — and tone: humble but not servile, seeking peace not comfort.

The Hopkins sonnet, called by its first editor "Carrion Comfort," similarly speaks of the temptations of despair leading to self-destruction, and of the struggle against despair leading to spiritual pride:

Not, I'll not, carrion comfort, Despair, not feast on thee;
Not untwist — slack they may be — these last strands of man
In me ór, most weary, cry *I can no more.* I can;
Can something, hope, wish day come, not choose not to be.
But ah, but O thou terrible, why wouldst thou rude on me 5
Thy wring-world right foot rock? lay a lionlimb against me? scan
With darksome devouring eyes my bruisèd bones? and fan,
O in turns of tempest, me heaped there; me frantic to avoid thee
and flee?

* l. 5 *reynes:* reins, kidneys, formerly thought to be the seat of feelings; compare this clause with Psalm 7:9: "Oh let the wickedness of the wicked come to an end; but establish the just: for the righteous God trieth the hearts and reins."

l. 10 *converted one, and three:* the reference is to the union of the Holy Trinity — Father, Son, and Holy Ghost — into one God; *converted* also describes the transposibility of subject and predicate of a proposition, so that the One (God) is Three and Three are One are equally valid, the three in one transposibility also applicable to "First, midst, and last," faith, hope, love, and judge, witness, advocate in ll. 11–12.

ll. 23–4 *wish for death / With holy* Paul: see, *e.g.,* Philippians 1:20–24, esp. 23: "For I am in a strait betwixt two, having a desire to depart, and to be with Christ; which is far better."

Why? That my chaff might fly; my grain lie, sheer and clear.
Nay in all that toil, that coil, since (seems) I kissed the rod,   10
Hand rather, my heart lo! lapped strength, stole joy, would laugh,
    chéer.
Cheer whom though? the hero whose heaven-handling flung me,
    fóot tród
Me? or me that fought him? O which one? is it each one? That
    night, that year
Of now done darkness I wretch lay wrestling with (my God!) my
    God.*

The tone here is clearly more intense — more personal, argumenta-
tive, exclamatory — than in the Jonson poem. This may be expressed
as essentially the difference between "dare I not complaine" and "I[,]
wretch[,] lay wrestling" or between "melancholy" and "Despair,"
carried throughout each poem by other elements. In "To Heaven,"
for example, the very couplet form, strictly observed (all couplets and
indeed most lines are stopped at the end with some form of punctuation), and the balance and antithesis of the line and sentence structure (for example, ll. 19 and 26) contribute to the air of precision, of
the making of fine distinctions even among intense emotions, of keen
self-examination. "Carrion Comfort," on the other hand, almost tears
the sonnet form apart with its variable line length; the frequent run-
on lines (ll. 2, 5, 6, 12, 13); heavy stopping, including ends of sentences,
within the line; not to mention the distorted, interrupted syntax,

---

* l. 1 *carrion comfort:* "comfort" is in apposition to "Despair"; "carrion" may be
either a noun or an adjective, indicating that Despair is both a comfort of dying flesh
and a comfort which itself feeds on death or the wish for death.

l. 2 *slack they may be:* slack [though] they may be

l. 4 *Can something:* Can [do] something; Hopkins is also, in this line and the
preceding, retaining the archaic sense of "can" — "know."

ll. 5–6 *why . . . rock?:* i.e., why would you rudely (roughly) rock on me your
right foot (with connotations of justice) that twists the world in pain (or, perhaps, the
foot that wrings worldliness out)?

ll. 10–11 *since . . . rather:* ever since, it seems, I accepted suffering, not imperson-
ally but from God's hand — perhaps more specifically, since accepting the authority
of the Church in kissing the bishop's hand (ring) in the ordination ceremony. In
Ezekiel 20:33–8 and such passages as Leviticus 27:32 and Micah 8:14, "rod" as "rule"
and even "makes suffer" and "hand" as "savior" or "protector" are virtually interchangeable.

repetition, parenthesis — all of this, of course, contributing to, or creating, the headlong, exclamatory tone.

In these instances tone is a concomitant part of the subject matter, detail, choice of words, sentence structure, meter, etc. We can speak of it as an aspect of the poem in itself but we cannot demonstrate its separate existence or its unique role in creating meaning. This is true of the tone of most discourse. There are occasions, however, in which it does seem to be a separate factor of meaning, and runs apart from or even counter to some or all of the other elements. Such separation can occur inadvertently in bad poetry, but it can also be an essential element in the sense or meaning of any discourse, qualifying, intensifying, or contradicting the apparent literal statement. Surely we understand something other than the literal statement of the following three sentences:

> If he shows up here, I'll die.
> Willie Mays is a pretty fair ballplayer.
> You're a fine one to talk.

We know the first statement is exaggerated; the speaker will not literally die. Such exaggeration is known as *overstatement* or *hyperbole*. We do not consider the second statement that of a madman or baseball ignoramus; we know the speaker means more than his words literally say. Such minimizing is known as *understatement* or *meiosis*. The third statement, we know, means not more or less than it says, but virtually the opposite. When it is as heavy-handed as this, it is known as *sarcasm,* but in general the reversal or serious qualification of a statement by tone is known as *irony.*

All of these terms assume a normative or "proper" response; that is, before we can say that something is overstated or understated we must have some conception of what constitutes the normal or right judgment (of Willie Mays as a ballplayer, for example). Such devices are most effective, therefore, when speaker and audience operate on common assumptions. Common assumptions derived from outside the poem are not essential, however: it is possible in a poem to use these devices and to show that the expected responses are not normative. Thus in Andrew Marvell's great love poem "To His Coy Mistress" the overstatement is identified in context as overstatement, primarily by the conditional or subjunctive mood — "Had we . . . would";

that very judgment itself, as we shall see, becomes evidence of the
speaker's common sense and sincerity and part of the effectiveness of
his argument, so that the device of overstatement is used to project a
tone of reasonableness:

To His Coy Mistress

Had we but World enough, and Time,
This coyness Lady were no crime.
We would sit down, and think which way
To walk, and pass our long Love's Day.
Thou by the *Indian Ganges'* side   5
Should'st Rubies find: I by the Tide
Of *Humber* would complain. I would
Love you ten years before the Flood:
And you should if you please refuse
Till the Conversion of the *Jews*.   10
My vegetable Love should grow
Vaster then Empires, and more slow.
An hundred years should go to praise
Thine Eyes, and on thy Forehead Gaze.
Two hundred to adore each Breast: 15
But thirty thousand to the rest.
An Age at least to every part,
And the last Age should show your Heart.
For Lady you deserve this State;
Nor would I love at lower rate.   20
      But at my back I alwaies hear
Time's wingèd Charriot hurrying near:
And yonder all before us lye
Desarts of vast Eternity.
Thy Beauty shall no more be found;   25
Nor, in thy marble Vault, shall sound
My ecchoing Song: then Worms shall try
That long preserv'd Virginity:
And your quaint Honour turn to dust;
And into ashes all my Lust.   30
The Grave's a fine and private place,
But none I think do there embrace.

> Now therefore, while the youthful hew
> Sits on thy skin like morning dew,
> And while thy willing Soul transpires   35
> At every pore with instant Fires,
> Now let us sport us while we may;
> And now, like am'rous birds of prey,
> Rather at once our Time devour,
> Than languish in his slow-chapt pow'r.   40
> Let us roll all our Strength, and all
> Our sweetness, up into one Ball:
> And tear our Pleasures with rough strife,
> Thorough the Iron gates of Life.
> Thus, though we cannot make our Sun   45
> Stand still, yet we will make him run.*

To make overstatements in the subjunctive mood — "Had we but . . ." — is to recognize them as overstatements and to imply that they are not true: "but we do not have World enough, and Time." Besides its force as argument, acknowledging the hyperbole establishes a tone of reasonableness or good sense. This tone does not, however, detract from the speaker's ardor as a lover: he wants to love her in this extravagant way and she deserves as much world and time as the overstatements describe. But the speaker is not a vegetable and has more than a merely vegetable soul: his sensitive soul, which man shares with animals but not with vegetables, makes him subject to

* Title: Neither *coy* nor *mistress* is used in its modern sense. The former meant both "quiet" and "disdainful" in the 17th century; the latter meant approximately "beloved."

l. 7 *Humber:* river in northern England which flows through Marvell's home town of Hull

l. 10 *Conversion of the Jews:* popularly assumed immediately to precede the Last Judgment

l. 11 *vegetable:* according to Renaissance faculty psychology, the lowest of the three souls (rational, sensitive, vegetable); it has the faculties of nutrition, growth and decay, and (asexual) reproduction.

l. 18 *show:* exhibit

l. 29 *quaint:* a pun; in addition to its usual adjectival meaning, it is here also the noun, meaning "pudendum."

l. 34 *dew:* a textual crux: 1681 edition reads "glew" which has been read as a variant of "glow" (*cf.* show-shew) and as the even then archaic "lew" ("warmth").

l. 40 *slow-chapt:* the meaning is doubtful, but usually read as "slow-jawed" (*cf.* slang "chops").

sexual passion, and his rational soul makes him conscious of the passage of time and the inevitable approach of death.

The second verse-paragraph, reasonable like the first, is more clearly ironic, almost cruelly realistic rather than hyperbolic: after death we shall certainly have time enough but not world enough, only a narrow grave, and, he says with wry understatement, "none I think do there embrace." The tone of the last verse paragraph is importunate, almost desperate. It is established in part by the frequent references to time — "Now . . . while . . . morning . . . while . . . instant," etc. — and in part by terms suggesting violence — "birds of prey . . . devour . . . roll . . . tear . . . rough strife." Had this violent passage come earlier in the poem it would have seemed more appropriate to a rape than to a seduction (some readers, indeed, see this poem as the final unmasking of the "bestiality" behind the tradition of the seduction poem in the seventeenth century). Coming where it does, however, after the reasonable though hyperbolic first and realistic second verse-paragraphs, in the frame of a logical argument, its importunity suggests not that passion has overcome reason but that it has been released by the logic and clear vision of the rational mind.

The tone of the first verse-paragraph of "To His Coy Mistress" is persuasively reasonable; only certain statements are hyperbolic, these are acknowledged as such, and the acknowledgment is used in establishing the reasonableness of the rest of the argument. This is not the case in much love poetry, as in this song by Ben Jonson:

> Doe but looke on her eyes! They doe light
>   All that *Love's* world comprizeth!
> Doe but looke on her hayre! It is bright
>   As *Love's* star when it riseth!
> Doe but marke, her fore-head's smoother   5
>   Than words that soothe her!
> And from her arched brows, such a grace
>   Sheds it selfe through the face;
> As alone, there triumphs to the life,
>   All the gaine, all the good, of the element's strife!   10
>
> Have you seene but a bright Lilly grow,
>   Before rude hands have touch'd it?
> Have you mark'd but the fall of the Snow,

> Before the soyle hath smuch'd it?
> Have you felt the wooll o' the Bever?   15
>   Or Swan's downe ever?
> Or, have smelt o' the bud o' the Bryer?
>   Or Nard i' the fire?
> Or, have tasted the bag o' the Bee?
>   O, so white! O, so soft! O, so sweet is shee! *   20

Are we then to assume, since the praise is undoubtedly somewhat overstated (indeed, a lady as white as new fallen snow might look a bit ill), that the lover is insincere? Surely not. The rationale behind this sort of exaggeration would seem to be that the lover is giving emotional rather than realistic equivalents: "this is how white, sweet, and soft she seems to me." As important as the rationale is the tradition or convention. Just as we understand that someone who says "I'll die" or "terrific" is neither speaking literally nor lying, that someone who asks "How are you?" is neither seeking a clinical diagnosis nor expressing lack of interest in our welfare, so within certain literary conventions norms of statements are established that cannot with justice be measured by standards from outside the tradition.†

Granting the terms of the tradition and granting the lover the legitimacy of emotional rather than realistic equivalents, we surely can retain certain standards of sense without demanding "modern" or realistic treatment. A poem that might raise questions of the degree to which we must accept all lover's hyperbole and internally established authority (within the poem and the tradition) is this song by Matthew Prior:

> If Wine and Musick have the Pow'r,
> To ease the Sickness of the Soul;

* This version is from the play *The Devil Is an Ass*. The same lines, divided after "strife," form the second and third stanzas of the fourth part of a work called "A Celebration of Charis in ten Lyrick Peeces." Lines 11–20 here also stand alone as a poem in manuscript. There is yet another manuscript version of "Charis" with variations in what are here lines 11–20 and two additional ten-line stanzas.

l. 18 *Nard:* aromatic plant, source of an ancient ointment

† A famous example of how an established convention can be ridiculed by treating it literally is Sir Walter Raleigh's "The Nymph's Reply" which "answers" Christopher Marlowe's "The Passionate Sheepheard to His Love," a poem written within the pastoral tradition. (See below, pp. 196–8. See, too, the discussion of Shakespeare's "My Mistres' eyes" later in this chapter.)

Let *Phoebus* ev'ry String explore;
And *Bacchus* fill the sprightly Bowl.
Let Them their friendly Aid imploy,   5
To make my *Cloe's* Absence light;
And seek for Pleasure, to destroy
The Sorrows of the live-long Night.

But She to-Morrow will return:
Venus, be Thou to-Morrow great;   10
Thy Myrtles strow, Thy Odours burn;
And meet Thy Fav'rite Nymph in State.
Kind Goddess, to no other Pow'rs
Let Us to-Morrow's Blessings own:
Thy darling *Loves* shall guide the Hours;   15
And all the Day be Thine alone.

That his beloved is the emotional equivalent of the nymph Cloe, that she is, in his lover's world at least, the favorite of Venus, we can, within the usual terms, accept. That Phoebus and Bacchus as gods of music and wine may be called upon to bring solace to the lover when the nymph has departed we may also discount into sense. But, even when we realize the eternity of a day or night to the lonely lover, that all this solace, all the vows, preparations for return, dedication of the day of the return, and the whole intensity of tone, is brought to bear on the occasion of "Cloe's" absence for one night, even the most sympathetic must find a bit strained. At some point, that is, the limits of the convention and our toleration of the vagaries of the lover will begin to buckle and hyperbole will approach the ludicrous.*

If convention can on the one hand make hyperbole acceptable it can equally make it absurd. So, in the *mock heroic* or *mock epic* much of

* We are speaking of a breakdown within the poem. There may also be a breakdown between the poem and its alleged subject matter, but this is harder to assess. To find that the historical Beatrice or Laura had piano legs or protruding eyes should not detract from the poems of Dante or Petrarch. Yet to find that Prior's "Cloe" was mistress of a pub and was, as R. B. Johnson says, "described by [Prior's] contemporaries in terms as unequivocal as they are unchivalrous," more than confirms our sense of the flaw in this poem. It is difficult to say just what such information does (or did for contemporaries) to the *tone* of the poem, difficult to say what it should do for the tone of the poem, but, for better or worse, once established, it is almost impossible to ignore in reading the poem.

the joke lies in the contrast between the inflated style and the ordinary subject matter; this is usually so obvious that no special knowledge of the convention is necessary — when, in *The Dunciad,* we see "Mighty Mother" linked to "Dunce the first," and the triad of "Dulness, Jove, and Fate" we know we are reading satire or comedy — but much of the additional fun comes from the echoes of the epic conventions of Homer, Virgil, and Milton, such as the invocation of the muse: "I sing. Say you . . ." The convention brings memories of matter previously treated in the form, and paradoxically, reduces the relatively trivial matter of the mock epic to even greater triviality.*

Even here, in what seems a rather obvious form of the use of tone to augment or qualify the literal statement, since by definition we are dealing with norms, we can encounter difficulty or uncertainty. When *is* matter "unworthy" of the epic form? Can the epic be "democratized," to deal with ordinary men? Can there be no attempt to elevate relatively simple materials to epic or near-epic stature? Are the following lines, which open "The Sofa" or first book of William Cowper's *The Task,* such an attempt, or are they ironic or mocking?

> I sing the Sofa. I, who lately sang
> Truth, Hope, and Charity, and touch'd with awe
> The solemn chords, and with a trembling hand,
> Escap'd with pain from that adventurous flight,
> Now seek repose upon an humbler theme: 5
> The theme though humble, yet august and proud
> Th' occasion — for the Fair commands the song.
>   Time was, when clothing sumptuous or for use,
> Save their own painted skins, our sires had none.
> As yet black breeches were not; satin smooth,   10
> Or velvet soft, or plush with shaggy pile:
> The hardy chief upon the rugged rock
> Wash'd by the sea, or on the gravelly bank
> Thrown up by wintry torrents roaring loud,
> Fearless of wrong, repos'd his weary strength.   15

* One difference between mock epic and parody is that parody mocks the manner itself whereas, despite the ambiguity of the name, mock epic does not mock the epic manner but only the matter in casting it in a form much too lofty and dignified for it; it is even more effective, of course, when the matter or subject pretends to great dignity and loftiness or worth.

Those barbarous ages past, succeeded next
The birthday of invention; weak at first,
Dull in design, and clumsy to perform.
Joint-stools were then created; on three legs
Upborne they stood. Three legs upholding firm   20
A massy slab, in fashion square or round.
On such a stool immortal Alfred sat,
And sway'd the sceptre of his infant realms:
And such in ancient halls and mansions drear
May still be seen; but perforated sore,   25
And drill'd in holes, the solid oak is found,
By worms voracious eating through and through.
    At length a generation more refin'd
Improv'd the simple plan; made three legs four,
Gave them a twisted form vermicular,   30
And o'er the seat, with plenteous wadding stuff'd,
Induc'd a splendid cover, green and blue,
Yellow and red, of tapestry richly wrought,
And woven close, or needle-work sublime.
There might ye see the peony spread wide,   35
The full-blown rose, the shepherd and his lass,
Lapdog and lambkin with black staring eyes,
And parrots with twin cherries in their beak.
    Now came the cane from India, smooth and bright
With Nature's varnish; sever'd into stripes   40
That interlac'd each other, these supplied
Of texture firm a lattice-work, that brac'd
The new machine, and it became a chair.
But restless was the chair; the back erect
Distress'd the weary loins, that felt no ease;   45
The slippery seat betray'd the sliding part
That press'd it, and the feet hung dangling down,
Anxious in vain to find the distant floor.
These for the rich: the rest, whom fate had plac'd
In modest mediocrity, content   50
With base materials, sat on well-tann'd hides,
Obdurate and unyielding, glassy smooth,
With here and there a tuft of crimson yarn,
Or scarlet crewel, in the cushion fix'd;

Clearly Cowper knows his subject is somewhat less than heroic. The
question is whether he is mocking his subject, shrinking it still
further, by putting it in the epic form, or attempting to domesticate
the epic form and show that "humble" subjects (he does not say
"trivial" subjects) are important, poetic, deserving of celebration. A
further question is whether we can read this poem as serious or
earnest regardless of what may or may not have been Cowper's intention. As we read more and more eighteenth-century poetry, for example, heavy as it is with inverted word order (in part because of the
rigid couplet form), Cowper's verse may seem relatively straightforward in its word order. Still, it will be difficult to so lull our modern
sensibilities as to read lines like "when clothing . . . Save their own
painted skins, our sires had none," or, "on three legs / Upborne they
stood," or, "these supplied / Of texture firm a lattice-work," without
just a hint of a smile. Further, it is perhaps natural that a poem about a
seat be prone to fundamental punning, but this poem does not seem
to exploit the possible double meanings and it is difficult to believe
that Cowper was fully aware of them. It is even more difficult to believe that he could have been totally unaware of them in such passages
as the following: "The slippery seat betray'd the sliding part / That
press'd it," the description of the poor who "sat on well-tann'd hides,"
or "our rugged sires" who did not complain of being "ill at ease behind," though "The ladies first / 'Gan murmur, as became the softer
sex." Subject aside, when the poem moves from the rather trivial (or
at least "humble") subject of the evolution of the sofa to the sententi-
ousness of lines 83–5, it borders dangerously on self-mockery — especially when coupled with the possibility of a howling pun in the last
clause: "so hard / T' attain perfection in this nether world." It is perhaps too much to ask even of the well-trained historical imagination
that it slough off its contemporary responses. We must try at least not
to transfer these responses to those operating within other conventions
and other norms, difficult though it may be to imagine a set toward
language and subject that could fail to see what we see and respond
as we respond.

When the diction of a poem calls for or expresses more emotional
response than the situation warrants, the tone is said to be *sentimental*. Prior's song and Cowper's "The Sofa" may both be so described. The word expresses a critical judgment about which there
may, naturally, be some disagreement, and a reader must acquire a

knowledge of conventions and changing diction if he is not to misjudge. Hyperbole need not be sentimental when, as in Jonson's "Doe but looke on her eyes!," it conveys convincingly an authentic response. One may argue that, precisely because lovers *are* sentimental, the poem is not; or one may argue that love in fact warrants such a response.

Sentimentality is not a question of subject matter, though certain subjects (cats, mothers, death) have surely called forth the largest percentage of poetry that is bad because it is sentimental. Think how sentimentally one could speak about a small bird, and then look again at the Keats and Hardy poems quoted earlier in this chapter to see how each poet has avoided the traps of sentimentality, however closely he may have skirted them: how — since his subject is not, in fact, the bird — he has presented a situation warranting the emotional response. One of the hallmarks of a superior poet is this ability to keep the emotional response consonant with the situation, to convince us that each is precisely what the other demands. One of the hallmarks of a sensitive reader is his ability — one, fortunately, that can be developed — to distinguish warranted from unwarranted emotional response, valid overstatement from sentimentality.

Like overstatement, understatement assumes a normative response. At times, as in Robert Frost's final line of his poem "Birches" — "One could do worse than be a swinger of birches" — that more is implied than is stated * is obvious even without reference to the context of the poem: one can, after all, be many other things — a murderer, a spitter in subways — "worse than . . . a swinger of birches." Even here, however, the context defines the precise nature and degree of understatement: in context the swinger of birches is one who gets away from the world awhile — but returns — a momentary escapist, with overtones suggesting the artist (in, for example, the description of the

---

* Understatement is clearly only a special kind of implication. It is at times difficult to draw a firm line between the two. In Wordsworth's "Michael," for example, the elderly shepherd, terribly disappointed in his lost son, goes to the site of the sheepfold he meant them to build together, "And never lifted up a single stone." This line closely resembles an understatement of his emotions; it seems more accurate, however, to treat it as simple implication since there is no emotion "stated" in any terms at all. Had Wordsworth written, "And had no joy in thinking of his son," or made some such muted reference to his grief, the line would more strictly qualify as understatement.

technique of the swinger). One can do worse, the speaker says, than escape in this manner.

On the other hand, the statement, "the sight was not so fair as one or two that I have seen elsewhere," divorced from a context may or may not be normative. When the sight is that of a friend in the throes of a lingering, painful, fatal illness, become an "it," as in the following poem by Edwin Arlington Robinson, the context shows the clause to be bitter understatement:

How Annandale Went Out

"They called it Annandale — and I was there
To flourish, to find words, and to attend:
Liar, physician, hypocrite, and friend,
I watched him; and the sight was not so fair
As one or two that I have seen elsewhere: 5
An apparatus not for me to mend —
A wreck, with hell between him and the end,
Remained of Annandale; and I was there.

"I knew the ruin as I knew the man;
So put the two together, if you can,   10
Remembering the worst you know of me.
Now view yourself as I was, on the spot —
With a slight kind of engine. Do you see?
Like this . . . You wouldn't hang me? I thought not."

On occasion the poet will not depend on general experience but on specific allusion to establish a norm external to the context of the poem itself. Not knowing the story of Belshazzar, one would read the following little poem by Emily Dickinson more or less at face value, unless, indeed, "immortal" and "Revelation's Wall" might be thought overstatements:

Belshazzar had a letter —
He never had but one —
Belshazzar's Correspondent
Concluded and begun
In that immortal Copy

> The Conscience of us all
> Can read without its Glasses
> On Revelation's Wall —

The allusion is, of course, to the fifth chapter of Daniel, in which
Belshazzar, son of Nebuchadnezzar, sees, in the midst of revelry, a
hand write a mysterious message on "Revelation's Wall." This supernatural message is scarcely a mere "letter." Only Daniel can interpret
the message, which says, in part, "Thou art weighed in the balances,
and art found wanting"— presumably the message we too can read
"On Revelation's Wall." That we can read it without our glasses is in
striking contrast to Belshazzar's search for an interpreter, and the
discrepancy perhaps measures the clarity of the message.

There is a rather special form of playing against the literary conventions that may be considered related to, though not strictly part
of, understatement. It consists in striving for realism and sincerity, as
it were, by negating conventional overstatements. The anti-
Petrarchanism of the later Renaissance, an attack on the highflown
hyperbole and conceits of the Petrarchan love poets, is perhaps the
best example of such debunking. Compare the Jonson and Prior
poems quoted earlier in this chapter, for example, with Shakespeare's
"Sonnet 130":

> My Mistres' eyes are nothing like the Sunne;
> Corrall is farre more red than her lips' red;
> If snow be white, why then her brests are dun;
> If haires be wires, black wires grow on her head.
> I have seene Roses damaskt, red and white,   5
> But no such Roses see I in her cheekes,
> And in some perfumes is there more delight
> Than in the breath that from my Mistres reekes.
> I love to hear her speake, yet well I know
> That Musicke hath a farre more pleasing sound;   10
> I grant I never saw a goddesse goe,
> My Mistres, when shee walkes, treads on the ground.
>   And yet by heaven I thinke my love as rare
>   As any she beli'd with false compare.

This description of the beloved is not truly understated, but the conventional hyperbole is so established in love poetry that to deny the

mistress coral lips, white breasts, etc., has some of the effect of understatement.

Irony is the most prevalent and certainly the most discussed device
for qualifying by tone.* It, too, is most safely identified within the
poem itself. Wilfred Owen, in a famous World War I poem describes
the horrors of death in war under the title *"Dulce et Decorum Est,"*
the full expression (. . . *pro patria mori*) meaning, "It is sweet and
fitting to die for your native land"; the contrast of detail and title
(the expression is repeated in full at the end of the poem) is enough
to reveal the irony, but Owen makes sure of his point by calling the
saying an "old lie":

Dulce et Decorum Est

Bent double, like old beggars under sacks,
Knock-kneed, coughing like hags, we cursed through sludge,
Till on the haunting flares we turned our backs,
And towards our distant rest began to trudge.
Men marched asleep. Many had lost their boots,   5
But limped on, blood-shod. All went lame, all blind;
Drunk with fatigue; deaf even to the hoots
Of gas-shells dropping softly behind.

Gas! Gas! Quick, boys! — An ecstasy of fumbling,
Fitting the clumsy helmets just in time,   10
But someone still was yelling out and stumbling
And flound'ring like a man in fire or lime.
Dim through the misty panes and thick green light,
As under a green sea, I saw him drowning.

In all my dreams before my helpless sight   15
He plunges at me, guttering, choking, drowning.

If in some smothering dreams, you too could pace
Behind the wagon that we flung him in,
And watch the white eyes wilting in his face,

* We are limiting the discussion here largely to *verbal irony*. There are other kinds,
the chief of which is *dramatic irony*, which usually involves the unwitting foreshadowing of his future by a character's own words. Thus, in Strindberg's *Lady Julie*,
Lady Julie mockingly says to her servant early in the play, "Don't worry, Kristin! I
shan't take your sweetheart away from you!" but by the end of the play she has taken
the valet Jean as a lover and has taken him away from Kristin.

His hanging face, like a devil's sick of sin,   20
If you could hear, at every jolt, the blood
Come gargling from the froth-corrupted lungs
Bitten as the cud
Of vile, incurable sores on innocent tongues, —
My friend, you would not tell with such high zest   25
To children ardent for some desperate glory,
The old lie: *Dulce et decorum est*
Pro patria mori.

Irony does not necessarily reverse meaning, that is, you cannot always turn the apparent meaning completely around and get the "real"
meaning. In the E. E. Cummings poem that follows, for example, the
denotation of "etcetera" is "and so on," and on its first appearance it
clearly suggests that we are to add other clichés attached to elderly
aunts. This undoubtedly suggests that the words "sweet old" are not
to be accepted literally, at face value, but it does not necessarily suggest that the speaker's aunt is the opposite of sweet and old. (Indeed,
the mother in the poem is treated rather more harshly than the aunt.)
Further, "etcetera" keeps shifting meaning, so that though it can be
read on the first two occasions to mean "and so on" it is not clear that
"to die etcetera / bravely" means "to die and so on" — nor does it
clearly mean "to die bravely and so on," a deliberate bit of playing
with word order, though this is a possibility. By the end of the poem
the meaning "and so on," a vague term suggesting an unspecified
series, comes to mean virtually the opposite of the generalized "and so
on," its specificity reinforced by the capital:

my sweet old etcetera
aunt lucy during the recent

war could and what
is more did tell you just
what everybody was fighting   5

for,
my sister

isabel created hundreds
(and

hundreds) of socks not to   10
mention shirts fleaproof earwarmers

etcetera wristers etcetera, my
mother hoped that

i would die etcetera
bravely of course my father used   15
to become hoarse talking about how it was
a privilege and if only he
could meanwhile my

self etcetera lay quietly
in the deep mud et   20

cetera
(dreaming,
et

    cetera, of
Your smile   25
eyes knees and of your Etcetera)

Irony, like other matters of tone, is at times difficult to identify
with absolute certainty. Sometimes the difficulty is a matter of different or changing mores; but it does happen that contemporaries
who speak the same language mistake each other's tone. What would
you say is the tone of the following poem by A. E. Housman?

1887

From Clee to heaven the beacon burns,
    The shires have seen it plain,
From north and south the sign returns
    And beacons burn again.

Look left, look right, the hills are bright,   5
    The dales are light between,
Because 'tis fifty years tonight
    That God has saved the Queen.

Now, when the flame they watch not towers
    About the soil they trod,   10
Lads, we'll remember friends of ours
    Who shared the work with God.

To skies that knit their heartstrings right,
    To fields that bred them brave,
The saviours come not home tonight: 15
    Themselves they could not save.

It dawns in Asia, tombstones show
    And Shropshire names are read;
And the Nile spills his overflow
    Beside the Severn's dead.   20

We pledge in peace by farm and town
    The Queen they served in war,
And fire the beacons up and down
    The land they perished for.

"God save the Queen" we living sing,   25
    From height to height 'tis heard;
And with the rest your voices ring,
    Lads of the Fifty-third.

Oh, God will save her, fear you not:
    Be you the men you've been,   30
Get you the sons your fathers got,
    And God will save the Queen.*

Frank Harris complimented Housman by telling him, "You have poked fun at the whole thing and made splendid mockery of it." The poet, however, was incensed: "I never intended to poke fun, as you

* l. 1 *Clee:* hill in Shropshire
ll. 7–8: Victoria was crowned queen in 1837.
ll. 19–20: reference for 1887 not clear; there was, however, a good deal of fighting along the Nile in the 1890's when Housman was writing *A Shropshire Lad,* in which this poem appears.
l. 20 *Severn:* river in Shropshire
l. 28 *the Fifty-third:* Shropshire Regiment of Infantry

call it, at patriotism, and I can find nothing in the sentiment to make
mockery of. I meant it sincerely. If Englishmen breed as good men as
their fathers, then God will save their Queen. I can only reject and
resent your — your truculent praise." *

Does Housman's response end all argument? Is the poet the supreme authority on the tone of his own work? Of course we cannot
lightly quarrel with Housman's statement of his intentions, but no
one, especially after Freud, can argue that we are always fully conscious of all our own intentions, and no one, before or after Freud,
could argue that the actuality of all our actions and utterances are
what we intended them to be. In the context of the frequently ironic
A Shropshire Lad and in the "cool," debunking twentieth century, it
is difficult to read such a "patriotic" poem without at least the suspicion of irony. And what if Housman the ironist were being supremely ironic in his straight-faced denial of irony?

As we see here and saw in "The Sofa," tone may, like final interpretation, defy certain definition, no matter how fully and intelligently
we read the text itself. It is perhaps less important to reach final agreement about the reading of a poem than it is to recognize the nature
of the disagreement, to distinguish statement from implication, what
can be demonstrated "on the page" from what can, in the final analysis, only be inferred.

THE MEANING OF FORM

One of the ways we know *The Dunciad* is satirical is by the appearance together of such groups of words as "Dulness, Jove, and Fate."
The sense is created by the nonsense or impropriety of the statement:
"Dulness" just does not "belong" with "Jove and Fate." There is nothing in the denotation or connotation of each word taken separately
or in the syntax itself that creates the tone or implies satire; the full
meaning, adjusted by tone, inheres chiefly in the relationship of the
words to the syntax: words that do not "belong together" are somehow together in parallel structure. The inappropriateness creates the
humor — and the meaning. This kind of creation of meaning by
bringing concepts together for an effect that neither would have apart
from the other we call *juxtaposition*.

We can see another example of juxtaposition at work in creating

* Quoted by Carl J. Weber in the Jubilee Edition of *A Shropshire Lad* (Waterville,
Maine, 1946), p. 109.

meaning in another line of Pope's, that in which he describes Queen Anne who "Dost sometimes counsel take — and sometimes Tea" (in "The Rape of the Lock"). We understand the meaning of each word taken separately, but the meaning of the line is not merely the sum of these individual meanings. We understand the structure of the sentence, but the grammatical or syntactical relationship of the words alone does not determine the full meaning of the line. The primary meaning — statement qualified by tone and context — lies in the ludicrous contrast of the serious "counsel" and trivial "Tea" forced together by the parallel structure heightened by the repetition of "sometimes." It is not merely that the words "counsel" and "Tea" are so incompatible as to be impossible to relate seriously in a passage — we might say, for example, that "on some mornings she takes counsel while on other mornings she relaxes and drinks tea with her friends" — it is the forcing of terms into equivalence and thus contrast by the structure which determines the meaning. We find the meaning, then, in the interrelationship of the words and structure brought out by their proximity, by, in short, juxtaposition.

The most compact and perhaps dramatic form of meaning through juxtaposition is in the figure known as *oxymoron,* a term derived from two Greek words meaning "sharp" and "foolish," and used to designate a brief expression that appears to be self-contradictory. Once again we can go to Pope for our example. In the Atossa passage quoted earlier he used an oxymoron composed of almost the very root words of the term: "Full sixty years the World has been her Trade, / The wisest Fool much Time has ever made." We reduce these apparent contradictions to sense initially by adjusting the meaning of one or both terms. Here, for example, we probably read "wisest" as "most experienced" or "most worldly wise"; Atossa, because she has devoted so much time to the world is, in this sense of the word, "wisest." However, she is not "truly wise" at all, is indeed a fool insofar as wisdom signifies deep understanding of the whole of life. We have been forced, be it noted, not only to adjust the term to make sense of the locution but to re-examine our conception of the term, to distinguish in this case "worldly wisdom" and "true wisdom."

An oxymoron need not be satiric or humorous in its appearance of self-contradiction. There is no humorous intent in Thomas Gray's famous phrase from "Elegy Written in a Country Churchyard": "Some mute inglorious Milton." The effect is startling but not particularly funny. We pause and readjust the meaning as we did in the

Pope expression: Milton was neither mute nor inglorious; we read "Milton," then, to mean "one who was *potentially* as great and glorious a poet as Milton." Here, too, the adjustment causes us to re-examine our conceptions of such qualities associated with "Milton" as "genius" and "greatness"; insofar as these qualities may be said to exist as entities in themselves they may exist as potential within an obscure illiterate farmer as well as in the realized potential of the renowned.

In expressions that are remote from the oxymoron, of course, we also select or adjust meaning by the relation of a word to its context. Alone, "fast" may mean many things; following "stuck" its appropriate meaning is selected. In such cases, however, meaning is not created by the juxtaposition, but one potential meaning is selected *and the rest are discarded.* The oxymoron in this regard operates more like the pun in that more than one meaning ("worldly wise," "truly wise") is retained. It differs from the pun in that its two or more meanings are not discrete or separable (as in Mercutio's "grave man," above p. 54), but are different aspects of the same general meaning and so force a re-examination of the full meaning of the term. It is the need for distinguishing two meanings of a term that justifies the "shock" value of the oxymoron. Even after one or both seemingly contradictory terms are redefined to produce "sense," the "old" sense of the term is retained and thus the appearance of self-contradiction and the startling effect are retained.

When such a seeming contradiction is more extended than a phrase it is called a *paradox.* The Atossa passage, for example, is full of paradoxes — indeed it is the portrait of a paradoxical nature — which culminate perhaps in the intensity of the paradox "Sick of herself thro' very selfishness." Here again, in order fully to appreciate the passage, we must accept (at least provisionally) the potential moral truth that excessive love of and concern for the self ("selfishness") can, and indeed might very well, lead to self-disgust or self-hatred. The apparently contradictory terms are adjusted to a sequential or causal relationship to make not only sense rather than nonsense but to create a moral insight.

Because the apparent self-contradiction of paradox causes us to stop and think, to do an intellectual double-take, as it were, it is extremely useful as a vehicle for new or unfamiliar "truths" or for breaking through verbal or conventional ways of looking at things to

a new view of reality or of the poet's vision. When we read, in Keats's
"Ode on a Grecian Urn," that "Heard melodies are sweet, but those
unheard / Are sweeter," we adjust the meaning by redefining a term,
as we do in the oxymoron, in order to grasp the sense. Keats helps us
here with the lines that follow — "play on; / Not to the sensual ear,
but . . . Pipe to the spirit . . ." — so that we readily redefine "melodies" to include imagined sounds. We then accept the possibility of
our imagining sounds sweeter than any we might actually hear. We
are now in the world of Keats's vision, in which the imagination can
create beauty or perfection beyond the ability of reality to imitate or
equal. The paradox has alerted us, in some measure by its failing to
"make sense" on first reading, and has forced us to adjust not only to
the phrase but to the vision of the universe on which it depends; it
has created the possibility of a range of truth or of insight beyond the
conventional and to some extent beyond the logical reach of the words.

Not all instances of juxtaposition which stop us in our reading or
call attention to themselves, which bring things together we do not
usually put together, which force us to re-examine our definitions or
perceptions of reality, which force comparison and contrast necessarily involve paradox. There are, for example, several instances of
non-paradoxical but inter-relating juxtaposition in this short poem by
Thomas Hood:

The Death Bed

We watched her breathing thro' the night,
    Her breathing soft and low,
As in her breast the wave of life
    Kept heaving to and fro.

So silently we seemed to speak,   5
    So slowly moved about,
As we had lent her half our powers
    To eke her living out.

Our very hopes belied our fears,
    Our fears our hopes belied —   10
We thought her dying when she slept,
    And sleeping when she died.

> For when the morn came dim and sad,
>   And chill with early showers,
> Her quiet eyelids closed — she had   15
>   Another morn than ours.

The reversal of subject and predicate in lines 9 and 10 is technically known as *conversion.* The effect of the interchangeability of
subject and predicate is to compress the two and bring them into a
relationship much closer than comparison, virtually to identity. Here
"hopes" and "fears" are by the process made almost indistinguishable,
which is precisely the intensity of comparison called for. At first glance,
however, one would think this union of hope and fear might be better
served by making line 10 perfectly parallel with line 9, "Our very
fears belied our hopes." Logically or syntactically this would be true,
but the inversion in the second of these lines juxtaposes (with identical pronouns) fears and hopes in so unusual a syntactical sequence
as to have almost the momentary effect of paradox — "Our fears our
hopes." Should we stop there the construction falls short of sense,
though the completed line makes perfect sense and the inversion of
verb and object is itself not unusual. The juxtaposition, with the little
jolt to normal expectations, serves still further to identify hope and
fear.

The last two lines of the third stanza, lines 11–12, involve that contrast between appearance and reality so dear to paradox, though there
is no appearance of contradiction to startle the attention and the whole
is qualified by "We thought" ("[though we were wrong]"), so that
the voice of the poem in the "now" of the poem (as opposed to the
past actions described in the poem) is no longer "fooled" by the appearance of dying and sleeping, and the two are never confused for
the reader. The structural device is something like that of conversion
though it does not involve transposing of subject and predicate but
of gerund and finite verb in the subordinate clause: "to die" in line 11
appears as a gerund and in line 12 as the verb in the subordinate
clause; "to sleep" in line 11 is the finite verb in the subordinate clause
and in line 12 the gerund. The parallelism is enforced by the reversal
of the roles of the two verbs and the result, as in conversion, is further
to link sleeping and dying so that the two, as is fitting in the context,
virtually become aspects of each other.

Juxtaposition, working through or beyond syntax, serves to bring dissimilar elements into meaningful relationship with each other, often with the effect of creating a new entity of meaning comparable to a chemical compound as opposed to a mere mixture.* Wisdom and foolishness are generally thought to be opposite qualities, but they are brought together in the oxymoron with the result not only of qualifying "true wisdom" but of creating the new entity of "wise foolishness," or that kind of foolishness that arises from too narrow a concentration upon social sophistication. (There are other forms of "wise foolishness," perhaps, created by the contexts of other oxymorons.) Similarly, Keats creates the "unheard melody." Less paradoxically, hopes and fears, also thought of as opposite emotions, are merged by juxtaposition into a new emotion (or an emotion newly and more accurately defined) in which the two interact to create a special form of anxiety. Sleep and death are not usually considered opposites, and indeed to compare them figuratively is rather trite; Hood, however, makes them opposite alternatives for the dying woman and then merges them literally so that the transition between the two states becomes indistinguishable and what is in effect a new intermediate state is created.

Juxtaposing means literally "placing next to"; we have extended this somewhat to include "near to," but the proximity of the related elements is an important factor in creating the new entity. This compression makes juxtaposition especially useful in the shorter forms like the epigram, as, for example, in this one by Sir William Jones:

> On parent knees, a naked new-born child,
> Weeping thou sat'st while all around thee smiled:
> So live, that sinking to thy life's last sleep,
> Calm thou may'st smile, whilst all around thee weep.

What are yoked or brought into close relationship here (with no notable help from syntax or structure) are not primarily the opposed states of weeping and smiling but the two brief vignettes of which weeping and smiling are a part: the crying baby surrounded by smiling friends and relations; the smiling dying man surrounded by

---

* We are here dealing with dissimilar but literal elements brought into relationship. The same principle of juxtaposition operates in the case of figurative language, though the elements brought into relationship are not both in the same sense literally there in the poem. See Chapter IV.

weeping friends and relations (our summary is more parallel than is the structure in the poem). At work here is not only something like conversion — the smiles move from the others to the auditor, the tears from the auditor to the others — but the juxtaposition of birth and death which helps create the moral meaning of the poem: life is short, joys and sorrows are transient, therefore live a virtuous life so that when its brief span is over you will be able to die peacefully (presumably sure of eternal life in heaven). It is primarily the juxtaposition of the contrasting scenes that creates the impression of the brevity of life which gives the imperative, "So live," its full meaning.

It will have been noticed that in many of the examples of juxtaposition, particularly in conversion and related forms involving reversal, one of the prime ingredients is *repetition* of words or phrases ("hopes," "fears") or repetition with some variation ("dying . . . slept," "sleeping . . . died"; "Weeping . . . smiled," "smile . . . weep"). When these repetitions are close together, let us say in the same or consecutive lines, we seem justified in treating them as elements of juxtaposition. They may occur, however, at intervals widely enough spaced so as not to be legitimately considered juxtaposed. Even so, the repetition of a term has the effect of recalling its previous occurrence, creating in the mind or memory something quite comparable to juxtaposition. In the last stanza of "The Death Bed," for example, "the morn" appears in the first line and "another morn" in the last; the repetition clearly calls for comparison, perhaps even a slight merging, of the two.

Repetition need not be spaced widely in a poem and need not be exact (as in the variation "dying . . . died"). Even when juxtaposed rather than spaced and virtually identical rather than varied, it most often, when used well, involves an increment of meaning, as when, in *King Richard III,* Queen Margaret catalogues Richard's crimes, hammering home the accusation:

> I had an Edward, till a Richard kill'd him;
> I had a husband, till a Richard kill'd him;
> Thou hadst an Edward, till a Richard kill'd him;
> Thou hadst a Richard, till a Richard kill'd him.

The repetition, even to the point of monotony, stresses the separateness, the individual acts, of the murders and yet the identical nature of each act and the accumulated guilt of the murderer. Similarly, the

six appearances of the word "happy" and the five of "forever" in the
third stanza of Keats's "Ode on a Grecian Urn" create the effect of
the static quality, the monotony that he sees as the fatal flaw in the
otherwise attractive world he has been led to imagine.

A subtler form of repetition with variation is involved in one of
Shakespeare's best-known sonnets, "Sonnet 116":

> Let me not to the marriage of true mindes
> Admit impediments, love is not love
> Which alters when it alteration findes
> Or bends with the remover to remove.

Here we are first forced to make a distinction between two meanings
of the same word ("love is not love") and then to distinguish variant
forms of words ("alters . . . alteration . . . remover . . . remove"):
the repetition with variation is clearly involved in the making of distinctions of meaning. In Yeats's "Byzantium," too, many words are
repeated time and again; attempting to understand the reason for
such repetition should help one's comprehension of this difficult
poem. We have already seen in Cummings' use of "etcetera" how the
change in context from one appearance of a word to another can
radically alter the meaning of that word yet bring the two meanings
together into a new entity.

The examples of repetition to this point have been occasional, unfixed by the form of the poem. There are forms, however, in which
the repetitions are highly patterned, occurring at fixed points in the
poem. Such a form is the *sestina,* adopted from the French, in which
the end-words of the six lines of the first stanza reappear at the ends
of the lines in each of the next five stanzas in varying, yet prescribed,
order, and three of these end-words appear at the ends of the three
lines of the abbreviated last stanza, the other three end-words appearing in the middle of these three last lines. Like all strict forms, the
sestina can strain the ingenuity of the poet; it is perhaps least un-
successful where the end-words are rather ordinary and flexible, as
exemplified in the following poem by Rudyard Kipling:

Sestina of the Tramp-Royal

> Speakin' in general, I 'ave tried 'em all —
> The 'appy roads that take you o'er the world.

Speakin' in general, I 'ave found them good
For such as cannot use one bed too long,
But, must get 'ence, the same as I 'ave done,   5
An' go observin' matters till they die.

What do it matter where or 'ow we die,
So long as we've our 'ealth to watch it all —
The different ways that different things are done,
An' men an' women lovin' in this world;   10
Takin' our chances as they come along,
An' when they ain't, pretendin' they are good?

In cash or credit — no, it aren't no good;
You 'ave to 'ave the 'abit or you'd die,
Unless you lived your life but one day long,   15
Nor didn't prophesy nor fret at all,
But drew your tucker some'ow from the world,
An' never bothered what you might ha' done.

But, Gawd, what things are they I 'aven't done?
I've turned my 'and to most, an' turned it good,   20
In various situations round the world —
For 'im that doth not work must surely die;
But that's no reason man should labour all
'Is life on one same shift — life's none so long.

Therefore, from job to job I've moved along.   25
Pay couldn't 'old me when my time was done,
For something in my 'ead upset it all,
Till I 'ad dropped whatever 'twas for good,
An' , out at sea, be'eld the dock-lights die,
An' met my mate — the wind that tramps the world!   30

It's like a book, I think, this bloomin' world,
Which you can read and care for just so long,
But presently you feel that you will die
Unless you get the page you're readin' done,
An' turn another — likely not so good;   35
But what you're after is to turn 'em all.

Gawd bless this world! Whatever she 'ath done —
Excep' when awful long — I've found it good.
So write, before I die, " 'E liked it all!"

We might look at the variations in the use of "all" as an example of the nature, range, and function of the repetitions in varying contexts in this sestina. On three occasions "all" is used to describe the aspects of life; in the first, second, and sixth stanzas "all" refers to the world's roads, "The different ways that different things are done," and the pages in the book that is the world. In the third stanza it is more or less thrown away in the idiom "at all" ("nor fret at all"), though because of its other appearances, perhaps, it has more of its original force of "everything," or, in this case, "any way (manner)." In the fourth stanza it modifies "life," and means "entire," and in the fifth stanza it has a similar denotation but refers to the whole situation involved in a steady or static job. Finally, in the last stanza it sums up all of life, and its all-encompassing force is, of course, enforced by all that "all" has referred to in the previous stanzas.

In addition to the repetition of individual words, there may be repetition of whole lines of a poem. When this occurs at regularly spaced intervals, and not merely in isolation to emphasize a point (as in the passage quoted from *Richard III*), the repeated line is called a *refrain*.

Perhaps the most effective use of the refrain occurs in those poems in which the meaning of the refrain changes though the words remain the same. There is an excellent example of this in the anonymous sixteenth-century ballad "Edward," as the increments of information change our understanding of the feelings expressed by the repeated names in the refrains. What we at first take to be the mother's concern for her son and his love for her is gradually converted, through the increasing intensity of the emotion expressed, into her wheedling self-concern and his crescendo of hatred:

Edward

"Why dois your brand sae drap wi bluid,
Edward, Edward,
Why dois your brand sae drap wi bluid,
And why sae sad gang yee O?"
"O I hae killed my hauke sae guid,
Mither, Mither,
O I hae killed my hauke sae guid,
And I had nae mair bot hee O."

5

"Your haukis bluid was nevir sae reid,
    Edward, Edward,   10
Your haukis bluid was nevir sae reid,
 My deir son I tell thee O."
"O I hae killed my reid-roan steid,
    Mither, Mither,
O I hae killed my reid-roan steid,   15
 That erst was sae fair and frie O."

"Your steid was auld, and ye hae gat mair,
    Edward, Edward,
Your steid was auld, and ye hae gat mair,
 Sum other dule ye drie O."   20
"O I hae killed my fadir deir,
    Mither, Mither,
O I hae killed my fadir deir,
 Alas, and wae is mee O!"

"And whatten penance wul ye drie for that, 25
    Edward, Edward?
And whatten penance wul ye drie for that?
 My deir son, now tell me O."
"Ile set my feit in yonder boat,
    Mither, Mither,   30
Ile set my feit in yonder boat,
 And Ile fare ovir the sea O."

"And what wul ye doe wi your towirs and your ha,
    Edward, Edward?
And what wul ye doe wi your towirs and your ha, 35
 That were sae fair to see O?"
"Ile let thame stand tul they doun fa,
    Mither, Mither,
Ile let thame stand tul they doun fa,
 For here nevir mair maun I bee O."   40

"And what wul ye leive to your bairns and your wife,
    Edward, Edward?
And what wul ye leive to your bairns and your wife,
 Whan ye gang ovir the sea O?"

"The warldis room, late them beg thrae life, 45
Mither, Mither,
The warldis room, late them beg thrae life,
For them nevir mair wul I see O."

"And what wul ye leive to your ain mither deir,
Edward, Edward? 50
And what wul ye leive to your ain mither deir?
My deir son, now tell me O."
"The curse of hell frae me sall ye beir,
Mither, Mither,
The curse of hell frae me sall ye beir, 55
Sic counseils ye gave to me O."

Without repetition, here is a translation of the Scots:

"Why does your sword so drop with blood,
Edward,
And why so sad go you O?"
"O I have killed my hawk so good,
Mother,
And I had no more but he O."

"Your hawk's blood was never so red,
My dear son I tell thee."
"O I have killed my red-roan steed,
That formerly was so fair and free."

"Your steed was old, and you have got more,
Some other grief you suffer."
"O I have killed my father dear,
Alas, and woe is me!"

"And what penance will you suffer for that?
My dear son, now tell me."
"I'll set my feet in yonder boat,
And I'll fare over the sea."

"And what will you do with your towers and your hall
That were so fair to see?"
"I'll let them stand till they down fall,
For here never more must I be."

"And what will you leave to your children and your wife,
    When you go over the sea?"
"The world's room, let them beg through life,
    For them nevermore will I see."

"And what will you leave to your own mother dear?
    My dear son, now tell me."
"The curse of hell from me shall you bear,
    Such counsels you gave to me."

Comparison of this dehydrated version with the original should teach the reader a good deal about the effect of repetition and refrain, here especially in building suspense. The implication is, of course, that his mother influenced him to murder his father, but the effectiveness of the poem goes far beyond the shock of this revelation. As we gradually come to realize who knows what, we realize too that the mother's original questions were seeking information behind the answers she already knew. The whole complex psychological interaction between the mother and the son is gradually revealed: the cloying power she has had over him and the desperation of her growing awareness that she has lost it; his attempt to avoid the issue and, under her relentless probing, his ultimate self-assertion. The repetition and refrain in no way impede the presentation of this effect; instead they are in large part responsible for it. The repetition of questions and answers is psychologically fitting, emphasizing the further situation implied behind the mother's insistence and the son's refusal to answer any more than the precise question asked. The lingering over the names, which seems at first to imply simple affection, comes to take on increasingly complex overtones as the mother clings to what she has lost and the son arrives finally at what must be said. The final "Mither, Mither," interrupting the impetus of the reiterated "curse of hell," has not been drained of its originally implied affection. The psychology is more complex than that, for the word continues to imply affection, though tortured now through its coexistence with hatred for and repulsion from the beloved individual. Repetition and refrain in this ballad do not merely fill out a musical pattern; they create its meaning.

Some of the effect of repetition is, one might say, "spatial," that is, it minimizes the other matter that appears between occurrences of the word, phrase, or line and thus juxtaposes these repeated elements or reminds the reader of the previous occurrences of them. An even larger part of the effect of repetition, however, is "temporal"; we not only juxtapose the occurrences in our minds or memories but we compare the contexts in which the occurrences appear. The variation of context, even when there is no variation in the repetition, is significant. The repetition is "temporal," too, in that sequence is vital. Even after reading "Edward" through, we cannot go back to the first appearance of "Mither, Mither," and endow it with the full weight of the last. It is the position of the last as last, getting the benefit and pressure of the previous occurrences, that creates its full meaning.

The refrain involves frequent and patterned repetition, the repetition of an entire line at rather fixed intervals. There are forms, relatively rare in English poetry, which involve even more frequent and more strictly patterned repetition of lines. One of these is the *villanelle*, also borrowed from the French, which has nineteen lines, the first of which reappears as lines six, twelve, and eighteen, and the third of which (rhyming with the first) reappears as lines nine, fifteen, and nineteen. (In addition, line two rhymes with lines five, eight, eleven, fourteen, and seventeen, so that there are but two sound-endings in the entire nineteen lines.) In so strict and artificial a form it is vital that the lines reappear as naturally as possible, and yet that the reappearance in differing contexts give new depth, range, or precision to the lines involved. In the following villanelle by Dylan Thomas, for example, the first and third lines are so closely related in import that they can be used almost interchangeably, lending some flexibility to the fixed form. The basic variation giving range is the use of the lines as imperatives in the first and last stanzas and as simple predicates elsewhere. The middle four stanzas, on the other hand, which do not vary syntactically, have the effect of accumulation, somewhat like the repetition involved in the lines from *Richard III* quoted earlier.

> Do not go gentle into that good night,
> Old age should burn and rave at close of day;
> Rage, rage against the dying of the light.
>
> Though wise men at their end know dark is right,
> Because their words had forked no lightning they   5
> Do not go gentle into that good night.

Good men, the last wave by, crying how bright
Their frail deeds might have danced in a green bay,
Rage, rage against the dying of the light.

Wild men who caught and sang the sun in flight,   10
And learn, too late, they grieved it on its way,
Do not go gentle into that good night.

Grave men, near death, who see with blinding sight
Blind eyes could blaze like meteors and be gay,
Rage, rage against the dying of the light.   15

And you, my father, there on the sad height,
Curse, bless me now with your fierce tears, I pray.
Do not go gentle into that good night.
Rage, rage against the dying of the light.

With the possible exception of the refrain, fixed forms involving
repetition of words, phrases, or whole lines are relatively uncommon
in English poetry. (We shall deal with fixed forms of meter and
stanza in Chapter VI.) On the other hand, occasional, unfixed
repetition with variation, along with juxtaposition, are everywhere
in English poetry as adjuncts to form and meaning. At times, indeed,
they are not so much adjuncts as creators of form and meaning, as
in the long poem by Henry Reed that follows. In each of the four
sections of this poem meaning is created by the juxtaposition of a
"lesson of war" and a fragment of more natural, especially sexual,
life. The fusion of the lessons of war (in the flat phrases of the instructor) and the acts of love (in the imagination of the rookie) is
further heightened by puns and other verbal devices; thus the very
epigraph from Horace is doubly relevant in that *duellis* (wars) appears in some Horatian manuscripts as *puellis* (girls). Other instances
of the same sort of dual verbal relevance within the poem may be
found in the titles and in such phrases as "easing the spring." In the
first and fourth sections in particular repetition in disparate contexts
culminates in the final stanzas with the bringing together of the
repeated phrases.

Lessons of the War

To Alan Michell

Vixi duellis nuper idoneus
*Et militavi non sine gloria**

1. Naming of Parts

To-day we have naming of parts. Yesterday,
We had daily cleaning. And to-morrow morning,
We shall have what to do after firing. But to-day,
To-day we have naming of parts. Japonica
Glistens like coral in all of the neighbouring gardens,   5
        And to-day we have naming of parts.

This is the lower sling swivel. And this
Is the upper sling swivel, whose use you will see,
When you are given your slings. And this is the piling swivel,
Which in your case you have not got. The branches   10
Hold in the gardens their silent, eloquent gestures,
        Which in our case we have not got.

This is the safety-catch, which is always released
With an easy flick of the thumb. And please do not let me
See anyone using his finger. You can do it quite easy   15
If you have any strength in your thumb. The blossoms
Are fragile and motionless, never letting anyone see
        Any of them using their finger.

And this you can see is the bolt. The purpose of this
Is to open the breech, as you see. We can slide it   20
Rapidly backwards and forwards: we call this
Easing the spring. And rapidly backwards and forwards
The early bees are assaulting and fumbling the flowers:
        They call it easing the Spring.

They call it easing the Spring: it is perfectly easy   25
If you have any strength in your thumb: like the bolt,

---

* Epigraph: Horace, *Odes*, III, 26 — "I have lived fit for the wars lately and acted
like a soldier not without glory." See last two lines of section IV of this poem.

And the breech, and the cocking-piece, and the point of balance,
Which in our case we have not got; and the almond-blossom
Silent in all of the gardens and the bees going backwards and
    forwards,
          For to-day we have naming of parts.   30

II. Judging Distances

Not only how far away, but the way that you say it
Is very important. Perhaps you may never get
The knack of judging a distance, but at least you know
How to report on a landscape: the central sector,
The right of arc and that, which we had last Tuesday,   5
          And at least you know

That maps are of time, not place, so far as the army
Happens to be concerned — the reason being,
Is one which need not delay us. Again, you know
There are three kinds of tree, three only, the fir and the poplar, 10
And those which have bushy tops to; and lastly
          That things only seem to be things.

A barn is not called a barn, to put it more plainly,
Or a field in the distance, where sheep may be safely grazing.
You must never be over-sure. You must say, when reporting: 15
At five o'clock in the central sector is a dozen
Of what appear to be animals; whatever you do,
          Don't call the bleeders sheep.

I am sure that's quite clear; and suppose, for the sake of example,
The one at the end, asleep, endeavours to tell us   20
What he sees over there to the west, and how far away,
After first having come to attention. There to the west,
On the fields of summer the sun and the shadows bestow
          Vestments of purple and gold.

The still white dwellings are like a mirage in the heat,   25
And under the swaying elms a man and a woman
Lie gently together. Which is, perhaps, only to say
That there is a row of houses to the left of arc,

And that under some poplars a pair of what appear to be humans
          Appear to be loving.   30

Well that, for an answer, is what we might rightly call
Moderately satisfactory only, the reason being,
Is that two things have been omitted, and those are important.
The human beings, now: in what direction are they,
And how far away, would you say? And do not forget   35
          There may be dead ground in between.

There may be dead ground in between; and I may not have got
The knack of judging a distance; I will only venture
A guess that perhaps between me and the apparent lovers,
(Who, incidentally, appear by now to have finished,)   40
At seven o'clock from the houses, is roughly a distance
          Of about one year and a half.

III. Movement of Bodies

Those of you that have got through the rest, I am going to rapidly
Devote a little time to showing you, those that can master it,
A few ideas about tactics, which must not be confused
With what we call strategy. Tactics is merely
The mechanical movement of bodies, and that is what we mean
          by it.   5
          Or perhaps I should say: by them.

Strategy, to be quite frank, you will have no hand in.
It is done by those up above, and it merely refers to
The larger movements over which we have no control.
But tactics are also important, together or single.   10
You must never forget that suddenly, in an engagement,
          You may find yourself alone.

This brown clay model is a characteristic terrain
Of a simple and typical kind. Its general character
Should be taken in at a glance, and its general character   15
You can see at a glance it is somewhat hilly by nature,
With a fair amount of typical vegetation
          Disposed at certain parts.

Here at the top of the tray, which we might call the northwards,
Is a wooded headland, with a crown of bushy-topped trees on;   20
And proceeding downwards or south we take in at a glance
A variety of gorges and knolls and plateaus and basins and saddles,
Somewhat symmetrically put, for easy identification.
        And here is our point of attack.

But remember of course it will not be a tray you will fight on,   25
Nor always by daylight. After a hot day, think of the night
Cooling the desert down, and you still moving over it:
Past a ruined tank or a gun, perhaps, or a dead friend,
Lying about somewhere: it might quite well be that.
        It isn't always a tray.   30

And even this tray is different to what I had thought.
These models are somehow never always the same; the reason
I do not know how to explain quite. Just as I do not know
Why there is always someone at this particular lesson
Who always starts crying. Now will you kindly   35
        Empty those blinking eyes?

I thank you. I have no wish to seem impatient.
I know it is all very hard, but you would not like,
To take a simple example, to take for example,
This place we have thought of here, you would not like   40
To find yourself face to face with it, and you not knowing
        What there might be inside?

Very well then: suppose this is what you must capture.
It will not be easy, not being very exposed,
Secluded away like it is, and somewhat protected   45
By a typical formation of what appear to be bushes,
So that you cannot see, as to what is concealed inside,
        As to whether it is friend or foe.

And so, a strong feint will be necessary in this connection.
It will not be a tray, remember. It may be a desert stretch   50
With nothing in sight, to speak of. I have no wish to be inconsiderate,
But I see there are two of you now, commencing to snivel.

I cannot think where such emotional privates can come from.
     Try to behave like men.

I thank you. I was saying: a thoughtful deception   55
Is always somewhat essential in such a case. You can see
That if only the attacker can capture such an emplacement
The rest of the terrain is his: a key-position, and calling
For the most resourceful manoeuvres. But that is what tactics is.
     Or I should say rather: are.   60

Let us begin then and appreciate the situation.
I am thinking especially of the point we have been considering,
Though in a sense everything in the whole of the terrain
Must be appreciated. I do not know what I have said
To upset so many of you. I know it is a difficult lesson.   65
     Yesterday a man was sick,

But I have never known as many as *five* in a single intake,
Unable to cope with this lesson. I think you had better
Fall out, all five, and sit at the back of the room,
Being careful not to talk. The rest will close up.   70
Perhaps it was me saying 'a dead friend,' earlier on?
     Well, some of us live.

And I never know why, whenever we get to tactics,
Men either laugh or cry, though neither being strictly called for.
But perhaps I have started too early with a difficult problem?   75
We will start again, further north, with a simpler assault.
Are you ready? Is everyone paying attention?
     Very well then. Here are two hills.

IV. Unarmed Combat

In due course of course you will all be issued with
Your proper issue; but until to-morrow,
You can hardly be said to need it; and until that time,
We shall have unarmed combat. I shall teach you.
The various holds and rolls and throws and breakfalls   5
     Which you may sometimes meet.

And the various holds and rolls and throws and breakfalls
Do not depend on any sort of weapon,
But only on what I might coin a phrase and call
The ever-important question of human balance,   10
And the ever-important need to be in a strong
        Position at the start.

There are many kinds of weakness about the body,
Where you would least expect, like the ball of the foot.
But the various holds and rolls and throws and breakfalls   15
Will always come in useful. And never be frightened
To tackle from behind: it may not be clean to do so,
        But this is global war.

So give them all you have, and always give them
As good as you get; it will always get you somewhere.   20
(You may not know it, but you can tie a Jerry
Up without rope; it is one of the things I shall teach you.)
Nothing will matter if only you are ready for him.
        The readiness is all.

The readiness is all. How can I help but feel   25
I have been here before? But somehow then,
I was the tied-up one. How to get out
Was always then my problem. And even if I had
A piece of rope I was always the sort of person
        Who threw the rope aside.   30

And in my time I have given them all I had,
Which was never as good as I got, and it got me nowhere.
And the various holds and rolls and throws and breakfalls
Somehow or other I always seemed to put
In the wrong place. And as for war, my wars   35
        Were global from the start.

Perhaps I was never in a strong position,
Or the ball of my foot got hurt, or I had some weakness
Where I had least expected. But I think I see your point.
While awaiting a proper issue, we must learn the lesson   40

> Of the ever-important question of human balance.
> It is courage that counts.
>
> Things may be the same again; and we must fight
> Not in the hope of winning but rather of keeping
> Something alive: so that when we meet our end,
> It may be said that we tackled wherever we could,
> That battle-fit we lived, and though defeated,
> Not without glory fought.*

45

Juxtaposition, repetition and variation, and related devices are not the only means of relating part to part or part to the whole poem — that is, of creating form. We have already looked at a few of the fixed forms (in the sense of "molds") like the villanelle and sestina into which the material can be "poured," and we shall see more of these in the chapter that deals with meter, rhyme, and stanzaic forms. The metrical and other fixed forms are by definition peculiar to poetry (that is, the definition of "villanelle" begins, "a poem in which . . ."; the definition of "sonnet" begins, "a poem in which . . . ," and so on). Juxtaposition and repetition and variation may have formal functions in prose as well as in poetry, though they are perhaps more prevalent and precise in poetry. There are other elements of form which are closely related to the material and its presentation irrespective of its appearance in poetry or prose. Thus temporal and causal indicators and manipulation of sequences of events is inherent in narrative, whether the narrative is in poetry or prose. Even in the few lines from the beginning of "Sohrab and Rustum" quoted earlier in this chapter, for example, time indicators mark the passage: ". . . morning filled . . . all night long / He had lain . . . But when . . ." and there would be even more but for the fact that in this passage Arnold frequently uses "and" rather than a more obviously temporal connector to indicate sequences. The logical structure or skeleton of argument, too, informs its material regardless of whether the argument is couched in prose or verse. We have already seen such a structure in Marvell's "To His Coy Mistress," in which the verse paragraphs represent the steps of the argument and are themselves marked by

* l. 25 *The readiness is all: Hamlet* V, ii

the logical indicators "Had we . . . ," "But . . . ," "Now, therefore . . . ."

It is important at this point to recall once again that form and content or meaning are not finally separable, that the logical structure of "To His Coy Mistress," for example, is not something imposed upon the poem or hung upon it ornamentally. The poem *is* an argument; its tone is that of reasonableness. To change the structure, to eliminate the logical connectives would be to make it a different poem. To assert the identity of form and content is, of course, to set up something like a standard of judgment. Though we cannot say that the structure of all poems should be logical, if "To His Coy Mistress" were in all other respects exactly the same poem it is now but the verse-paragraphs were divided elsewhere we might well consider the failure of the divisions of the poem to coincide with the divisions of the argument a flaw, though it might be a flaw in the typography rather than in the poem and would be relatively minor in any case. (We would prefer the last three lines of "Philomela," for example, to be set apart from those that precede it, for reasons made clear in the discussion of that poem.)

If form and content are, ideally, one, we can approach form through analysis of content and content or meaning through a scrutiny of form. So it is that in this book we begin with an approach to meaning and here end the first part with a discussion of form, while, in the second part, we approach poems primarily through form and end by approaching meaning. So, too, we can approach an individual poem. Very early in the first chapter, for example, in discussing Robert Bridges' "Nightingales" with the primary intention of understanding its most literal, prosaic statement, we found we had to relate the division of the poem into three stanzas to its statement. We discovered, you will remember, that if the poem were merely the statement of the speaker and the response of the nightingales the third stanza would be superfluous or, at best, asymmetrical or a violation of the principle of the identity of form and content. The consideration of the possible function of that final stanza led to an understanding of the poem not merely as statement-response but as statement-negation-counterstatement turning the poem back on itself and creating much of its meaning out of that turning back.

In the chapters that follow, through study of analogy, imagery, and prosody, we shall learn how to understand more fully the modes of creating meaning in poetry. Our understanding should grow increasingly full and profound, but we shall never be able to say finally, definitively, for all time, what even the shortest and simplest of poems "means." We learn to enter new areas of experience, not a room full of pigeon-holes.

From Form to Meaning

IV
Analogy and Image

INTERACTION

Asked to describe the difference between the original poem and a reordered prose version or paraphrase, many readers can only say, "The prose version hasn't the same force," or, "The ideas are about the same but the paraphrase just doesn't *work*." As we have seen in the previous chapters, the ideas or statements in the reordered and clarified versions of a poem are only approximately the same as those in the original, for the changes in words and word order have inevitably meant changes in meaning. Next, then, we must look for the sources of poetry's power to involve readers in experience, to move them. What makes poetry "work"? What does a poem have in addition to the statement that may be reordered in prose?

Consider these familiar lines:

> My Luve is like a red, red rose,
> That's newly sprung in June . . . .

Even if the two lines were unknown to us and were written out as one, most of us would immediately recognize that line as poetry. Asked why, we would probably mention the rhythm and the comparison of the beloved with a rose. It is worth noting at once that both of these poetic traits are relative, not absolute: prose has rhythms, but the rhythms of poetry are more consistent; prose may include analogies, but poetry hardly exists without them. Leaving the whole subject of sound patterning until later, let us now think of analogies in general and their uses in poetry in particular.

The most obvious way to compare two objects (or qualities, or actions) is to say that one is like the other: my beloved is like a rose. Such a statement is called a *simile,* which may be defined as an explicit comparison of terms essentially unlike,* and which may be recognized by its use of the words *like* or *as.*† These lines all contain similes:

> Say to the Court it glowes,
>   and shines like rotten wood . . . .

> The stupid Fishes hang, as plain
> As *Flies* in *Chrystal* over t'ane . . . .

> Then felt I like some watcher of the skies
> When a new planet swims into his ken . . . .

> If any state be enviable on earth,
> 'Tis yon born idiot's, who, as days go by,
> Still rubs his hands before him, like a fly,
> In a queer sort of meditative mirth.

> To get to sleep in latitudes called upper
>   Is difficult at first for Englishmen.
> It's like being sent to bed before your supper
>   For playing darts with father's fountainpen . . . .

A simile may be brief, like these, or it may form the basis of a whole poem, as in this sonnet by Edmund Spenser in which the

---

* The statement "Your necktie is like mine" is not a simile because neckties, however dissimilar, are essentially the same.

† The simple comparative construction with *than* suggests a simile but is not a true one:

> "when god decided to invent
> everything he took one
> breath bigger than a circustent . . . ."

In so far as the breath is being compared, by implication, to a circus tent, the statement is like a simile. Actually, however, the size of the one is being compared to the size of the other; the qualities being compared are thus essentially the same and the statement is not a true simile. "I wandered lonely as a cloud" is a true simile because not just degrees of loneliness but "I" and "cloud" are being compared. We can say "I, like a cloud, wandered lonely"; we cannot say "The breath, like a circus tent, is bigger."

INTERACTION

speaker compares himself to a huntsman and his "dear" to a "deer"
that came to him of its own accord only after he stopped chasing it:

> Lyke as a huntsman after weary chace,
>> seeing the game from him escapt away,
>> sits downe to rest him in some shady place,
>> with panting hounds beguilèd of their pray:
> So after long pursuit and vaine assay,   5
>> when I all weary had the chace forsooke,
>> the gentle deare returned the selfe-same way,
>> thinking to quench her thirst at the next brooke.
> There she beholding me with mylder looke,
>> sought not to fly, but fearless still did bide: 10
>> till I in hand her yet halfe trembling tooke,
>> and with her owne goodwill hir fyrmely tyde.
> Strange thing me seemd to see a beast so wyld,
>> so goodly wonne with her owne will beguyld.

Everyday speech is full of similes, many so common that, given the
first half, anyone can supply the rest: he was dead as a . . . ; she
was as pretty as a . . . ; her eyes were as blue as . . . . Obviously any
poet who used such conventional similes would run the risk of
sagging into banality. The trouble with a trite expression is that it
insulates us from experience: we do not see *doornails* (who still
knows what a doornail is?), *pictures,* or *the sky* when we hear the
similes they occur in, so the words cannot be said to be working
efficiently. How many people who use the expression "crazy as a
loon" know both what a loon is and what it does that led to a meaningful comparison?

There is nothing wrong with a trite comparison, however, if the
poet can so rearrange his statement of it that we re-experience its
original force. This is what Burns succeeds in doing. The analogy
between a girl and a rose is so stale that we are insulated from seeing
the rose, but Burns makes us re-experience it through convincing us
that he is not merely and half-heartedly using a traditional comparison
but is himself awake to its full effect. The repetition insists upon the
color sufficiently to make it vivid, and "newly sprung" and "June"
suggest that he is talking about a particular rose (and a particular
girl) so that the comparison has a fresh impact.

If the direct comparison is omitted from a simile, and one object is not said to be like, but simply to be, the other, the result is a *metaphor:* my beloved is a rose. Though the statement identifies one object with the other — and, taken literally, the idea is nonsensical — in practice we usually recognize without difficulty an implied comparison which we do in fact understand. "You rat!" we say (with the tone of voice conveying anything from hatred to affection), or "You're a clod." A metaphor may therefore be defined as an *implicit* comparison, and may be recognized by its speaking of one object (or quality, or action) as though it were another (essentially unlike it*). Thus we are using metaphors if we say that the racehorse *flew* around the track or that the little boy held up his grimy *paws*.

A metaphor is a compressed comparison. It brings something new into being (a flying horse, a boy with paws), and so is "creative," while the simile merely calls attention to an existing similarity (a boy with hands like paws). A simile says to us, "Now *compare* this with that." A metaphor, on the other hand, says, "*See* this as that." Its compression, then, is not just in its economy of words, but in its appearing to bypass the intellect. The metaphor acts; the simile warns us that it is acting.

These lines all contain metaphors:

> To you, my purse, and to non other wight
> Compleyne I, for ye be my lady dere! †

> But thy eternal summer shall not fade . . . .

> Love is a sickness full of woes . . . .

> And the hapless Soldier's sigh
> Runs in blood down Palace walls.

> For your brain is on fire — the bedclothes conspire
> of usual slumber to plunder you . . . .

A metaphor, like a simile, may be brief, or the basis of a whole poem. When a metaphor is extended for a number of lines, it will usually turn into the special kind of metaphor called a symbol, which we will discuss later.

* The statement "My beloved is a beautiful girl" — whether or not it is true — is not a metaphor because "beloved" and "girl," in this sentence, are actually the same object.
† *wight:* person

Everyday speech is full of expressions which started as metaphors but in which the new thing has been so successfully created that we no longer refer back to the implied comparison. Without consciousness of the original metaphor, we speak of the eye of a needle, the mouth of a river, the leg of a table, the wing of a building, or a branch of the family. These vestigial metaphors now function merely as acceptable denotations and thus, since they have in effect been swallowed by our common speech, they do not raise the problem of banality.*

It would seem on first thought that both similes and metaphors simply explain unknown objects or feelings by comparing them to others that are known. Thus, if asked to describe what happens when we learn that A ("My Luve") is like B ("rose"), we might say that the unknown, A, has been given the meaning of — or defined in terms of — the known, B. Our understanding of B, we suppose, creates our understanding of A. But the action of a simile or metaphor is more complex. Though B gives meaning to A, A simultaneously modifies B; the process is not a simple action but an interaction. At the same time that the rose tells us something about the girl, the girl modifies our responses to — controls the connotations of — the rose. Each term exerts a control on the other. "My Luve" is not in every way like "a red, red rose, / That's newly sprung in June." We are not, in this poem, asked to consider her thorns. We are not asked to see her with curling petals and a green stem. In other words the comparison is not a one-way boulevard open to all traffic; while the B-term explains the A-term, the A-term places limits on our response to the B-term. Though there are many connotations of the rose that are relevant, such as visual suggestions of beauty, freshness, and blushing, and suggestions of fragrance, the primary effect of this simile arises from the comparison of two emotional responses. Attempting to write out what precisely is being compared to what, we might arrive at some such statement as this: I respond to (the presence or the thought of) my beloved as one responds to the general effect of a fresh, red rose.

* They are not clichés as the conventional similes are, for to be a cliché an expression need not only be common but must also call attention to itself as in some way excessive or pretentious. What makes it trite is the fact that an intended ornament is so obviously shopworn. "Hello" and "Good-bye," no matter how often repeated, have not become clichés; "Long time no see," and "See you later, alligator" became clichés almost immediately.

Similarly, in the line "I wandered lonely as a cloud," while the cloud intensifies the loneliness, the loneliness and the wandering create the particular cloud. This is not just any cloud; it must be a slow-moving cloud in a sky that is otherwise almost clear. The remainder of the simile — "That floats on high o'er vales and hills" — adds height and a vague landscape to the general idea but has in fact less effect on the connotations of "cloud" than does the A-term, "I wandered lonely." The effect of the comparison results not from a simple action but from a complex interaction.

Such interactions are the very core of poetry's effect. Direct analogies — similes and metaphors — as prominent as they may be in poems, are but examples of a more general process introduced in Chapter III: the juxtaposing, or placing next to each other, of two or more components (whether they be images, rhythms, ideas, sounds — any components that can be brought into poetry) which then interact with each other. The experience that comes from a poem is not a simple experience of "this," or even of "this in the light of that," but always of "this and that in relation to each other." And the interaction both heightens and modifies the original terms, involving both a comparison and a contrast. In the previous chapter we have seen how juxtaposition can create new relationships and meanings. This same principle is at work in the juxtaposing of elements in similes and metaphors: "I wandered lonely as a cat" creates a meaning of "wandered lonely" different from that of Wordsworth's line and, incidentally, creates a cat different from that of "The owl and the pussy cat." Though similes and metaphors provide the clearest examples, it is essential to recognize that the process goes on continually in poetry even though no formal figures of speech are present.

Perhaps the briefest example of this direct interaction is to be found in a six-character poem by the eighth-century Chinese poet Tu Fu (pronounced Doo Foo):

Blue	Smoke	War
White	Bones	Men

Complete translation into English requires certain obvious additions:

Blue is the smoke of war;
White are the bones of men.

Here there is no simile or metaphor, no direct comparison, either explicit or implicit. There are only two simple statements. And yet almost everyone who encounters this poem testifies to its compelling power, its grasp upon his imagination, its ability to stir his emotions. What is the source of this power? It can only come from the inter-action of the two statements with each other, or, to be more exact, of each word with each of the other five.

Can we be more specific? There are certain direct relationships to which we can point. That the colors somehow interact is obvious: blue and white, color and non-color, yet consonant. Had the first character in the Chinese been that for "black" there would be a stronger contrast — and a less effective, indeed a different, poem. Though "blue" and "white" contrast, they are also similar: they are both cool; there is a modulation between them and not simply a direct clash. In "smoke" and "bones" there is a decided contrast of textures, the soft and ephemeral beside the hard and durable. But the interaction of these connotations surely reminds us that the bones are a remnant of something else that was ephemeral, the flesh that clothed them or, simply, "men." The interactions between these first pairs of words suggest that there are also interactions between "war" and "men" — and so there are — but any paraphrase is apt to be rigid, limiting, and oversimplified. To insist upon a cause-and-effect re-lationship between "men" and "war," "war" and "bones," is to enforce a meaning that goes beyond the direct statements of the poem. The most we can say here is that "war" is both human and inhuman, that "men" are both intrinsic to it and extraneous to it, enveloped by it and yet separable from it.

But even these relationships do not adequately account for the effect of the poem; the interactions go beyond pairs of words to whole concepts — the first three Chinese characters as a unit and the second three as a unit. Compared with each other, the two lines imply two kinds of distance. "Blue is the smoke of war" puts a spatial distance between the war and us (both speaker and audience). The connota-tions are rather of distant haze and small campfires than of the chaos of immediate battle (as they might have been had that first word been "black"). "White are the bones of men" implies a temporal distance between the event and us. Literally, present smoke could only relate to future bones, present bones only to past smoke. Either way — or, more simply, with its images building as they must on memory and the imagination — the poem is contemplative; the distance is not only spatial and temporal but philosophical. Hence the total inter-action creates an experience of pensive insight rather than experiences of active horror, or dedication, or revulsion, such as might lead to avoidance or protest and such as would result from more directly personal involvement in the time or place of the battle. The action of the poem is contemplation; the contemplation is a result of the total complex interaction of the six characters, or words.

Perhaps this is not to say more than that every word both contributes to and is controlled by the context in which it appears. This fact is as evident in prose as it is in poetry, though poetry tends to exploit these interactions more thoroughly than does prose.

Before returning to direct analogies, let us consider a further brief example of the power of juxtaposed statements. Here is a well-known, though anonymous, early sixteenth-century English poem:

> Western wind, when wilt thou blow,
> The small rain down can rain?
> Christ, if my love were in my arms
> And I in my bed again!

As in Tu Fu's poem, there is no simile and no metaphor. A question and an exclamation are brought together to interact with each other. Why? What are the relationships between them?

The question and the exclamation each express a desire, and, in order to relate the desires, readers often resort to inventing a plot for the poem: the speaker, students have frequently told us, is a sailor becalmed in mid-ocean, praying for the wind that will take him home to his beloved. This brief plot, be it noted, not only goes beyond what the poem says; more importantly, it fails to account for one whole line, one-fourth of the poem. The sailor might well want a wind, but why should he also long for rain? Nor is it even a question of "also": the wind is desired for the sake of the rain: "Western wind, when wilt thou blow / [so that] The small rain down can rain?" Readers at this point in the discussion sometimes reach for the Ancient Mariner's "Water, water, every where, / Nor any drop to drink," or, more frequently, turn the speaker into a farmer and further complicate the plot. But such inventions, going far beyond legitimate inferences, are not the way to account for the effect of the poem.

A question and an exclamation, each expressing a desire — how do they relate to, or affect, each other? Two longings, a longing for a wind bringing "small rain," and a longing to return home to "my love . . . in my arms / And I in my bed. . . ." Despite the frequent student paraphrase "praying for the wind," not the first but the second longing is heightened by the exclamation "Christ," which derives its force from that area of emotional intensity in which profanity and prayer are almost indistinguishable. And this mixture, at once sacred and profane, which is close to the emotional essence of intense human love, directly conveys the profound nostalgia of the lover for his beloved. But what has this nostalgia to do with the weather unless there is some cause-and-effect relationship? It is this doubt that leads to the invention of such plots as we have ruled out.

The relationship is not one of cause and effect but one, again, of interacting connotations. The process is not to invent a plot that does not exist and cannot be tested in the poem, but to seek in the juxtaposition of wind, rain, and love, as they are qualified in the poem, potentially meaningful common elements, like those of "wandered lonely" and "cloud" in Wordsworth's line. The rain desired, the rain to be brought on the western wind (in the British Isles, the moist wind off the ocean), is the "small" rain which fosters growth, as opposed to the destructive rain of a heavy storm. The filaments that tie the halves of the poem together are connotations of desired fertility and creativity. The general drought implied by the question becomes an unspoken metaphor for the condition of the lover, the personal drought implied by the exclamation. The lover's longing is profoundly, and openly, sexual, but not obscene, for the interacting connotations emphasize what is natural and gentle and creative, what is central to life itself. Thus the power of this essentially simple poem comes from juxtaposing two expressions of basic human needs, the connotations of which control and intensify each other.

The brief poems just discussed have each presented a single pair of statements and thus each depends upon a single primary interaction. Obviously, longer poems can be much more complex, with every simile or metaphor an individual interaction, and all of these interacting with each other. Though every line, clause, phrase, or, indeed, word in a poem in fact interacts with every other, some of these relationships will of course be more important than others, and even some longer poems may be dominated by a primary interaction. The single simile of the Spenser sonnet "Lyke as a huntsman" is an example. Donne's poem "The Flea," in spite of the complications of the precise argument, gains its effect primarily from the interaction between the aim of the elaborate argument and the incongruous insect on which it centers. The effect of "Richard Cory" comes from E. A. Robinson's sudden substitution of a new contrast in the character of Cory himself, replacing the contrast between Cory and the townspeople which, until the last two lines, had seemed to be the point of the poem:

Richard Cory

Whenever Richard Cory went down town,
We people on the pavement looked at him:
He was a gentleman from sole to crown,
Clean favored, and imperially slim.

And he was always quietly arrayed,   5
And he was always human when he talked;
But still he fluttered pulses when he said,
'Good-morning,' and he glittered when he walked.

And he was rich — yes, richer than a king —
And admirably schooled in every grace: 10
In fine, we thought that he was everything
To make us wish that we were in his place.

So on we worked, and waited for the light,
And went without the meat, and cursed the bread;
And Richard Cory, one calm summer night,   15
Went home and put a bullet through his head.

By adding one additional fact, one final line, Robinson forces the reader to refocus all that he had accepted earlier.

The next poem, by A. E. Housman, is an example of a more complex series of interactions:

To an Athlete Dying Young

The time you won your town the race
We chaired you through the market-place;

Man and boy stood cheering by,
And home we brought you shoulder-high.

To-day, the road all runners come,   5
Shoulder-high we bring you home,
And set you at your threshold down,
Townsman of a stiller town.

Smart lad, to slip betimes away
From fields where glory does not stay   10
And early though the laurel grows
It withers quicker than the rose.

Eyes the shady night has shut
Cannot see the record cut,
And silence sounds no worse than cheers   15
After earth has stopped the ears:

Now you will not swell the rout
Of lads that wore their honours out,
Runners whom renown outran
And the name died before the man.   20

So set, before its echoes fade,
The fleet foot on the sill of shade,
And hold to the low lintel up
The still-defended challenge-cup.

And round that early-laurelled head   25
Will flock to gaze the strengthless dead,
And find unwithered on its curls
The garland briefer than a girl's.

Running through this poem, beginning with the pictures of the
runner being brought home "shoulder-high" on two differing occasions — being brought, that is, to two quite different "homes" —
is the unexpected contrast of death as victory with life as inevitable
defeat. This interaction with its resultant irony is clear: it is good to
have died in triumph since there is no way from victory but the way
down. Yet, clear as it is, this irony is not sufficient to account for the
full effect of the poem. It might be revealing to pick out those words
or lines that seem to go beyond the central contrast and thus to add

other elements to the final interaction. We will return to this poem later.

IMAGES

In order to talk more explicitly about the uses of analogies and other interactions in poetry, it is necessary now to clarify another central concept, the poetic image.

Most readers of Burns's lines will say that, in some way or other, they "see" the red, red rose. Words "call up" objects; our imaginations are prompted to picture an actual rose. Of course, could they be compared directly, the pictures formed by any two readers would be found to differ in most details — some would be vivid and precise, every petal in place, some would be vague, and no two would be exactly alike. The definition of a word is a set of substitute words; the *image* it creates is a picture in the mind. Though two readers may agree upon a definition, their images will still differ.

The pictures we form depend upon our knowledge, experience, and memories: we can call up no picture of a pangolin (or a schnauzer, or a rose) if we have not seen one, or a picture of one, or had it described to us. If we have seen only one hookah, the picture we form when we hear the word will probably be a memory of that one experience (and may bring along details irrelevant to the new context, such as a caterpillar and a toadstool, if our one experience of "hookah" was with Alice in Wonderland); if we have seen many, the picture we form will be a composite based on our many experiences. Though we may never have seen a polar bear, we easily picture one by combining our memories of "white" with our memories of "bear." However, though the result may be adequate for our needs at the moment — though it may result in a correct definition — it will be only a rough approximation of an adequate image. The Roman snout of a polar bear, for example, is quite unlike the teddy bear snub we may have supplied from our memories; the color is uneven and not at all like the blue-white of new snow.

In other words, the precision of our picture depends upon the precision of our memories and the range of our experience. The more we have observed and read, absorbed and attempted to understand, the more experience we have, the readier we are to recognize the nuances that differentiate one event from all others. A boy in love for the first time "doesn't know what is happening to him"; he is confused and "can't straighten things out"; he "doesn't know what it all means." A newcomer to baseball sees no difference in the delivery of two pitchers. A geologist sees an area's prehistory in what, to a layman, are just hills. We notice only a fraction of the phenomena available to our senses; though it sounds strange when said this way, we can go along from day to day failing to experience our own experience. Nothing can be apprehended in itself; any new idea, event, or object can only be apprehended against whatever background we bring to it. If our past experiences have been vague, our present experiences will suffer; words will call up only imprecise associations and the pictures formed in our imaginations will inevitably also be vague.

But the fact that the pictures formed by any two readers will always differ does not alter the more important fact that, for both, words can create the sensation of seeing (or seeming to see) an object not actually present. Such a sensation is called an *image* or, more precisely, a *visual image*. When we speak of "an image" in poetry, however, we are likely to be speaking of the words that give rise to the sensations rather than of the sensations themselves which, as psychological events, vary from one individual to another or indeed from time to time in the same individual. "Image," denoting a word or group of words, is not (as we are using it) synonymous with "simile" or "metaphor." These figures of speech often, though not necessarily, include two images. "My Luve" hardly exists visually for most readers, although for some strong visualizers she may; the "red, red rose, / That's newly sprung in June," at all events, is in itself an image, though it is but one term of the simile.

Images are words, or groups of words, which denote things or the qualities of things, words with the power to elicit imagined sensory reactions. By such definition, any concrete noun is an image: "ballot box" but not "democracy," "sweetheart" but not "adoration." It is easy to see that the more specific the noun, the more vivid the potential reaction. (Consider this progression: creature, animal, bird, water bird, duck, mallard drake.) Although it is true that any concrete noun is an image, poetic images are more often phrases, or even whole sentences, than single words. Adjectives are sometimes of more importance to an image than the unobtrusive (but essential) noun or pronoun they modify ("He is tall and bald.").

So far, then, we might say — as is indeed often said — that an image is simply a word-picture; however, this definition is too limited. Visual images, the most common variety, may be word-pictures, but there are as many varieties of imagery as there are physical senses. Individuals differ vastly in their sensitivity to various types of image (as they do in their sensitivity to types of physical events, to odors, say, or noises), but each of the traditional five senses — sound, touch, smell, and taste, as well as sight — can be appealed to through the imagination. Here are examples:

VISUAL   All in a hot and copper sky,
The bloody Sun, at noon,
Right up above the mast did stand,
No bigger than the Moon.

And higher than that wall a circling row
Of goodliest trees, loaden with fairest fruit,
Blossoms and fruits at once of golden hue,
Appeared, with gay enamelled colours mixed . . . .

And Marian's nose looks red and raw . . . .

AUDITORY   And now 'twas like all instruments,
Now like a lonely flute . . . .

Shrieking voices
Scolding, mocking, or merely chattering,
Always assail them.

TACTILE   Her lost moist hand clings mortally to mine.

I shall go shod in silk,
And you in wool . . . .

I am sleepy, and the oozy weeds about me twist.

OLFACTORY   There in the fragrant pines and the cedars dusk and dim.

Lilies that fester smell far worse than weeds.

GUSTATORY   When you came, you were like red wine and honey . . . .

Then to the Spicy Nut-Brown Ale . . . .

In listing images related to each of the primary senses, we have not yet exhausted the varieties of imagery. There are subdivisions of these five, such as *onomatopoeia,* an auditory image in which the words imitate the intended sound ("bow-wow," "crash," or, the usual example, "And murmuring of innumerable bees"), and there are others appealing to additional senses. The image of felt warmth or cold is not merely a question of touch but of a separate temperature sense. Images of motion may be visual ("He is waving his hands, he is wagging his head, / He has certainly found a Snark"), but there is also the image of bodily participation in a motion:

> I sprang to the stirrup, and Joris, and he;
> I galloped, Dirck galloped, we galloped all three . . . .
>
> My instep arch not only keeps the ache,
> It keeps the pressure of the ladder-round.
> I feel the ladder sway as the boughs bend.

Note in the first example how the rhythm strengthens the image. In the second example the swaying of the ladder is an image not only for us but for the speaker, who is no longer on it. Such images of felt motion, formed with verbs or verbals, are called *kinesthetic images* — "kinesthesia" being the sense which gives us an awareness of our own bodily tensions and muscle movements. (Bodily tension and not motion is the essential ingredient of a kinesthetic image: the image of a weight held motionless in the hand is kinesthetic.) Images of motion seen or heard but not felt are called *kinetic.*

It should be clear from these few examples that images rarely appeal to only a single sense. The heat of Coleridge's "bloody Sun" is more than visual; the "oozy weeds" or the "red wine and honey" can be seen as well as felt or tasted. The categories are not to be used as pigeon-holes; they simply illustrate the variety of claims that words can make upon our imaginations.

There is a mixing of the senses in some images, however, that goes beyond their normal, simultaneous participation. This mixture occurs in any image that explicitly demands the exercise of some sense not literally capable of responding, as when we are asked to taste a sound, to see an odor or, perhaps, to hear some abstract mental state. These are called *synesthetic images.* For example:

Silence will fall like dews,
On white silence below.

       But here there is no light,
Save what from heaven is with the breezes blown . . . .

I cannot see . . .
  . . . what soft incense hangs upon the boughs . . . .

No matter, so I taste forgetfulness . . . .

Silence is not visual, and thus cannot be white. In its context in Elinor Wylie's poem, the image both condenses the visual and aural effects of a snowscape and creates a visual metaphor of silence itself. Light cannot be blown, incense (the fragrance of flowers) seen, or forgetfulness tasted; though such images mingle sense impressions in a way that is, logically, impossible, they can be most effective sensory metaphors.* And such metaphors are not limited to poetry: responsible critics will speak of the color of a musical tone or the texture of prose.

Just as our senses constantly interact in response to everyday phenomena — we know the chops for dinner by the sizzle and the aroma as well as by their appearance and their taste, each of these sensations reinforcing the others — so do images interact in a poem. In Frost's "After Apple-Picking," for example, the kinesthetic image of swaying on a ladder is made especially vivid by its following immediately upon the particular image of pressure on the instep arch. Our attention is shifted from the feet to a motion involving full bodily balance; yet by the same movement the image of pressure on the contact point between the body and the swaying ladder is intensified.

The relation of images to each other is of more importance to a poem than is the vividness of any particular image. At the same time, however, it is the quality, not the quantity, of its images that matters. The fact is that we do not stop to consider every glimmer of an image

* Most images which mix the senses can, in fact, be accounted for logically by applying such technical terms as *synecdoche* ("soft incense," a part, stands for "flowers," the whole, and the flowers may hang upon boughs), *metonymy* ("the laughing crown" stands for an amused king), or *ellipsis* ("No matter, so I taste [the wine which leads to] forgetfulness"). But, however well these terms explain the logic involved, they do not explain away the immediate metaphorical impact of the synesthetic images, just as the logical redefinition of "wisest" does not explain away the impact of the apparent contradiction in the oxymoron "wisest fool" discussed in the preceding chapter.

as we read. Some potential images must be held to a minimal effect
by the poet and others emphasized if his poem is not to be a mere
clutter of sense impressions. In fact, it is quite possible for an image
to be too vivid and thus to interfere with, or even destroy, what would
seem to have been the intended effect of the poem. Sometimes this
may be due to the poet's having been at least momentarily inept (as
when Crashaw writes of the cherub who sips from the waters of Mary
Magdalene's tears, and adds the repellent idea that his song "Tastes
of this breakfast all day long"), but sometimes it is apparently due
to the poet's having been carried away by an image, admittedly impressive or beautiful, which unfortunately overpowers the context
in which it appears. An image is a means of poetic communication,
of the creation of precise meaning; it is not an end in itself.

POETRY WITHOUT IMAGES

Critics, and poets too, have sometimes spoken of images as though
they were the primary units — or even the whole — of poetry. That
such is not true is apparent in the simple fact that there is a poetry
almost without images, a poetry of statement, of abstract idea, whether
serious or satiric:

> The mind is its own place, and in itself
> Can make a Heaven of Hell, a Hell of Heaven.

> *Shadwell* alone, of all my Sons, is he
> Who stands confirm'd in full stupidity.
> The rest to some faint meaning make pretence,
> But *Shadwell* never deviates into sense.

> Time present and time past
> Are both perhaps present in time future,
> And time future contained in time past.
> If all time is eternally present
> All time is unredeemable.   5
> What might have been is an abstraction
> Remaining a perpetual possibility
> Only in a world of speculation.
> What might have been and what has been
> Point to one end, which is always present.   10

Here there are no images to speak of, but only a fanatic would deny that Milton, Dryden, or Eliot was writing poetry.

Images appeal to the senses; poetry can also appeal directly to abstract reason. There have been poets, in fact, who have considered any appeal to the senses to be necessarily discreditable, and an appeal to reason an appeal to what is noblest in man. We need not here evaluate differing theories of what poetry *ought* to be; we need only recognize that there is a wide range within what poetry *is*. Naturally the distinction between poetry of statement and poetry of image is, again, not absolute but relative. What is basically poetry of statement uses images; poetry stressing images rarely exists without statements. Poets usually appeal both to reason and to the senses, though we must recognize tendencies to favor one or the other.* We have discussed various forms of statement in the preceding chapter; we mention the subject again here to remind you that, in discussing the uses of images, we are not discussing all of poetry. With that warning, we should look now at a number of poems which do depend to a great extent upon their images, not in order to categorize the images according to kinds, but to see how they interact. Having done this, we can, in the next chapter, turn to various common uses of image and analogy.

INTERACTING IMAGES

Even in poetry in which images are of primary importance, there is something more than the image, as difficult as that "something more" may be to define. Image must be distinguished from both idea and feeling, either of which may be tied to an image but is not identical with it. Even stripped of such intellectual or emotional accompaniments, however, the image is more than a bare sense perception. For one thing, its medium of expression is language, which we think of as essentially meaningful. Perhaps it is enough to say that the precisely rendered sensory impression will, when it stands alone, suggest that it has meaning, whether or not that meaning can

---

* It is probably true that, in the total interaction that creates poetry, there is a roughly algebraic balance such that a poem without images must have a strong or regular rhythmical pattern, while increasing vividness of imagery will sustain decreasing regularity of sound pattern, one powerful poetic element replacing another.

be stated. It is, in fact, not the meaning itself but the experience of
meaningfulness that is important here; this experience is the "something more." We take this experience to be the point of William
Carlos Williams' well-known but badly mistreated poem:

The Red Wheelbarrow

so much depends
upon

a red wheel
barrow

glazed with rain
water

beside the white
chickens

Though readers are frequently fascinated with this poem, they just
as often don't know what to make of it. Asked to discuss it, some will
discourse on the importance of wheelbarrows to agricultural economy
— and we once received a lengthy student paper written to prove that
the poem was a complex presentation of sexual passion through the
symbolic use of "red" and "white," which "obviously" stand for the
passionate male and the virginal female. But, when they have finished,
these same readers will usually agree that somehow the poem seems to
have escaped, somehow they have lost contact with it. It is not their
fault entirely for, in pushing for a meaning which they feel it must
have, they are merely following the demand of any verbal communication as strengthened here, in particular, by the apparent demand of
the first four words. The poem, as brief as it is, begins with a claim
that something is important; in order to meet the claim, they resort
to dragging additional meaning into the poem. Submitting again to
an encounter with those first four words in context, they can usually
be shown that "so much depends / upon" is not to be taken as an
evaluation of the wheelbarrow but rather as a part of the very experience of seeing it so vividly.

Williams has presented a precise visual impact. The colors are pristine; the scene is fresh. In spite of the rain, these chickens are not bedraggled: the rainwater glaze heightens the red of the wheelbarrow, preparing the contrast which heightens the white of the chickens; the brilliance of the colors in turn keeps the rainwater clear and clean, not drenching cold or muddy. "so much depends / upon" is not, then, a statement about the wheelbarrow but a statement re-creating in words the experience of seeing it (or anything) so vividly. A brilliantly realized, exact image conveys both a sense impression and an impression of meaningfulness. An impression of meaningfulness is not the same thing as a meaning. We may have a profound sense — perhaps indeed the very basis of our sanity — that the world has meaning, that what we see and do is coherent and important, and yet we may remain totally unable to formulate that meaning. A poetic image usually reaffirms the experience of meaningfulness which accompanies any vivid perception.

Though it is certainly a fact that most of us delight in a vivid image, ultimately we are not satisfied with an image in isolation, however vivid it may be. We want a context for the image; we want the interaction that is a poem. (Williams' first four words provide such a context by making his poem not just an image but, explicitly, a poem about the image-experience.) Even the Japanese *haiku,* that brief poetic form which is apt to seem entirely image, will be found, when successful, to set up an interaction between two images, between an image and an abstract idea or, at least, between one moment and the next.* *Haiku* — indeed any poems — should be encountered one at

* "The *hokku* (or more properly, *haiku*) is a tiny verse-form in which Japanese poets have been working for hundreds of years. Originally it was the first part of the *tanka,* a five-line poem, often written by two people as a literary game: one writing three lines, the other, two lines capping them. But the *hokku,* or three-line starting verse, became popular as a separate form. As such it is properly called *haiku,* and retains an incredible popularity among all classes of Japanese.

"There are only seventeen syllables in the *haiku;* the first and third lines contain five, the second line seven. There is almost always a key word giving the season of the year — directly or by inference. (This is a short-cut, costing the poet only one or two syllables, whereby the reader can immediately comprehend the weather, the foliage, the bird and insect life, and the emotions traditional to the season — factors which almost always are important in the poem.) But there is also, in a good *haiku,* more than a mere statement of feeling or a picture of nature: there is an interior switch in viewpoint . . . ." Peter Beilenson, *Japanese Haiku,* The Peter Pauper Press (Mount Vernon, N.Y., 1956). The five haiku in the text below are Mr. Beilenson's translations from this same volume.

a time, not in bunches, as it is necessary to set them down here. But, looking at each of these poems individually, the reader should quite readily recognize the two images, or the image and the idea, which interact to create poems as vastly different in effect as the first and the last of these:

> Plume of Pampas grass
> > Trembling in every wind . . .
> > > Hush, my lonely heart.

> Black cloudbank broken
> > Scatters in the night . . . now see
> > > Moon-lighted mountain!

> Don't touch my plumtree
> > Said my friend and saying so . . .
> > > Broke the branch for me.

> Carven gods long gone . . .
> > Dead leaves alone foregather
> > > On the temple porch.

> Buddha on the hill
> > From your holy nose indeed
> > > Hangs an icicle.

The visual image of the grass plume reinforces the idea of the lonely heart; the moment of the cloudbank is replaced by the moment of the mountain's first visual impact; the friend's words contrast with his actions; in each brief poem there is an interaction of image with image or image with idea.

Now we are ready to look at the interacting effects of images within a few somewhat longer poems, the first by Tu Fu:

Passing the Night in a Pavilion by the River

> Darkness claims the mountain path
> Leading to this high room beside the water gate.
> Thin clouds rest on the cliffs;

A lonely moon turns in the waves.
Cranes fly past in silence
While sated wolves howl.
Not sleeping, I worry about the wars,
Lacking the strength to put the world in order.*

The poem is simple and direct and therefore the relationships among the interacting elements are comparatively obvious. Six lines presenting images precede two lines presenting a direct statement of the speaker's condition. The images, then, may be expected to relate to that condition, not as substitutes for it or to be equated with it (the wolves "standing for" the war), not necessarily (nor even probably) as cause and effect, but as emotionally consonant, so that the images and the statement of the condition reinforce each other, allowing us to participate in the experience. Presumably the poet chose to mention these details rather than other possible details (the furnishings of the room, for example, or his reason for being there) because he expected them to create the experience he wished to convey.

The first two lines, though they present two visual images (three, if the room and the water gate are separated), differ in approach, and thus in effect, from lines three through six. Each of the four central lines briefly presents a direct image; the first two lines are somewhat more abstract. "Darkness" is not as concrete a noun as "clouds," "moon," "Cranes," or "wolves," all four of which are material objects (though one may quibble about "clouds"). "Claims" is a more abstract verb than are "rest," "turns," "fly," or "howl," all four

---

* We should perhaps explain why we include so many oriental poems in a volume for English-speaking readers. We are, of course, happy to call attention to a magnificent body of poetry, but that is not a sufficient motive. Translations from oriental languages have a particular usefulness. Just because the structure of Chinese, for example, differs so vastly from that of English — lacking many of our overt grammatical distinctions but adding tonal variations to our already complex range of sound patterns — the translator is left with little beyond image and idea that can be carried over from one language to the other. Translators working from languages more akin to English often attempt to carry over similar sound-patterns and are thus involved in selecting English words that will compromise between the new sound and the meaning of the original. In a poem translated from the Chinese, images and ideas, less compromised, can be studied more or less independently of other poetic elements. However, it must be admitted that, without knowledge of the Chinese, we can only discuss the effect of the English words, which will necessarily convey an experience differing from that conveyed (to one who can read it) by the original poem.

of which are physical actions (though "rest" is, more precisely, an absence of physical action). "Darkness claims the mountain path" is a metaphor that goes beyond simple presentation of the visual image by making a statement about the relationship of the darkness and the path: the path now belongs to the darkness which is taking possession of it. What, precisely, any reader "sees" as a result of this line will depend of course upon what memories are roused by the words "mountain path," perhaps modified not only by the darkness but also by memories of Chinese paintings, since the fact that this is a Chinese poem will of itself exert some controls over a sensitive reader. Thus the primary effect of the image is likely to be determined by the more concrete noun, even though that noun is the object and not the subject in the action, even though the line actually asks us to see the darkness more vividly than the path it dominates.

The second line is grammatically subordinate to the first — the whole of it functioning as an adjective modifying "path" — but the images, though perhaps no more precise (since we are given few details about the room and may not know what a water gate is), are nevertheless more direct. "Leading to" suggests a view of the path from its beginning; "this" brings us quickly to the other end of the path (with the possible implication that the speaker has just traversed it) and provides a vantage point from which the subsequent images are perceived. "High" may describe either the shape of the room or its location, or both. The first is suggested by the immediate effect of the adjective upon the noun, the second by the continuing influence of "mountain path." Readers may imagine various forms of (presumably oriental) rooms, but the fact is that the first two lines, which introduce us to the world of the poem, sketch that location with the briefest of strokes. The following four images, though also brief, are much more specific.

That the darkness has claimed only the path is implied by the third line, which presents something to be seen at a distance, while the fourth line adds the moonlight that enables us to see. But these logical effects are subsidiary to the more direct impact of the actual pictures, the wisps of cloud stationary against the cliffs above the gently flowing river in which the reflected moon appears to revolve slowly. The image "A lonely moon turns in the waves" is both concise and precise, including every necessary control against misreading. That the river flows gently is, for example, necessitated by the "turning" of the moon: were the waves at all violent the reflection would disintegrate. "Lonely" is here a visual effect (as well as, of course, an emotional effect); the moon is lonely in part because it is not, in this poem, the mistress of the night sky but a reflected light subject to the action of the water. The moon appears lonely because, also, the perceiver is lonely.

This decisive image, almost literally the poem's center, dominates the others. The visual loneliness of the moon, and the loneliness of the speaker thereby implied, strengthen the suggestions of isolation already latent in the first two lines, the remote room, the path now too dark to be followed. The clouds are "thin," ephemeral, existing now but threatened with disintegration at any moment, like the reflection in the waves. They too, like the moon and the speaker, are out of their proper element; their insubstantiality is directly heightened in contrast with their background, the cliffs on which they rest.

As the potent fourth line interacts with our memories of the preceding three, so also does it heighten particular aspects of those following. Cranes are gregarious birds noted for their singularly loud and resonant voices and for the constancy of their calling to each other in flight. Thus there is within the fifth line a kind of self-contradiction that renders the silence ominous. The image is explicitly auditory — for silence can only be heard, or rather not heard — but it is also implicitly visual, adding the moving cranes, as shadows or silhouettes, to the backdrop of darkness, clouds, cliffs, and moon-reflected-in-the-river — for only if seen could silent cranes be noticed. Into the silence of the passing cranes comes the howling of wolves (for even though "while" implies simultaneity, we must read the lines consecutively) and we would expect an intensification of the threatening overtones, but, though these overtones remain, there is a specific control placed upon them by the information that these wolves are "sated." Presumably, if we knew enough about the howling of wolves, the adjective would serve to modify the quality of the howl — the implication being that there is a difference between the howls of a hungry and a sated wolf. Even without such knowledge (and even if there were in fact no such difference) we accept the poet's statement as it affects the overtones. The howling of sated wolves is less an immediate threat than it is a reminder of a threatening force which has triumphed and still exists. The silenced cranes retain at least their power of flight; the speaker is isolated, confined, motionless.

After such preparation of emotion and attitude, the last two lines fall easily into place. They add information we did not have — that the speaker is troubled specifically about "the wars" and about his personal inadequacy, the helplessness of any lone individual who longs to bring order out of the world's chaos — but this information by itself would be an ineffective statement of fact; the context of images adds the situational and emotional overtones that make of this fact an experience. All coheres: the spiritual and the physical isolation, human helplessness, thin clouds, lonely moon, silent cranes, with sated wolves and wars haunting the imagination. The speaker is not threatened by any physical danger; he is not a soldier but rather a civilian in wartime at a time when war was not the immediate threat to all civilians that it is now. The experience of the poem, created by the precision of the language rendering its images and by the interacting of those images with each other and with a statement of the speaker's condition, is an experience of a man's awareness of human isolation and helplessness in the face of moral dislocation.

Now, having looked at a poem in which the imagery is central to the creation of an experience, let us consider a very different poem, by Archibald MacLeish, in which the imagery accompanies a logical framework of statements and abstract ideas. Though this poem does conclude by emphasizing the experience of a particular image, that experience also concludes an argument, and the various other images in the poem, though they naturally interact, are consciously played down and kept subordinate to the central argument:

"Not Marble nor the Gilded Monuments"

The praisers of women in their proud and beautiful poems,
Naming the grave mouth and the hair and the eyes,
Boasted those they loved should be forever remembered:
These were lies.

The words sound but the face in the Istrian sun is forgotten.   5
The poet speaks but to her dead ears no more.
The sleek throat is gone — and the breast that was troubled to listen:
Shadow from door.

Therefore I will not praise your knees nor your fine walking
Telling you men shall remember your name as long   10

As lips move or breath is spent or the iron of English
Rings from a tongue.

I shall say you were young, and your arms straight, and your mouth
    scarlet:
I shall say you will die and none will remember you:
Your arms change, and none remember the swish of your garments,   15
Nor the click of your shoe.

Not with my hand's strength, not with difficult labor
Springing the obstinate words to the bones of your breast
And the stubborn line to your young stride and the breath to your
    breathing
And the beat to your haste   20
Shall I prevail on the hearts of unborn men to remember.

(What is a dead girl but a shadowy ghost
Or a dead man's voice but a distant and vain affirmation
Like dream words most)

Therefore I will not speak of the undying glory of women.   25
I will say you were young and straight and your skin fair
And you stood in the door and the sun was a shadow of leaves on
    your shoulders
And a leaf on your hair —

I will not speak of the famous beauty of dead women:
I will say the shape of a leaf lay once on your hair.   30
Till the world ends and the eyes are out and the mouths broken,
Look! It is there!

The poem begins with a generalization, a statement of the boast made
by any number of "praisers of women" that the beloved would be
made immortal by the poetry praising her. MacLeish's title is the first
line of "Sonnet 55" in which Shakespeare so boasts. The images, even
when one is alert for them, almost escape notice. The noun-phrases
in the first line — "praisers of women" and "their proud and beautiful poems" — hardly involve the senses, though a strong visualizer
might insist that he sees the poets or their poems, and the slow rhythm
of the line may create an auditory suggestion of the "proud and beau-

tiful poems." The nouns in the second line, referring to objects more readily imagined — "mouth," "hair," "eyes" — are also general. Only "grave mouth" is at all specific, and this phrase too is applicable to many women, not just to an individual. In fact, we are not asked to picture a woman but to recognize that all these love poets were limited to "Naming," to representing objects by use of words. That the words are not the objects themselves is the point of the first two stanzas, and this point is furthered by keeping the images general. In spite of the poets' high claims for their praise, those they loved are not remembered. (Or, more precisely, they are remembered only as abstract characters in a pseudo-biographical fiction. The words cease to have any relevance to the actual person who was beloved: even the most specific image merely creates a picture for the reader, and the reader's picture has little relation to the woman of whom the poet wrote.)

In the second stanza, the speaker explains his general denial by moving out of the plural into a single instance of the loss — but the poet and the woman are unidentified and thus still representative. Though the words of the poem remain, the woman is dead. To suggest simultaneously both the loss of individuality and its former existence, the vague noun "face" is given geographical placement "in the Istrian sun." Not actual precision but an effect of precision is the result: there is a sound of particularity, but no vividness. Without reference to a historical atlas, few could locate Istria, and, even knowing where it is, few would find it helpful in giving features to this particular face. It may, of course, add such connotations as go with southern Europe, the Mediterranean, the Adriatic (though it is the sun and not the face that is Istrian), but primarily it serves to convince us that there once *was* a now unrecapturable woman of whom the poet wrote. At the same time, the connotations of "sun" contrast with the meanings of "dead" and "gone" to reinforce the sense of loss. If the modifying phrase "in the Istrian sun" thus lends a somewhat deceptive sense of individuality to the "face," the modifying phrase "that was troubled to listen" renders "breast" abstract; it is a conceptual breast, the location of the feelings, rather than a material object of visual beauty. The most distinct image in the stanza, "Shadow from door," objectifies the emotion of loss, not the woman. At her most distinct, she is no more than a shadow.

"Therefore" — this being so — the speaker quite logically will refrain from praising his own beloved. In his very denial of his intention, of course, he is insinuating that which he denies (a rhetorical device known as *apophasis*). The "knees" and the "fine walking," we are to realize, are well worthy of praise, and to imply this is, in effect, to praise them. The distinction developed through the next stanzas is that between praising, which he has rejected as ineffective, and simple naming, statement of unadorned fact: "I shall say you were young . . . I shall say you will die . . . ." In spite of this logical distinction, however, the images push us finally beyond simple naming. We become increasingly aware, not of the actual woman, but of the speaker's love for her, as particular images interact with the knowledge of ultimate loss.

It might be helpful, for purposes of analysis, to consider the images in the third, fourth, and fifth stanzas logically, according to subject, rather than chronologically. There is, for example, a group of metaphors related not to the speaker's beloved but to his medium, poetry itself: "the iron of English / Rings from a tongue"; writing poetry involves "Springing" ("bending," "forcing"), with "hand's strength" and "difficult labor" (metaphorical here as bodily, rather than mental, toil), "the obstinate words . . . And the stubborn line . . . And the beat." (Note how "Springing," though it comes two stanzas later, carries the mind back to "iron of English / Rings" both through the sound-echo of "Rings" and through the logical relationship — English words being the obstinate iron that must be sprung.) A metaphor first appearing, then, as an auditory image for the sound of English, reappears as a kinesthetic image suggesting the intractability of the materials of poetry. Here we have the opposite of the popular stereotype of limpid verse flowing easily from a languid poet; the metaphor demands respect both for the refractory nature of the medium and for the manliness of the medium's master. The logic of the argument, however, is that not even such mastery is sufficient to create a memory of the beloved in anyone who has not known her.

The images related to the beloved may be divided between those that follow the demands of the speaker's logic by simply naming, and those that strain against that logic by pushing us through the "names" to a sense of an actual woman. Thus in the fourth stanza we move from the general images, "young," "arms straight," "mouth scarlet," to three images with more telling effects. The first of these, three innocent-sounding words, "Your arms change," expands grammatically and visually into an image of horror that is all the more effective for its understatement. "I shall say you will die . . . [I shall say] Your arms [will] change. . . ." "Change," an abstract word, is capable of creating a graphic image of decay in this syntactical and emotional context. The other two images, "the swish of your garments," "the click of your shoe," though also close to simple naming, vividly suggest ephemeral sounds and are thus much less general in their effect than were the first three images in the stanza.

Just as "Your arms change" recalls and contrasts with the preceding image "your arms straight," so "the bones of your breast," in its suggestion of a firm rib cage in a flesh-and-blood woman, contrasts with the abstract "breast that was troubled to listen" of the vague woman in the second stanza. There are a number of such repeated images in the poem, some for the sake of contrast, some for the sake of reiterating the argument. "Shadowy ghost" in the sixth stanza recalls "Shadow from door," not to contrast with it but because the parenthetical sixth stanza repeats the argument of the first two. We are brought back to the earlier argument by this repetition of image and idea; we proceed from it by repetition of syntactical structure: the "Therefore" which begins the seventh stanza takes off from the same point in the argument as did the "Therefore" beginning the third. We are logically in the same place, but only logically. The images intervening between the two "Therefore's" have not changed the argument — they have not brought the speaker's actual beloved to our minds — but they have convinced us that she exists and, in his anguished recognition that it is impossible to "prevail on the hearts of unborn men to remember," convinced us that the speaker loves her deeply. Even though we cannot picture the precise woman, we can share the experience of love heightened by the sense of irrevocable loss.

The new conclusion to be drawn from the argument is, "Therefore," not identical with the first. Poetry, it is true, cannot give immortality to an individual, but, as this poem has been demonstrating, there remains something that it *can* do very well indeed: it can communicate (or, more precisely, create) an emotional experience. Thus the new argument is not the earlier "I will not praise . . . I will say . . . ," but "I will not speak of the undying glory of women. / I will say. . . ." The thing to be said is almost identical: "young and straight and your skin fair" recalls, with just enough variation to keep it vital, "young, and your arms straight, and your mouth scarlet." Given this near identity, what then is the difference between the two arguments? It is the recognition that the effectiveness of the naming comes not from the avoidance of praise but from the avoidance of abstract generalizations: "the undying glory of women," "the famous beauty of dead women." The effectiveness comes from the precision of the image, which can convey not a precise picture of the beloved but a keen realization of the emotion of loving her. The seventh stanza moves from the completely abstract "undying glory of women," through simple naming, "young and straight and your skin fair," to a visual image that becomes increasingly exact as detail is added to detail: "And you stood in the door and the sun was a shadow of leaves on your shoulders / And a leaf on your hair — " (Note how "door," "sun," and "shadow" repeat, and thus gather into this image the connotations of, earlier images in the poem.) Here, with this new detail, the speaker, having found how (and what) it is possible for him to communicate, breaks off and makes a new beginning: what communicates is not an abstract generalization, but a sharply focused detail, "the shape of a leaf lay once on your hair." Abstract praise disperses in the mind, but the concrete image is creative, conveying the experience of an otherwise ephemeral moment. Till all is ended and men can neither see nor speak, the poet's image exists, always as fresh as before, always capable of being re-experienced. "Look! It is there!" The poet cannot give immortality to his beloved, but he can create an immortal image that will "prevail on the hearts of unborn men" to experience an emotion corresponding to his own.

Both Williams' and MacLeish's are poems *about* images as well as poems which use images; the effectiveness of what they say is, as it should be, dependent to a greater degree upon the effectiveness of their images than upon the cogency of their statements, though the MacLeish poem does in fact present an argument. We would not have the reader draw from our discussion the conclusion that poems using images are necessarily about images. We have chosen such poems for analysis here merely in order to have the advantage of approaching our subject from two directions at once. Other poems to which one could return for fruitful consideration of the effect of interacting images might be "Ode to a Nightingale," "Carrion Comfort," "To His Coy Mistress," "Lessons of the War," or "The Darkling Thrush." For poems in which images are dominant, one might look, in any standard anthology, at Shakespeare's songs (especially "Spring" and "Winter" from the end of *Love's Labour's Lost*), at Keats's other odes (especially "To Autumn"), or in one of the collections of Chinese or Japanese poems (especially, perhaps, Arthur Waley's translations of the "Five 'Tzu-yeh' Songs," "Li Fu-jēn," or "Lo-yang"). Imagery is so pervasive in poetry that to suggest individual poems is probably unnecessary, but these are a few whose images might hold particular interest at this point.

V

Uses of Images and Analogies

Images, similes, and metaphors may serve a variety of purposes and, indeed, usually serve several at the same time. In this chapter, we will try to distinguish a few of the (not always separable) ways in which images and analogies are related to the poems in which they appear — as decoration, illustration and clarification, explanation, or creation — and we will then be in a position to discuss several specific varieties of metaphor, including the symbol.

DECORATION

One of the most common assumptions about images is that they are purely decorative, that they are "pretty pictures" added to poems to "make them pretty." That this is not our assumption should be obvious, since it is but one form of what we have called the "sugar-coated-pill" theory of poetry. However, even though one believes images serve more important purposes, he cannot deny that they enrich, enliven, even "decorate" a poem by inducing pleasurable sense impressions. What, then, is wrong with calling them decorative?

The word "decorative" is objectionable when it not only denotes that imagery is attractive but implies that it has been "added" to a poem which could make the same statement (have the same meaning) without it, that it has been added merely to embellish what might otherwise be dingy. In this sense, "decorative images" would be detachable from the poem in which they appear; without them, the poem, though it might not be as pretty, would still say the same thing.

We should look, therefore, at some poems in which the images have been considered decorative in the sense here rejected. In such a poem the images are usually attractive, plentiful, and brief (since development of any particular image tends to give it an emphasis beyond decoration): their apparent purpose is to add pleasant sensations to whatever statement the poem is making. In looking for examples, we turn naturally to Elizabethan lyrics, for it was an Elizabethan fashion to load poems with sensory images which critics have frequently called decorative. Consider, then, this song by Thomas Nashe:

> Spring, the sweete spring, is the yere's pleasant King,
> Then bloomes eche thing, then maydes daunce in a ring,
> Cold doeth not sting, the pretty birds doe sing,
>> Cuckow, jugge, jugge, pu we, to witta woo.
>
> The Palme and May make countrey houses gay,   5
> Lambs friske and play, the Shepherds pype all day,
> And we heare aye birds tune this merry lay,
>> Cuckow, jugge, jugge, pu we, to witta woo.
>
> The fields breathe sweete, the dayzies kisse our feete,
> Young lovers meete, old wives a-sunning sit;   10
> In every streete these tunes our eares do greete,
>> Cuckow, jugge, jugge, pu we, to witta woo.
>> Spring, the sweete spring.*

What Nashe's poem presents would hardly appear to be more than a collection of pleasant images for "the sweete spring," with a refrain of four traditionally onomatopoeic images of bird songs. Note that each of five of the lines includes two complete images, and (except that the third line of each stanza introduces the refrain) none of the images extends for more than a line. The brief images in this little

---

* l. 5 *Palme:* willow, laurel, yew, or any of a number of other native English shrubs or trees. Since actual palm branches were not available, a variety of substitutes were used in churches on Palm Sunday and came to be called "palm."

    May: hawthorn or spirea

l. 7 *aye:* ever, continuously;

    lay: song

catalogue might seem merely embellishments on the celebration of spring. They are surely decorative: they do add attractive sensations to the simple central idea. The question is, are they detachable? Would the poem say the same thing without these images?

No. If we excise them, the statement that remains says only that spring is the best time of the year. The images do not merely garnish that idea, like parsley that can be shoved aside; they add to it. The original poem says, roughly, that spring is the best time of the year because flowers make the fields and houses beautiful, because the weather is good, because young and old can enjoy the outdoors and thus there is heightened fellowship, because the music of birds and shepherds is merry. The difference is not just that between an ineffective and an effective statement; it is a difference in actual meaning.

If, instead of excising them, we attempt to substitute other, equally attractive images traditionally associated with spring, we discover that these specific images are essential to this specific meaning. For example, in place of the opening line of the final stanza we might substitute "The woods breathe sweete, the violets kiss our feete . . . ." "Woods" and "violets" are no less attractive and no less related to spring than are "fields"and "dayzies." But, though they may be equally ornamental and relevant in themselves, they do not fit so well into the poem. They violate the coherence of the other images and their connotations. It is difficult to define this violation without appearing to exaggerate, but we might say, for example, that the connotations of "woods" and "violets" bring shadow and seclusion into what is otherwise all sunlight and companionship. In addition to being attractive or delightful, Nashe's images are coherent. Nor do they add something to the poem; they *are* the poem (which cannot be said to exist apart from them). Nashe did not choose them to decorate his meaning — nor even to "express" it. They are part of his meaning; any change in them changes what it is about spring that he is celebrating.

The situation differs in this next poem, by Christopher Marlowe:

The Passionate Sheepheard to His Love

Come live with mee, and be my love,
And we will all the pleasures prove

That vallies, groves, hills and fieldes,
Woods, or steepie mountaine yeeldes.

And wee will sit upon the Rocks,   5
Seeing the Sheepheards feede theyr flocks,
By shallow Rivers to whose falls
Melodious byrds sing Madrigalls.

And I will make thee beds of Roses,
And a thousand fragrant poesies,   10
A cap of flowers, and a kirtle,
Imbroydred all with leaves of Mirtle;

A gowne made of the finest wooll
Which from our pretty Lambs we pull;
Fayre linëd slippers for the cold,   15
With buckles of the purest gold.

A belt of straw and Ivie buds,
With Corall clasps and Amber studs:
And if these pleasures may thee move,
Come live with mee, and be my love.   20

The Sheepheards' Swaines shall daunce and sing
For thy delight each May-morning:
If these delights thy minde may move,
Then live with mee, and be my love.*

Here there is a request quite separable from the images. They are
not the request as Nashe's images are the celebration; they are sense
impressions aimed at making the request attractive. Since they are in
fact added to the request, are they not decorative in the sense we have
rejected?

No, they are not: they are added to the request not merely as orna-
ments to delight the reader, but as promises or arguments to convince
the speaker's beloved. They are not simply decorative; they are horta-
tive: they urge toward a particular course of action. The speaker's

* l. 2 *prove:* test, try out; demonstrate through action
l. 8 *Madrigalls:* part songs for five or six voices
l. 11 *kirtle:* skirt or gown
l. 12 *Imbroydred:* ornamented (not necessarily with needlework)
l. 18 *studs:* ornamental knobs
l. 21 *Swaines:* lads, lovers

"Melodious byrds," "beds of Roses," and "Amber studs" are not mere embellishments, but inducements. There is a logical purpose — or at least an apparent motive — behind their attractiveness. One stanza of Sir Walter Raleigh's well-known answer to Marlowe's poem, "The Nymph's Reply to the Shepherd," will show that an effective rebuttal to the shepherd's argument cannot merely choose new images to deny the invitation (as it might if the images were "detachable"), but must deal with the very same images, disposing of them in some way that will demonstrate the fallacy in the original argument:

> Thy gownes, thy shooes, thy beds of Roses,
> Thy cap, thy kirtle, and thy poesies,
> Soone breake, soone wither, soone forgotten:
> In follie ripe, in reason rotten.

That both Nashe's and Marlowe's poems contain images of "shepherds" and "lambs" suggests another distinction that ought to be briefly mentioned here. Modern readers frequently consider the images in such poems "decorative" because they find them "artificial." This is not to say that shepherds do not exist, but only that they have never existed as they appear in the idyllic world of pastoral poetry, where they spend all their days in dancing, piping, and courtship. Since such images appear to have no other possible relation to his daily life, the reader is apt to consider them merely decorative. The poetry is pretty, perhaps, but he can hardly take it seriously.

This isn't the place to undertake a full defense of pastoral poetry,* but we would point out that even if the judgment "artificial" were to apply to such poetry, it would not thereby automatically follow that the images within that convention were merely decorative. That is to say, whether or not we think the idealized bucolic world of such poetry has any relevance to human life, the images used within such poems will only be decorative in our rejected sense if they are independent of — additional to — the statements the poems make. We

---

* As does any other art, pastoral poetry uses its own conventions to transpose selected human interests into coherent patterns. We touched upon some of the issues raised by the reading of conventional poetry in the discussion of overstatement in Chapter III. Here we might remind the reader that to treat pastoral details literally is to ignore important aspects of implication and tone and is equivalent to erroneous inference. The pastoral tradition is, admittedly, out of fashion and modern readers are apt to be sated with a very little of it.

hope we have shown, in these somewhat typical examples, that they are not.

Before leaving the subject, let us give two further examples of ways in which apparently decorative images may serve other purposes. The first two stanzas of the first of the poems that follow — written perhaps by Anthony Munday — are apt to seem unsatisfactory upon a first reading largely because of the images. These comparisons are conventional, even trite; they are exaggerated (and this is conventional too) almost to the extent of throwing doubt upon the sincerity or good sense of the speaker; they are one-dimensional (only in its whiteness is snow relevant, only in its straightness is cedar) and heterogeneous (snow, cedar, glass, and roe deer have little in common with each other). For all these reasons, we are apt to be impatient with what appears to be an unconvincing catalogue of merely decorative comparisons.

But then we reach the final stanza and discover, in the agreeable surprise of its sudden reversal, that the poet was anticipating and even taking advantage of our response. There is comedy in the fact that a complete switch in estimation occurs with no switch in the syntactical pattern: she is —er than —. The abusive comparisons are just as exaggerated as the praise, and the juxtaposition of opposite exaggerations is humorous. But there remains a further surprise — the reversal reversed with a second "Yet"— when the speaker, in spite of what he has just said, ends up exactly where the first stanzas had led us to expect. (The final couplet is, in fact, a multiple, sexual pun, which would have been obvious to its original audience but would require lengthy historical explanation for a modern reader.) The lover's conventional praises are first exposed for the nonsense they are, if read literally, and then shown to be irrelevant to the fact that, whatever common sense might admit, he is nevertheless trapped by his love. It is as if the poet had written the plea of Marlowe's passionate shepherd and Raleigh's nymph's reply and had then carried the argument a step further: he has apparently used conventional and decorative imagery deliberately, setting up a false response and then using that response to clinch the true one:

> I serve a Mistres whiter than the snowe,
> Straighter than Cedar, brighter than the Glasse,
> Finer in trip and swifter than the Roe,

More pleasant then the Feeld of flowring Grasse,
> More gladsome to my withering Joyes that fade   5
> Than Winter's Sun or Sommer's cooling shade.

Sweeter than swelling grape of ripest wine,
Softer than feathers of the fairest Swan,
Smoother than Jet, more stately than the Pine,
Fresher than Poplar, smaller than my span,   10
> Clearer than Beautie's fiery pointed beam,
> Or Icie cruste of Christalle's frozen stream.

Yet is shee curster than the Beare by kinde,
And harder-harted than the agëd Oke,
More glib than Oyle, more fickle than the winde,   15
Stiffer than steel, no sooner bent but broke.
> Loe, thus my service is a lasting sore:
> Yet will I serve, although I dye therfore.*

The second example, a song by the poet-musician Thomas Campion, both starts with an apparent absurdity —"There is a garden in her face"— and then goes on to use images and comparisons so trite that they ought to fail even to decorate: "Roses and white lillies," lips like cherries, teeth of pearl. But the fact is that Campion's lyric retains its charm and its images their freshness, in part because the poet, having introduced his images in the first stanza, keeps them integral by returning to and developing each of them as he proceeds. The flowers reappear as the daintier, but cooler, "Rose-buds" of the second stanza; the "Garden" itself, as "A heav'nly paradice," is later guarded by "Angels" who protect "sacred" fruit. The value of the fruit is in-

* l. 2 *the Glasse:* a mirror
l. 3 *trip:* tripping, stepping lightly
l. 10 *smaller than my span:* smaller, presumably around the waist, than the circle he can make with his two hands
l. 11 *Beautie's fiery pointed beam:* a ray of light emanating from a blinding beauty? (perhaps a personification of "Beauty" itself)
l. 12 *Christalle's frozen stream:* not the more obvious "frozen crystal stream," a clear frozen brook, but a crystal which is, metaphorically, a frozen stream on which its outer surface is the icy crust
l. 13 *by kinde:* by nature (may modify either "shee" or "Beare")
l. 15 *glib:* slippery

creased as the poem develops: beginning with the low-keyed "none may buy," its worth is insisted upon by "nor Peere nor Prince can buy" until it finally becomes "sacred"— beyond price and theft. And, of course, the cherries are the primary continuing metaphor, reappearing in each stanza and heightened by the clever turn in the refrain. Cutting across the crescendo of praise comes the cry of the common street-vendor with cherries of his own to sell. There is a proper limit — a "Till" — to this woman's unavailability: no man may have her lips and love until he is prepared to yield his own:

> There is a Garden in her face,
> Where Roses and white lillies grow;
> A heav'nly paradice is that place,
> Wherein all pleasant fruits doe flow.
>> There Cherries grow which none may **buy**   5
>> Till Cherry ripe themselves doe cry.
>
> Those Cherries fayrely doe enclose
> Of Orient Pearle a double row,
>> Which when her lovely laughter showes,
> They looke like Rose-buds fill'd with snow.   10
>> Yet them nor Peere nor Prince can buy,
>> Till Cherry ripe themselves doe cry.
>
> Her Eyes like Angels watch them still;
> Her Browes like bended bowes doe stand,
>> Threatning with piercing frownes to kill   15
> All that attempt with eye or hand
>> Those sacred Cherries to come nigh,
>> Till Cherry ripe themselves doe cry.

Once more images sometimes considered merely decorative because of their traditional prettiness turn out to have other relations to the poem. Such is almost inevitably the case; imagery cannot be "added to" a poem without becoming an integral part of the final effect.

To assume that an image may be used merely to decorate is to assume that the poem, or the line in which it appears, is a statement plus an effect (a pill plus its coating) such that a paraphrase without the image, though less "pretty," would "mean" the same as the line including it. Any image, decorative or not, will qualify, if only slightly, will alter or clarify by its very specificity the statement of which it is a part.

> O, for a draught of vintage! that hath been
>   Cool'd a long age in the deep-delvèd earth,

and

> O, for a draught of vintage! that hath been
>   Cool'd a long age in the deep-delvèd earth,
> Tasting of Flora and the country green,
>   Dance, and Provençal song, and sunburnt mirth!

are two different cups of wine. Images are frequently (though not necessarily) attractive in themselves and therefore do add to the pleasure conveyed by a poem. However, mere decorativeness is not enough, and an image inevitably adds to the effect of the poem in some other way at the same time. An image is, in the grammarian's sense, "restrictive," so that the statement it adorns, if stripped of it, becomes in fact a different statement. What would be likely to happen if a poet set out to decorate his work is that incongruous, uncontrolled meanings would enter with the images to rip apart any fabric of coherent statement in the poem.

ILLUSTRATION AND CLARIFICATION

Probably the most usual purpose served by images is that of helping to make a meaning vivid — to illustrate it or clarify it — through making some portion of it palpable to the senses. (We speak now of images not involved in analogies; images so involved are illustrations of a more complex kind, which we shall call explanations.) We have already inspected a number of examples in showing that their images were not merely decorative. "Sweete spring" is a relatively abstract concept until Nashe provides the images to illustrate or clarify just what it is about spring that he is celebrating. Similarly, Marlowe's "Melodious byrds" and "Corall clasps" are images serving to make the shepherd's offered "pleasures" more specific and thereby more tempting.

Lest, by our choice of Elizabethan poems, we seem to be suggesting that illustrative images belong to a particular period, let us provide two modern examples here. When you consider the wide range of attitudes that might be taken toward Louise Bogan's subject, her poem is a fine example of the way in which the choice of particular illustrations serves to limit a poem's meaning:

Women

Women have no wilderness in them,
They are provident instead,
Content in the tight hot cell of their hearts
To eat dusty bread.

They do not see cattle cropping red winter grass,   5
They do not hear
Snow water going down under culverts
Shallow and clear.

They wait, when they should turn to journeys,
They stiffen, when they should bend.   10
They use against themselves that benevolence
To which no man is friend.

They cannot think of so many crops to a field
Or of clean wood cleft by an axe.
Their love is an eager meaninglessness   15
Too tense, or too lax.

They hear in every whisper that speaks to them
A shout and a cry.
As like as not, when they take life over their door-sills
They should let it go by.   20

Just as Nashe's images clarify his concept of spring, Bogan's images clarify her concept of woman's shortcomings. Note that each statement about women implies the contrary about men, so that the poem does not merely define women but defines a psychological difference between women and men. The final sentence is therefore ironic, for the "life" women "take over their door-sills" refuses to "go by," just as women cannot "let it." Men may have the wilderness in them, but men and women have also a need for each other, whatever their shortcomings.

Wallace Stevens called his poem "A Postcard from the Volcano," and the title suggests the poet's sense of living on the verge of catastrophe. His poem is not about the catastrophe itself, however, but about the joy of living heightened by the sense of ultimate loss (whatever the cause of that loss):

A Postcard from the Volcano

Children picking up our bones
Will never know that these were once
As quick as foxes on the hill;

And that in autumn, when the grapes
Made sharp air sharper by their smell   5
These had a being, breathing frost;

And least will guess that with our bones
We left much more, left what still is
The look of things, left what we felt

At what we saw. The spring clouds blow   10
Above the shattered mansion-house,
Beyond our gate and the windy sky

Cries out a literate despair.
We knew for long the mansion's look
And what we said of it became   15

A part of what it is . . . Children,
Still weaving budded aureoles,
Will speak our speech and never know,

Will say of the mansion that it seems
As if he that lived there left behind   20
A spirit storming in blank walls,

> A dirty house in a gutted world,
> A tatter of shadows peaked to white,
> Smeared with the gold of the opulent sun.*

Children in the future, finding our bones, will not realize (in part because they are children) how alive we once were. ("Quick," in the third line, in addition to meaning merely "swift," means "vigorous," "energetic," "with keen perceptions," "lively"; the adjective once meant simply "alive," as the noun still does —"the quick and the dead.") It is the images — the smell of grapes making the sharp autumn air sharper, the lungs (though metaphorically the bones) "breathing frost" — which make this sense of life vivid. Similarly, at the end of the poem, it is the image of the ruined house "Smeared with the gold of the opulent sun," which makes most clear the (prenuclear-fission) idea, already present in the very existence of the "Children" and their "budded aureoles," that the luxuriant beauty of the physical world will survive (and make more poignant) any individual loss. There is of course more to be said about this poem, as indeed there is about any of the poems we discuss so briefly. For the moment we are concerned only with indicating how its images help to clarify its meaning.

Images offer clarity of various sorts. Most obviously, a visual image may offer a clear picture and, as already discussed, comparable effects may be created for the other senses. This is sensory clarity. An image may also, simultaneously, create (or contribute to creating) a mood or an emotional experience. In addition to its visual and auditory effect, the image "Cranes fly past in silence" conveys both a sense of isolation and a vague threat which, in the context of Tu Fu's "Passing the Night in a Pavilion by the River," contributes forcibly to the emotion of loneliness and the mood of helplessness. This is emotional clarity of a sort, but a distinction must here be made.

The abstract terms we used to describe the emotional effect of the cranes — "a sense of isolation and a vague threat" — and even those describing the effect of the poem as a whole — "the emotion of loneliness and the mood of helplessness" — are at best vague and ap-

---

* l. 17 *Still weaving budded aureoles:* an "aureole" is a radiance surrounding a sacred individual or a halo around his head. These children are perhaps making crowns of flowers which they wear like halos, but the connotations bathe the children in light.

proximate. Two individuals confronted with the same situation or experience will inevitably feel somewhat differing emotions, even though at times they may use the same name for their responses. Moreover, emotions are notoriously "mixed." "Loneliness," for example, seldom if ever exists in a pure state; it is most often accompanied by other emotions — at times an emotion we might call "fear," at other times an emotion we might call "sadness," at still other times both of these and others as well. Some emotional states, indeed, involve emotions we think of in the abstract as opposites, as in that state made up of "fear" and "hope" described in Thomas Hood's poem "The Death Bed," quoted in Chapter III. "Emotional clarity" in an image, then, comes not through the fact that the image will necessarily call up identical emotions in all readers, nor through the fact that the image will be clearly identifiable by one of the general names for emotions, but through the fact that the image does, in its context, provide a precise stimulus, not only for a sensory but for an emotional response.

An image can also contribute to intellectual clarity, though only in relation to a statement and not as an isolated sense perception. For example, in MacLeish's " 'Not Marble nor the Gilded Monuments,' " as discussed in the preceding chapter, the image "a leaf on your hair" conveys not only sensory clarity (a vivid picture) and emotional intensity (an experience of love heightened in this ephemeral moment of beauty) but, through these, intellectual clarity — understanding of a rational proposition through illustration of it. The statement is that the poet, though he cannot offer personal immortality, can create an immortal poem which can speak to "the hearts of unborn men"; the image of the leaf demonstrates such effectiveness and thus helps give meaning to the generalization. A sense perception, even an emotionally colored sense perception, is not an idea, but it may illustrate an idea or, in the best poetry, may be the experiential basis from which an idea may be abstracted.

Clarification or illustration — and not simple decorativeness — is the proper (and usual) purpose served by individual images.

EXPLANATION

With the image that is explicitly involved in furthering the reader's understanding, we move away from simple illustration to what may be called explanation. Though there is no hard line between what il-

EXPLANATION 207

lustrates and what explains, we are calling explanatory any images involved in analogies. An image involved in an analogy does not lose its sensory and emotional effects, but necessarily takes on an additional intellectual significance. An analogy affirms a relationship, and our apprehension of that relationship is a process of understanding as well as of perceiving and feeling.

A simile is an overt explanation: A is like B. (A metaphor is also an explanation, without calling attention to the fact.) The complex interaction between the two terms, of which we have already spoken, involves more than sensory connotations (the blush and fragrance of the rose) and emotional tone (the joy of seeing the rose); to some degree it involves evaluation (in their superlative beauty, the woman and the rose are worthy of comparison). The B-term may be chosen to gain approval or disapproval for the A-term, to magnify or disparage its worth. Compare, for example, this first stanza of Poe's "To Helen" with the brief poem by Ezra Pound that follows it:

> Helen, thy beauty is to me
>   Like those Nicéan barks of yore,
> That gently, o'er a perfumed sea,
>   The weary, way-worn wanderer bore
>   To his own native shore.*

∽

> As a bathtub lined with white porcelain,
> When the hot water gives out or goes tepid,
> So is the slow cooling of our chivalrous passion,
> O my much praised but-not-altogether-satisfactory lady.

(Note that it is not merely the choice of the B-term itself, but the choice of diction and connotative details that determines the evaluation.) A simile involves perception, feeling, and judgment, all three of which interact in any simile, though their relative importance can differ vastly from one simile to another.

If a simile is to explain something it also involves understanding; we must know *how,* or in what particular, A is like B. In Campion's poem, it is not simply "Her eyes are like angels" but "Her Eyes like Angels watch. . . ." The next simile is "Her Browes like bended bowes doe stand, / Threatning. . . ." Each explains a relationship

* l. 2 *Nicéan:* from Nicaea, an ancient Bithynian city in what is now Turkey

between a part of the woman's face and the continuing image of the garden of paradise: the eyes act as the guardian angels (with connotations of angelic beauty); the brows threaten (and are shaped) like the angel's weapons.

As an example of a simile as explanation, consider the opening lines of John Donne's poem "A Valediction: Forbidding Mourning":

> As virtuous men pass mildly away,
>   And whisper to their soules to goe,
> Whilst some of their sad friends doe say,
>   The breath goes now, and some say, no:
>
> So let us melt, and make no noise,
>   No teare-floods, nor sigh-tempests move . . . .

The simile asks us not merely to perceive a picture or to feel an emotion, but to understand a particular way of conducting oneself which, since it is the way of "virtuous men," it asks us to approve. The key word is "mildly," and this is emphasized by the subsequent contrast with "noise," "teare-floods," and "sigh-tempests." This way of dying "mildly," almost imperceptibly, is the B-term of a comparison for which the A-term is itself a metaphor, "So let us melt." (As the poem proceeds, it ultimately becomes clear that its subject, the A-term of the simile, is not the lovers' deaths but a simple parting for which death — through skillful choice of ambiguous terms — is itself a strongly implied, though never actually stated, metaphor.) The B-term image, a little drama explaining a way of dying, offers more clarity to the intellect than to either the senses or the emotions.

Let us, for the sake of the contrast between them, consider two modern poems that use similes to explain the same subject, the mind. The first, by Richard Wilbur, presents a single simile and uses it to explain a variety of aspects of the mind. After exploring these possibilities, the poet reconsiders his simile, finds it inadequate, and goes beyond what is possible for the material objects in order to explain a further potentiality of the mind:

Mind

Mind in its purest play is like some bat
That beats about in caverns all alone,

Contriving by a kind of senseless wit
Not to conclude against a wall of stone.

It has no need to falter or explore;   5
Darkly it knows what obstacles are there,
And so may weave and flitter, dip and soar
In perfect courses through the blackest air.

And has this simile a like perfection?
The mind is like a bat. Precisely. Save   10
That in the very happiest intellection
A graceful error may correct the cave.

Note how the poem moves from the disparagement of mind implied in "some bat" to the respectful recognition that the mind's very errors can bring about advancement. The bat's environment is independent of the bat, but the mind's is subject to the mind conceiving it.

The second poem, by Marianne Moore, is more complex, mingling a variety of similes and metaphors, sensuous images and abstract explanations, to interpret a particular aspect of the mind. Moore's meticulous images demand readers of wide experience; her readers must know not only of the kiwi, Herod, and the music of Scarlatti, but — for the fullest understanding — must also know the peculiar properties of the kiwi's beak and feathers, the story of the promise that cost the life of John the Baptist, and the probable quality of a particular pianist's rendering of Scarlatti. Even without this special knowledge, however, a reader can perceive both Moore's awe in contemplating the mystery of the mind ("Enchanting" and "enchanted"), and the exactitude of explanation for which she strives. While Wilbur's poem asks us to consider the ramifications of a single image, Moore's focuses numerous explanations upon one subject. Her title is an integral part of her first sentence:

The Mind Is an Enchanting Thing

is an enchanted thing
        like the glaze on a
katydid-wing

subdivided by sun
    till the nettings are legion.   5
Like Gieseking playing Scarlatti;

like the apteryx-awl
    as a beak, or the
kiwi's rain-shawl
        of haired feathers, the mind   10
        feeling its way as though blind,
walks along with its eyes on the ground.

It has memory's ear
    that can hear without
having to hear.   15
            Like the gyroscope's fall,
            truly unequivocal
because trued by regnant certainty,

it is a power of
    strong enchantment. It   20
is like the dove-
        neck animated by
        sun; it is memory's eye;
it's conscientious inconsistency.

It tears off the veil; tears   25
    the temptation, the
mist the heart wears,
        from its eyes — if the heart
        has a face; it takes apart
dejection. It's fire in the dove-neck's   30

iridescence; in the
    inconsistencies
of Scarlatti.
        Unconfusion submits
        its confusion to proof; it's   35
not a Herod's oath that cannot change.

Occasionally it will not be clear just what it is that a simile explains.
When this is so, the comparison is usually being made for the sake of
its complimentary or derogatory connotations. For example, in the

opening lines of an anonymous sixteenth-century song, "Though Amaryllis dance in green / Like Fairy Queen . . . ," it is not clear whether the simile modifies "Amaryllis," "dance," "in green," or all three of them. It adds connotations perhaps of daintiness, beauty, sovereignty, and, though the exact point of comparison is ambiguous, the effect is rather enhancing than disparaging. More often, however, the point of comparison is clear, as in the common comparative construction with "than" (not a true simile) which tells exactly in what respect one term surpasses the other: "I serve a Mistres whiter than the snowe, / Straighter than Cedar, brighter than the Glasse. . . ."

Explanation of the point of comparison is not always immediate. When it is withheld, the slight mystery or doubt that arises in the reader's mind opens him to more awareness of the images' connotations. Here, for example, are the openings of two poems, the first from Christina Rossetti's "A Birthday," and the second from Francis Quarles's *"Hos Ego Versiculos"*: *

> My heart is like a singing bird
>> Whose nest is in a watered shoot;
> My heart is like an apple-tree
>> Whose boughs are bent with thickset fruit;
> My heart is like a rainbow shell   5
>> That paddles in a halcyon sea;
> My heart is gladder than all these
>> Because my love is come to me.

∽

> Like to the damaske Rose you see,
> Or like the blossome on the tree,
> Or like the dainty flowre of May,
> Or like the Morning of the day,
> Or like the Sunne, or like the shade,   5
> Or like the Gourd that Jonas had,
>> Even such is man, whose thred is spunne,
>> Drawne out and cut, and so is done.

---

* Quoted from a story in which Virgil is said to have claimed authorship of a disputed poem with the statement *"Hos ego versiculos feci"*: I made these verselets. Quarles is claiming authorship of his own poem which, much copied and expanded by other poets, had appeared in print before he himself had intended.

The Rose withers, the blossome blasteth,
The flower fades, the morning hasteth,   10
The Sunne sets, the shadow flies,
The Gourd consumes, and man he dies.

In each passage there is a series of comparisons made before we are
given an explanation. In Rossetti's we know that bird, apple-tree, and
shell are being compared to the heart, but we wait to be told in what
way they compare; in Quarles's we have seven B-terms before we are
given the A-term, man, and the explanation. In each, the withholding
of information serves to keep us alert to possibilities.

In spite of these similarities, the Rossetti stanza is not, we think,
as successful as the Quarles passage, and an attempt to discern why
this is so may be instructive. Rossetti's images are, in effect, better than
the use she makes of them. "Singing," in the first simile, along with
the connotations of mating and domesticity that go with "nest," might
well suggest joy as the point of comparison between heart and bird,
but, without the poet's explanation, joy would probably not occur to
many readers as the common link between laden apple-tree and heart
or between heart and paddling shell (is it a boat? or a sea shell?). Nor
is the comparison, when it is pointed out with the graceless word
"gladder," likely to strike us as particularly apt or revealing. The mind,
considering these images as it awaits the explanation, finds richer
relationships among them than the poet allows. Nor does "gladness"
seem appropriate to either apple-tree or shell; the abstract statement
does not do justice to the ideas latent in the concrete images. The poet's
images are hampered by the idea she has set out to illustrate. Her
three diverse images are redundant because they are held to a limited
(and even false) point of comparison and are not allowed to bear their
full weight.

Quarles, though his approach is no less redundant, allows his images
full connotative weight and achieves variety through several means.
He withholds not merely the explanation but the A-term itself until
the multiplication of B-terms raises our curiosity to know what these
diverse images may have in common. Then, having supplied his A-
term, he reverses the expectation aroused by pleasant connotations and
explains the point in a series of staccato phrases which complete each
image with its own appropriate verb rather than summarizing them
all with some such abstract "catch-all" verb as "ceases" or "passes

away." To exaggerate the difference in effect between the conclusions of the two passages, one might say that Quarles hammers relentlessly at grim variations on his intentionally disagreeable point, gaining conviction through repetition of his logic, while Rossetti retrieves her slight intended emotion from images that have almost overwhelmed it.

Behind such comparisons as Rossetti's lies the so-called *Homeric simile,* one in which a lengthy description is developed around what may be only a single point of comparison. It is named, obviously, from the fact that such similes are common in Homer's *Iliad* and *Odyssey.* For example, to quote from Pope's translation, here is the Trojan attack on the walls around the Greek ships:

> Their ardour kindles all the Grecian powers;
> And now the stones descend in heavier showers.
> As when high Jove his sharp artillery forms,
> And opes his cloudy magazine of storms;
> In winter's bleak uncomfortable reign,   5
> A snowy inundation hides the plain;
> He stills the winds, and bids the skies to sleep;
> Then pours the silent tempest thick and deep;
> And first the mountain-tops are cover'd o'er,
> Then the green fields, and then the sandy shore;   10
> Bent with the weight, the nodding woods are seen,
> And one bright waste hides all the works of men:
> The circling seas, alone absorbing all,
> Drink the dissolving fleeces as they fall:
> So from each side increased the stony rain,   15
> And the white ruin rises o'er the plain.
>   Thus godlike Hector and his troops contend
> To force the ramparts, and the gates to rend. . . .

The stones fell like snow: the B-term of this comparison has been developed by the poet into a dozen lines of description. Modern readers are apt to object to the way in which such Homeric descriptions tend to become independent of the A-terms to which they are being compared. Thus, though the stoning of the walls may well be compared to a "snowy inundation" which "hides the plain," it is hardly a "silent tempest" of "dissolving fleeces," and the "mountain-tops," "green fields," and "nodding woods" add images of no particular relevance to the battle. The softness of the metaphorical "dissolving fleeces" is, in fact, in direct contrast with the more effective metaphor, "stony rain," which follows it immediately and brings us back from the extended and somewhat parenthetical description of the snow storm. The simile concludes most effectively, however, as the A- and B-terms coalesce in the final image: "And the white ruin rises o'er the plain."

Homeric similes, particularly in long narrative poems, have purposes other than the merely local comparison however: their details serve to establish the whole "world of the poem." Part of the meaning of the *Iliad,* for example, comes from the contrast of the battles with the natural world and the everyday lives of men at peace, which are brought into the poem primarily through its similes.

Though we may prefer similes with fewer irrelevant details (and may in fact consider many Homeric similes decorative in the pejorative sense of bringing in incongruous meanings), we must acknowledge the existence of a tradition in which it has been considered quite proper to base an extended image on a limited comparison. We must recognize a Homeric simile when one appears and must not attempt to force all of its details into the service of the A-term. In fairness to Homer, it should be pointed out that many of his extended similes are in fact relevant in most, if not all, of their details. For example, here, also in Pope's translation, is his description of Ulysses' startling appearance when, having been washed up, naked and half-drowned, upon the coast of Phaeacia, he rises from his sleep and comes down the riverbank, frightening the handmaids of Nausicaa:

> As when a lion in the midnight hours,
> Beat by rude blasts, and wet with wintry showers,
> Descends terrific from the mountain's brow;
> With living flames his rolling eye-balls glow;
> With conscious strength elate, he bends his way,   5
> Majestically fierce, to seize his prey
> (The steer or stag;) or, with keen hunger bold,
> Springs o'er the fence, and dissipates the fold.
> No less a terror, from the neighbouring groves
> (Rough from the tossing surge) Ulysses moves;   10
> Urged on by want, and recent from the storms;
> The brackish ooze his manly grace deforms.

Here most of the details of the B-term can be seen to be relevant, not to Ulysses' intent but to the impact of his appearance upon the "frighted virgins" who suppose themselves "his prey." Such a simile as this, in which all or most of the details of the B-term explain the A-term in one way or another, carries more weight — expresses more meaning (since all of the details are working simultaneously in relation to both terms) — than does the somewhat libelously named Homeric simile in which the details make contact with and explain the A-term at only a single point. A simile, because it is essentially an explanation, demands our understanding; our minds, when reaching out to understand a relationship, are distracted by blind alleys and incongruities and are stimulated by multiple points of correspondence.

But the two terms of a simile could obviously coincide completely only if something were compared to itself. The best similes bring together terms sufficiently unlike to avoid being obvious, but sufficiently alike to provide a recognizably congruent explanation. This congruence involves perception, feeling, evaluation, and understanding, as we have attempted to show, and it pleases the more as it involves the more aspects of the image.

When the explanation provided by a comparison surpasses simple congruence to become ingenious, calling attention to itself by the cleverness with which its details are put to use, the comparison is called a *conceit*. Once again no firm line can be drawn between what does and what does not qualify: it is a question of judging whether a comparison is ingenious or simply apt. Most readers would agree that Campion's "There is a Garden in her face" is built on a conceit; they might disagree about Wilbur's comparison of the mind with a bat. Here, at any rate, are two further examples about which there should be no disagreement. The first, taken from Andrew Marvell's poem "A Dialogue Between the Soul and the Body," follows a pattern quite common to conceits: a trite comparison is given new life by adding other comparisons logically proceeding from it. Here the not uncommon comparison of the soul to a prisoner in the body is expanded ingeniously, not to say brilliantly:

> O who shall, from this Dungeon, raise
> A Soul inslav'd so many wayes?
> With bolts of Bones, that fetter'd stands
> In Feet; and manacled in Hands.

Here blinded with an Eye; and there   5
Deaf with the drumming of an Ear.
A Soul hung up, as 'twere, in Chains
Of Nerves and Arteries and Veins.
Tortur'd, besides each other part,
In a vain Head and double Heart. . . .   10

The second, by John Lyly, quoted in its entirety, describes a supposed gambling game between the speaker's beloved, Campaspe, and Cupid, which starts with kisses and becomes increasingly costly for the loser:

Cupid and my Campaspe play'd
At Cardes for kisses, Cupid payd;
He stakes his Quiver, Bow and Arrows,
His Mother's doves and teeme of sparows;
Loses them too; then downe he throwes   5
The corrall of his lippe, the rose
Growing on's cheek (but none knows how),
With these the cristall of his Brow,
And then the dimple of his chinne:
All these did my Campaspe winne.   10
At last, hee set her both his eyes;
Shee won, and Cupid blind did rise.
O Love! has shee done this to Thee?
What shall (Alas!) become of mee? *

The central conceit is a metaphor showing love for Campaspe to be a dangerous game. Details of the wagers are used to account ingeniously for Campaspe's competence (with Cupid's weapons she may capture whom she chooses), for the mystery of her character (admitting both doves and sparrows), for her beauty (her best features having come from the very face of Love), and lastly for Cupid's traditional blindness. Whether Campaspe is simply lucky or, as the poem would seem to imply, quite in control of the cards, the final couplet shows the speaker's awareness that he is helpless before such power. He apparently lacks even the choice of refusing to play.

* l. 4 *His Mother's doves and teeme of sparows:* the doves and sparrows associated with Venus, the mother of Cupid, traditionally symbolize two aspects of love, the faithfully conjugal and the promiscuously lustful.

The so-called Homeric simile and the conceit are both extended comparisons, but they are otherwise quite different. In the Homeric simile, the B-term is extended, as it were, to explain itself, making contact with the A-term at only one major point. The statement made by a Homeric simile can often be reduced to a briefer equation — the stones covered the beach like snow. (Remember that the statement may be so reduced, however, only at the cost of changing the meaning.) In the conceit, the B-term is extended with further comparisons to explain (ingeniously) additional aspects of the A-term, with which it is in almost constant contact. The details of a conceit are all part of the equation. There are, of course, infinite gradations between these two poles, and the brief comparison may range similarly from the simple, or even obvious, to the ingenious, exaggerated, or even outlandish. All are varieties of explanation.

CREATION

The images we have been discussing have all been brought into their poems in order to provide explanations. They have all been subordinate to the concepts being explained, either in the literal sense that they have been grammatically subordinate ("Helen, thy beauty is to me / Like those Nicéan barks . . ."), or in the sense that an apparent controlling idea has determined the image ("Chains / Of Nerves" has come into the poem via the idea that the soul is a prisoner in the body). When the process is reversed, and the concept appears to arise from the image, the result is an image we would call creative rather than explanatory.

In calling an image creative, we are speaking of its use in the poem, not necessarily of the creative process in the poet. The creative image is not grammatically subordinate; in a short poem, it is likely to appear first and the concept — if stated at all — to follow. The poet's own mind may have started with either the image or the concept and worked toward the other, or both may have come to him at once. We cannot be certain how he may have come by his poem, but we can describe the syntax of his images. We are calling "creative" any image that appears in a poem as a sense perception independent of any illustrative or explanatory role, and then leads to some further development in the poem. It may first appear as an object perceived by someone speaking in the first person, or as an object described in the second person. The further development may occur in any of a number of ways. The most obvious (and perhaps least creative) is that in which the image leads into a direct statement of ideas. The poet gives an image and then philosophizes about it, or uses it as the basis of a little sermon. This poem by Ralph Waldo Emerson is an example:

The Rhodora

In May, when sea-winds pierced our solitudes,
I found the fresh Rhodora in the woods,
Spreading its leafless blooms in a damp nook,
To please the desert and the sluggish brook.
The purple petals, fallen in the pool,   5
Made the black water with their beauty gay;
Here might the red-bird come his plumes to cool,
And court the flower that cheapens his array.
Rhodora! if the sages ask thee why
This charm is wasted on the earth and sky,   10
Tell them, dear, that if eyes were made for seeing,
Then Beauty is its own excuse for being:
Why wert thou there, O rival of the rose!
I never thought to ask, I never knew:
But, in my simple ignorance, suppose   15
The self-same Power that brought me there brought you.

This direct way of developing a creative image is basic to some of the best, as well as to much of the worst, poetry written. The danger, which Emerson cannot be said to have escaped, is always that the idea may seem much too large for, too small for, or too remote from, the image (as Christina Rossetti's "gladder" is both remote from and smaller than the full effect of her images). Much popular verse follows this pattern, and many readers, unwilling to separate their acceptance of the stated idea from an evaluation of the poem, fail to recognize how fulsomely the image has been described or how blatantly the idea has been added to it. To be fully successful, such a poem should end with an idea no weightier than the image is capable of leading the reader to re-experience. Even so fine a poem as Keats's "Ode on a Grecian Urn" has been criticized because it ends with the

direct statement of an idea some have felt is an unjustified development of the images provided by the speaker's experience of the urn.
Here, from approximately the same time as Emerson's poem is another
which is more successful simply because the idea stays much closer
to the object being considered. These are four sections from the second
part of Tennyson's long poem "Maud":

I

See what a lovely shell,
Small and pure as a pearl,
Lying close to my foot,
Frail, but a work divine,
Made so fairly well   5
With delicate spire and whorl,
How exquisitely minute,
A miracle of design!

II

What is it? a learned man
Could give it a clumsy name.   10
Let him name it who can,
The beauty would be the same.

III

The tiny cell is forlorn,
Void of the little living will
That made it stir on the shore.   15
Did he stand at the diamond door
Of his house in a rainbow frill?
Did he push, when he was uncurl'd,
A golden foot or a fairy horn
Thro' his dim water-world?   20

IV

Slight, to be crush'd with a tap
Of my finger-nail on the sand,
Small, but a work divine,
Frail, but of force to withstand,

> Year upon year, the shock   25
> Of cataract seas that snap
> The three-decker's oaken spine
> Athwart the ledges of rock,
> Here on the Breton strand!

Even though Tennyson's lines use such dangerously vague and euphonious diction as "lovely," "pure," "divine," "delicate," "exquisitely," and "miracle," they are not as pretentious as Emerson's with his affectation of "simple ignorance." The image, in Tennyson's stanzas, is described somewhat insistently, but the idea is the more convincingly present for being understated and held to the terms of the particular image rather than made too general. The reader is free to generalize, but Tennyson does not force the generalization upon him.

Restraint is, in fact, essential to the successful development of a creative image by means of a direct statement of an idea. If the idea overwhelms the image, the relation between them ceases to be convincing. In one of A. E. Housman's best-known poems from *A Shropshire Lad*, this restraint is clearly exemplified:

> Loveliest of trees, the cherry now
> Is hung with bloom along the bough,
> And stands about the woodland ride
> Wearing white for Eastertide.
>
> Now, of my threescore years and ten,   5
> Twenty will not come again,
> And take from seventy years a score,
> It only leaves me fifty more.
>
> And since to look at things in bloom
> Fifty springs are little room,   10
> About the woodlands I will go
> To see the cherry hung with snow.

Here, in contrast with Tennyson's stanzas, not only the idea but the image itself is stated with restraint. The only word comparable to the loaded diction of Tennyson's lines is "Loveliest." This word, with its initial emphasis, demands a strongly emotional response, but that response is sustained only by the reader's image formed upon such matter-of-fact words as "bloom," "bough," "woodland," and "white," as well as such connotations of purity and reverence as might accompany the suggestion that the trees are "Wearing white for Eastertide." To interact with this image, Housman then states an idea which — though it has clearly occurred to the speaker as a result of experiencing the image — is also presented factually. Take from a man's Biblical allotment of years the speaker's twenty and simple arithmetic leaves him fifty. One word alone in the second stanza conveys the intended judgment of this fact: "It *only* leaves me fifty more." In the context of the beauty of the trees, he is most aware of the brevity of life. The restrained conclusion of this interaction of beauty with brevity is a simple announcement, following the direct statement of the idea like the "therefore" of a syllogism: "About the woodlands I will go / To see the cherry hung with snow."

We have known readers who, distrustful of so direct and restrained a poem, have attained a false complexity through turning the whole first stanza into a metaphor about the trees in winter, taking the brief metaphor of the final line ("snow") as confirming "fact." Such inversion stems primarily from an ingrained distrust of directness in poetry. The poem is fully effective if we accept the "now," the "bloom," and the "Eastertide" of the first stanza as the given basis of the image — as the "situation." To turn this into a winter poem is to detract from both the present loveliness of the trees and the idea of the brevity of "Fifty springs." "Snow" is not a fact confirming an earlier unhinted metaphor, but a metaphor which adds its own connotations of brevity and seasonal change to the statement made by the poem.

And yet the suspicious reader's decision that this is a winter poem may be excused by the coherence of the details. The metaphoric "snow" exists in an actual spring. The boy who is now twenty — the conventional springtime of life — thinks of his revisiting the trees annually for fifty years — to the winter of his life. The "idea" of the poem is the brevity of life, so brief that twenty and seventy are juxtaposed, as are spring and winter, blossoms and snow — so brief that spring almost *is* winter. Thus the full, almost "factual" force of the metaphoric snow is another example of how intimately image and idea are related: the image here is inseparable from the statement, and statement from image.

Housman's poem is a most successful example of restraint in the development of a creative image by means of the direct statement of an idea. The full idea is, in fact, held to a subordinate clause ("since to look at things in bloom / Fifty springs are little room") in which it is stated in terms of the particular speaker's age. Once again it is in such generalization as occurs in the reader's response that the idea achieves its full development.

Another way in which creative images are frequently developed is that in which they lead into a direct comparison. Here there is much less danger of divorce between image and conclusion because the comparison necessarily keeps the reader's mind on the image. In "The Bear," Robert Frost develops a double comparison rather than the usual single comparison of two terms. His opening description of a wild bear leads to a simile comparing man with a caged bear. Thus the reader carries all three — wild bear, caged bear, and man — in mind at once:

The Bear

The bear puts both arms around the tree above her
And draws it down as if it were a lover
And its choke cherries lips to kiss good-by,
Then lets it snap back upright in the sky.
Her next step rocks a boulder on the wall   5
(She's making her cross-country in the fall).
Her great weight creaks the barbed-wire in its staples
As she flings over and off down through the maples,
Leaving on one wire tooth a lock of hair.
Such is the uncaged progress of the bear.   10
The world has room to make a bear feel free;
The universe seems cramped to you and me.
Man acts more like the poor bear in a cage
That all day fights a nervous inward rage,
His mood rejecting all his mind suggests.   15
He paces back and forth and never rests
The toe-nail click and shuffle of his feet,
The telescope at one end of his beat,
And at the other end the microscope,
Two instruments of nearly equal hope,   20

And in conjunction giving quite a spread.
Or if he rests from scientific tread,
'Tis only to sit back and sway his head
Through ninety odd degrees of arc, it seems,
Between two metaphysical extremes.   25
He sits back on his fundamental butt
With lifted snout and eyes (if any) shut,
(He almost looks religious but he's not),
And back and forth he sways from cheek to cheek,
At one extreme agreeing with one Greek,   30
At the other agreeing with another Greek
Which may be thought, but only so to speak.
A baggy figure, equally pathetic
When sedentary and when peripatetic.

Modern man's relation to Greek metaphysics is surely just as far from
the creative image of the wild bear as is Emerson's faith from the
rhodora. But there is not the same divorce between image and idea
because Frost describes man's actions in terms fitting the image of the
caged bear, swaying from haunch to haunch; and this interminable
and futile action is, in turn, retroactively compared with the "uncaged
progress" of the wild bear.

The interaction between the beauty of the natural world and the
brevity of man's life is present in Robert Herrick's "To Daffadills" as
it is in Housman's "Loveliest of trees." In Herrick's poem, however,
there is a direct comparison of the brevity of man's life with the brevity
of the flowers':

To Daffadills

Faire Daffadills, we weep to see
    You haste away so soone:
As yet the early-rising Sun
    Has not attaind his Noone.
        Stay, stay,   5
    Until the hasting day
        Has run
    But to the Even-song;
And, having pray'd together, we
    Will goe with you along.   10

> We have short time to stay, as you;
> We have as short a Spring;
> As quick a growth to meet Decay,
> As you, or any thing.
> We die,   15
> As your hours doe, and drie
> Away
> Like to the Summer's raine;
> Or as the pearles of Morning's dew,
> Ne'r to be found againe.   20

At first "we weep" only for the brevity of the daffodils' lives, secure in the knowledge that our own are longer. This implied contrast renders the following exaggerated comparison all the more effective. (The hyperbole is not apparent until the second line of the second stanza; the first line means not "Our time is as short as yours" but only "We also have little time.") Our longer time is none too long; our "spring" is as short, our "growth to meet decay" as quick. Realization of the brevity of our own lives interacts with the originally implied contrast to make the daffodils' lives seem all the briefer. Note that Herrick calls the daffodils "Faire" but does not describe them directly at any point in the poem; his stress on their impermanence heightens our ideas of their beauty. However, because the two concluding explanatory images — "summer's rain" and "pearls of morning's dew" — come from the same area of natural experience, they serve to augment the general image of the flowers in spite of the fact that, grammatically, they are unrelated. The creative image thus dominates the poem, gathering the subordinate images to itself.

Because the clearest explanatory images are in similes, it would not be surprising to find the creative image related to metaphor. We said when first discussing it that metaphor is itself creative, bringing, as it were, something new into being (a boy with paws) rather than merely calling attention to an existing similarity (hands like paws). In fact, however, metaphors, like similes, involve explanatory images and none of the creative images we have considered have been actual metaphors. The explanatory image is part of an analogy; the creative image could be considered either implied metaphor or else the reverse of metaphor.

As implied metaphor the creative image is fairly easy to understand. It is an image that, with the slightest touch, could be turned into a metaphor. Frost's wild bear is not, syntactically, a metaphor for the freedom man would like to have, but it suggests such a metaphor and very slight syntactical changes would make it one. In this way the creative image can be seen to have an efficacy very like that of metaphor though it is, syntactically, the reverse. In an actual metaphor, the idea of relationship has created an explanatory image: it is an idea of his character that leads to calling a man a fox. (Again we are not speaking of the process in the poet's mind, but of the syntax of his poem.) In the poems we have just been considering, an initial image creates an idea, as though attention to an actual fox led to thoughts of the man. In metaphor, some concept of relationship has received expression; in the creative image, some concept is latent, awaiting further development in the poem or inference in the reader.

We have looked at two ways in which creative images may be developed — through direct philosophizing and through direct comparison. There remains yet another use of the creative image, and it is potentially the most creative of the three (which is not to say that its success is guaranteed). We speak now of the poem in which no development is stated, but the image is simply presented to the reader, who must be sensitive to its implications. Such an image must bear its full weight in the poem, for there is no additional statement to support it. This is not, however, a mere matter of omitting a statement that might be present; it is a matter of there being no statement that could do justice to the image, no statement that would not limit its effectiveness. For this creative image is complete in itself, a concrete object or situation presented directly to the reader and taking precedence over any idea that might arise from it. One form of this image is the poem presenting, without comment, a situation which, in its details and overtones, captures the essence of a personal relationship. This poem by Theodore Roethke is just such an image, a bittersweet memory of a boy's relationship to his father:

My Papa's Waltz

The whiskey on your breath
Could make a small boy dizzy;
But I hung on like death:
Such waltzing was not easy.

We romped until the pans   5
Slid from the kitchen shelf;
My mother's countenance
Could not unfrown itself.

The hand that held my wrist
Was battered on one knuckle;   10
At every step you missed
My right ear scraped a buckle.

You beat time on my head
With a palm caked hard by dirt,
Then waltzed me off to bed   15
Still clinging to your shirt.

Such a poem is self-contained; it does not "stand for" anything else. Therefore comment tends to be superfluous, though one can point to certain details in order to call attention to some of the implications that justify calling it a creative image. The image is one of a father playing with his son before bed, and the past tense adds a sense of loss to our awareness of the boy's love for his father — yet the poem is not sentimental, for the father's playfulness was almost too rough, and the boy's world was not free of pain. "Such waltzing was not easy." For whom? For any of them: for the father, with whiskey on his breath; for the boy, hanging on like death; for the mother, disapproving. Nor is life itself easy in this poem, in spite of affection: a knuckle has been battered; the child's ear is chafed in the very act of playing, by the very expression of affection; and the father's palm is "caked hard by dirt" — reminding us, perhaps (and one can immediately see how much more effective the direct image is than such a spelling out of one of its implications), that the waltz is an interval while labor is unremitting. Yet these are but the poem's grounding in "fact," the recognition of common reality which interacts with and lends depth to the primary effect of the poem, the boisterous fun, the masculine exuberance of this affectionate father. The image conveys, better than any statement can, the mingled feelings involved — both at the time and now, in memory — in a particular family relationship.

Here, for contrast, is another creative image, a poem by Stanley Kunitz presenting, without comment, a very different waltz:

The Waltzer in the House

A sweet, a delicate white mouse,
A little blossom of a beast,
Is waltzing in the house
Among the crackers and the yeast.

O the swaying of his legs!   5
O the bobbing of his head!
The lady, beautiful and kind,
The blue-eyed mistress, lately wed,
Has almost laughed away her wits
To see the pretty mouse that sits   10
On his tiny pink behind
And swaying, bobbing, begs.

She feeds him tarts and curds,
Seed packaged for the birds,
And figs, and nuts, and cheese;   15
Polite as Pompadour to please
The dainty waltzer of her house,
The sweet, the delicate, the innocent white mouse.

As in a dream, as in a trance,
She loves his rhythmic elegance,   20
She laughs to see his bobbing dance.*

There is nothing boisterous or masculine about this waltz: it is diminutive, delicate, even trifling. The poem at first seems perhaps somewhat overwrought about a subject so trivial, but then we begin to realize that this excessive approval is in keeping with the lady's preoccupation and is, indeed, central to the poem.

The diction is insistently flaccid: "sweet" (twice), "delicate" (twice), "little blossom," "swaying" (twice), "bobbing" (three times), "beautiful," "kind," "blue-eyed," "pretty," "tiny," "pink," "dainty," "innocent." The cumulative effect is ironic. The lady's preoccupation with something so insignificant is seen to be clearly significant itself as it

* l. 16 *Pompadour:* the Marquise de Pompadour, one of the pampered and powerful mistresses of King Louis XV of France

interacts in turn with one additional detail — "lately wed" — and we realize that there is something decidedly unpleasant about the overtones of the whole situation.

Once again, it is difficult not to be heavy-handed in attempting to state the implications of an image that can only be damaged through categorical interpretation. Put baldly, the lady's excessive interest in the waltzing mouse, at a time when one might expect unreserved interest in a husband, suggests that the marriage is in some way unhappy. In this context, certain details become particularly pointed, though it is important to see that the poet is not concerned to define the trouble but rather to create an image that conveys its actuality. This "beast" which delights her is no brute, but "A little blossom of a beast"; she laughs beyond reason at its sitting and begging on its "tiny pink behind." The comparison with Madame de Pompadour is especially productive of connotations and suggestions which enrich the image. The mere mention of her name amidst all this dainty prettiness may recall to an informed reader the delicately rococo canvases of her court painters, Boucher or Fragonard. While this comparison reinforces the effect of elegance and charm, it also reinforces the overtones of sensuality and decadence, for these were painters who created idyllic images in a rotten society, and Madame de Pompadour's politeness and her patronage of the arts masked a greed for power that led immediately (or so popular history would have it) to one war and ultimately toward the French Revolution. There is, in addition, the contrast between Pompadour's pleasing a king and this lady's eagerness to please a dancing mouse. It is here, just as the mingled delicacy and sensuality are most firmly established, that the poet adds (and thus emphasizes) a further detail while otherwise repeating his first line, the "sweet" and "delicate white mouse" becoming "The sweet, the delicate, the innocent white mouse."

It is possible to theorize beyond this, while still remaining faithful to the details of the poem. It is possible to suggest that the woman might be so amused by such innocence because it is foreign to her experience. Is it, then, that she is herself so far from innocent? or that the mouse is such a contrast to her husband? The poem does not say, and to pursue the questions further is to become entangled in an exercise of ingenuity. What Kunitz has written is not a case study from the files of a marriage clinic but a poem that is a creative image of a particular individual.

Though the creative image without explicit comment must be complete in itself, it occasionally also functions as the B-term of a metaphor. We recognize other metaphors because, like the "snow" on Housman's cherry tree or the "paws" on the boy, they have been substituted where something else would have been expected; we recognize these images as metaphors because, though they are not substitutes within any other expectation, their implications push us beyond the literal.

A well-known song from Shakespeare's play *The Tempest* is a fine example of this use of the creative image:

> Full fadom five thy Father lies,
> Of his bones are Corrall made:
> Those are pearles that were his eies,
> Nothing of him that doth fade,
> But doth suffer a Sea-change
> Into something rich and strange:
> Sea Nimphs hourly ring his knell.
> > *Burthen: ding dong.*
> Harke now I heare them, ding-dong, bell.*

Admittedly, this song's context in *The Tempest* adds depth to its full effect. Even apart from that context, however, the poem is effective. Made up of a group of images describing the miraculous "Sea-change" of a drowned human being — a beloved human being — into "something rich and strange," it concludes with no stated idea or comparison. Yet, in addition to the interactions within the poem — that between the human body and the rich substance it becomes (eyes-pearls), for example, or that between the emotionally related hearer ("thy Father") and the speaker ("I") — there is a further interaction: that between the poem as a B-term and the A-term which it implies.

What the poem clearly implies is not a particular A-term but rather the existence of some A-term or other. It is quite likely that readers would disagree about any A-term suggested, but few readers would

---

* l. 1 *Full fadom five:* five full fathoms [deep]

l. 2 *are Corrall made:* the verb has been attracted to the plural of the preceding noun, "bones."

l. 8 *Burthen:* burden, a chorus or refrain. In the theatre, the words "ding dong" were presumably sung (repeatedly) by off-stage voices. The final line is the original singer's response.

deny that the poem implies a meaning beyond the stated image. Why should this be? If we cannot point to a precise A-term here — and if we have argued against the assumption of "hidden meanings" — how can we maintain that the image of the "Sea-change" implies more than is stated?

We have already suggested that any vivid image implies its own "meaningfulness" and such is, in part, what is happening here — but only in part. This poem implies a further meaning for two primary reasons: first, it deals with something happening after death, a mystery we are accustomed to approaching metaphorically, and, second, it contradicts the natural process and thus invites attempts at explanation. We can imagine, all too vividly if we wish, the decomposing of a drowned body. In contrast, this poem offers a *re*-composing into "something rich and strange," a body transformed into an artifact of unimaginable splendor. Unwilling to accept this transformation as a literal report, we find our minds reaching out for other, metaphorical, explanations.

If he means something else — the next question obviously runs — why does the poet not state his meaning? Why does he give us only half a metaphor?

He has, in the first place, given us a whole metaphor, not a half. Remember that a metaphor is, by definition, an *implicit* comparison: we are given only the "paws"; it is the context that supplies us with "hands" as the A-term. Here there is also a context, a literal sea-change, a literal death, which renders the "rich and strange" sea-change metaphorical. But the first question is more important: why does he not state his meaning?

The answer must be that he *has* stated his meaning. The poem *is* his meaning (or he would have said something else). Any philosophizing about his image will only detract from, or limit, the full experience it can provide. Any formulation of the meaning of death is itself an arguable opinion. This poem does not present an argument about death but a comprehensible response to death. Here is death, not as a horror, not as a state of Christian blessedness (these are "Sea Nimphs," not angels), but as a mysterious transformation into something of lasting value. We could say much more, or nothing more. We could think of this change as a re-entry of the body into the natural processes of the world (which do, in the sea, eventuate in coral and pearls); we could think of this change as the transformation of our memories of a beloved person who has died; we can turn the metaphor in any of numerous directions and, so long as they keep contact with the image, tone, and grammar of the poem, they will be valid. To have added a little statement of the "meaning" of the image would have been to destroy much of its meaning.

There are, however, definite limits to the possible meaning of this poem. It is not merely a stimulus to the free imagination, which may then make anything it wishes out of it. The meaning is controlled by subject and statement. The poem is, for example, a metaphor for a view of death. It may be — it is — amenable to a variety of interpretations, but all these interpretations must present views of death. We have heard it otherwise interpreted. We have heard, for example, an interesting discussion of this poem as a metaphor for poetry, with metaphor itself the "Sea-change" that commutes everyday words into the opulent language of a poem. As interesting as this is, we must say that the critic was not interpreting Shakespeare's poem, but *using* it for a purpose of his own. It can be used the more readily because Shakespeare's creative image is now a created concept: the phrase "sea change" has entered our language and our better dictionaries to denote any profound metamorphosis, especially one involving a great increase in excellence or value. When a metaphor standing for some such abstract idea has thus entered the language (as opposed to the purely descriptive metaphors that also have entered the language — *e.g.,* the mouth of the river), it may truly be said to have become a symbol, though it was originally a creative image. Or, put another way, one might say that the metaphor is a creative image in Shakespeare's poem, but a symbol when anyone else uses it. Before defining and discussing the poetic symbol, however, we must introduce briefly several other related varieties of metaphor.

PERSONIFICATION AND ALLEGORY

Any metaphor that attributes human characteristics to something that is not human is said to *personify* its object. Inanimate objects, abstract ideas, or subhuman creatures may any of them be personified. Here are three examples:

> Lightly stepped a yellow star
> To its lofty place
> Loosed the Moon her silver hat
> From her lustral Face . . . .

> Can Honor's voice provoke the silent dust,
> Or Flattery soothe the dull cold ear of Death?

> For I will consider my Cat Jeoffrey.
> For he is the servant of the Living God, duly and daily serving him.
> For at the first glance of the glory of God in the East he worships
>   in his way.

Naturally there is a philosophical question involved in the last of these. If one were to believe that a cat is capable of worship (or even of worship "in his way"), the verb would be neither personification nor metaphor. An example of the personification of a subhuman creature about which there could be no question would be Ogden Nash's rooster who "swaggers by with his hands in his pockets." It is also interesting philosophically that, though "personification" is a common literary term, we have no word like "animalification" to describe the comparable (if not identical) process by which a lifeless object is given the attributes of a beast — as when Emily Dickinson writes of a railroad train, "I like to see it lap the Miles —/ And lick the Valleys up —/ And stop to feed itself at Tanks — . . ."

Probably the commonest form of personification in poetry is exemplified in our second quotation, that form in which abstract concepts are made to act as human beings. This process is very close to one logical basis of mythology, in which Venus is primarily a personification of love, or Neptune a personification of the ocean. But mythology is subject to extensive development — theological, historical, artistic — and its basis in personification is often almost lost with the figures functioning less as metaphors than as characters with particular biographies. We would make the distinction here between mythological characters with names of their own (Apollo, Zeus, Thor) and personifications that are capitalized abstract nouns (Love, Honor, Patience).

We call a single instance a personification; we call an extended narrative using personifications one of the forms of *allegory*. "Extended" is, of course, a relative term. For example, the personifications in the last six lines of the following sonnet by Michael Drayton, might (if they stood alone) be considered a little allegory, though the term is usually reserved for longer narratives:

> Since ther's no helpe, come let us kisse and part;
> Nay, I have done: you get no more of me,
> And I am glad, yea glad with all my heart
> That thus so cleanly I my selfe can free,
> Shake hands for ever, cancell all our vowes,   5
> And when we meet at any time againe,
> Be it not seene in either of our browes
> That we one jot of former love reteyne;
> Now in the last gasp of Love's latest breath,
> When, his pulse fayling, Passion speechlesse lies,   10
> When Faith is kneeling by his bed of death,
> And Innocence is closing up his eyes,
>> Now if thou wouldst, when all have given him over,
>> From death to life, thou might'st him yet recover.*

It is not the brevity of the metaphor here, however, that would keep us from calling it an allegory. It could only be so called out of the context of this poem. Here the metaphor follows eight lines that set up the explicit situation apart from the metaphor; in a true allegory the metaphor *is* the explicit situation, even though it is clearly also a metaphor.

An allegory is a continued metaphor, a narrative in which the characters, actions, or events refer to individual elements of a complex A-term. When these characters are personified abstractions, they allow the poet to dramatize the nature of man. Man's life might, for example, be allegorized either as a theological drama in which the Soul is tempted by Sins and aided by Virtues, or as a psychoanalytic drama in which the Ego struggles with the Id. But an allegory need not involve personification: the characters might be representative types — the Doctor, the Poor Man — in an allegory about contemporary society, or they might stand for actual individuals in, say, a politically motivated allegory. Dryden's "Absalom and Achitophel,"

---

* Readers have frequently misread these last six metaphorical lines, littering them with as many cadavers as close *Hamlet;* it is therefore worth mentioning that the third-person pronouns all refer to the single dying individual, though he has been given two names, "Love" and "Passion."

for example, is a satirical allegory by which Dryden apparently hoped
to aid the legitimate heir to the throne, the Duke of York, through
attacking his enemies, the Earl of Shaftesbury (Achitophel) and the
Duke of Buckingham (Zimri), who were partisans of the King's
illegitimate son, the Duke of Monmouth (Absalom). Dryden's allegory is noteworthy primarily as a series of satirical portraits. The
most famous of allegorical poems in English, however, Spenser's *The
Faerie Queene,* is much more complex. The allegory is not a rigid
one-for-one correspondence but a more fluid relationship in which a
character may simultaneously represent both an abstract virtue and a
historical individual, while varying aspects of the same historical
individual may be represented by different characters in the story.
Gloriana is both glory (which may be earthly or divine) and Queen
Elizabeth; Elizabeth is also represented by Belphoebe, who is simultaneously chastity. But Gloriana and Belphoebe, are also themselves,
characters in Spenser's fiction, not mere counters for Elizabeth's
glory and chastity, and the poem is best understood not by substituting concepts for its characters but by responding as we would to the
connotations and interactions of any complex fiction.

An allegory may, in other words, be as rigid or as fluid as is appropriate to the system of thought the author wishes to present.
Allegory implies systematic thought; however, it need not imply any
lack of subtlety. The bare outlines of an allegory are apt to appear
unsophisticated, a distressingly oversimple categorization of life, but
the effectiveness of the allegory lies in what the artist does with it,
rather than in the fact that one set of terms has been substituted for
another. Modern dissatisfaction with allegory has arisen, in large
part, because some authors and many readers have been satisfied with
the mere creation or identification of an allegorical framework rather
than pushing on to an understanding of what can be done within
that framework.

It must be admitted, however, that allegory invites ingenuity, chal-
lenging an author to see how many details he can fit into his scheme;
therefore, it is not surprising that many allegories, especially perhaps
the briefer ones, might also be considered conceits. The following
stanzas are Section IV of T. S. Eliot's "East Coker":

> The wounded surgeon plies the steel
> That questions the distempered part;

> Beneath the bleeding hands we feel
> The sharp compassion of the healer's art
> Resolving the enigma of the fever chart.   5
>
> Our only health is the disease
> If we obey the dying nurse
> Whose constant care is not to please
> But to remind of our, and Adam's curse,
> And that, to be restored, our sickness must grow worse.   10
>
> The whole earth is our hospital
> Endowed by the ruined millionaire,
> Wherein, if we do well, we shall
> Die of the absolute paternal care
> That will not leave us, but prevents us everywhere.   15
>
> The chill ascends from feet to knees,
> The fever sings in mental wires.
> If to be warmed, then I must freeze
> And quake in frigid purgatorial fires
> Of which the flame is roses, and the smoke is briars.   20
>
> The dripping blood our only drink,
> The bloody flesh our only food:
> In spite of which we like to think
> That we are sound, substantial flesh and blood—
> Again, in spite of that, we call this Friday good.   25

Here, with no capitalized abstractions, the allegory is clearly not a group of interacting personifications but simply an extended metaphor, differing from the usual conceit only in the fact that it has a cast of characters, each of whom has direct reference to a particular concept of its own. The "wounded surgeon" with "bleeding hands" is Christ; "we" are the patient; the "dying nurse" is the Church; the "ruined millionaire" is Satan; the poem is an ingenious presentation of a particular view of the meaning of Good Friday. Note that not only the characters but other details — the "distempered part," the "sickness" itself, the "hospital," "paternal care," "bloody flesh," "substantial" (reminding us of "transubstantial"), and more — may be seen to have individual meanings within the theological conceit.

How do we make these identifications? How do we know, in the first place, that we ought to make them? We make them because the details of the poem force them upon us. Though "wounded surgeon" suggests paradox, it is not this phrase that informs us we are dealing with allegory, but rather the addition to it of the third line, in which we find that we must conceive of ourselves as patients under a surgeon with "bleeding hands." The rapid mental search for the sense of such a statement leads into the allegory. We may first try to read "bleeding" as "bloody," perhaps, but too many difficulties soon pile up. When we get to "Adam's curse" we are alerted to possible religious implications. From then on it is a matter of recognizing how the other details fit, with the hospital identified specifically, and the final phrase of the poem a confirmation of the whole.

The primary danger posed by the existence of allegory, as a matter of fact, is not that of a reader's failing to make the identifications, but that of his approaching all poems as though they were allegories. We gave an example of this wholesale symbolmongering in our introduction, a student interpretation of Frost's "Stopping by Woods." (The owner of the woods is God; his house in the village is the Church; the horse is the Common Man, etc.) While the details in the Eliot poem seem grotesque on the literal level (e.g., "The dripping blood our only drink"), and so demand interpretation, nothing in Frost's poem demands allegorical interpretation in order to achieve sense. Too often readers invent allegories merely to satisfy themselves that the poem they are reading "says something really important."

It is true that there have been allegories so completely disguised, or so esoteric, that they have been intended to hide their meanings from any but the initiated. The disguise is sometimes adopted for safety's sake, allegory tending to be a convenient form under totalitarian governments. And it is true that some allegories that were once transparent now require historical annotation. But, in spite of these possible exceptions, it is on the whole a safe assumption that a poem which is an allegory will make that fact clear in some direct way, either through identification of some of its characters (as through the naming of personifications) or through the multiplicity of indicative detail. In the absence of such clear directions, the reader should resist making allegorical interpretations. He will otherwise prove himself ingenious at the expense of proving himself deluded. If there is any ingenuity involved, it should be the poet's and not the reader's.

SYMBOLS

A *symbol* is something that stands for something else. Thus one can say that a certain combination of marks on a page, $, is a symbol for the word "dollar," that the word "dollar" is a symbol for a particularly marked piece of paper, and that such a piece of paper is a symbol for a particular quantity of gold buried at Fort Knox. (Some economists might extend this by saying that the gold is itself symbolic, but we can stop here, having made our point.) When we use the word "symbol" in discussing the literary use of language, we are usually not referring to arbitrary marks like $, &, +, or — (which can be set apart from symbols by calling them *signs*), nor are we usually referring to the fact that each combination of letters that we call a word is a symbol for a concept (a thing, an action, a relationship, etc.); we use the word "symbol" to designate a particularly compact form of metaphor.

In this use of the word, a symbol is a metaphor in which a simple B-term stands for a complex A-term. The cross (whether we mean the word in a poem or a material object) is a symbol for the paradoxes of humanity and divinity, of suffering and redemption at the heart of Christianity. The elephant and the donkey are symbols for massive political parties which, through evolution on precinct, county, state, and national levels, in fact embrace numerous delicate compromises and outright contradictions. Such a symbol provides both a convenient verbal (or visual) shorthand and a focus for such emotions of faith, loyalty, love, or scorn, or hatred, or indifference, as the individual may feel for whatever he comprehends of the complicated idea for which it stands.

A literary symbol is thus perhaps the richest form of metaphor. Therefore to speak of such a symbol as "standing for" an idea, however complicated, is to belie it through attempting to divide what is indivisible. To substitute an abstraction for the symbol, just as to reorder a poem into prose, may clarify a statement but only at the expense of reducing its meaning. The meaning is not outside the literary symbol, which stands for it: the symbol is the meaning. Though we must, for the sake of clarity, continue to speak of A-term and B-term, in the symbols of the finest poetry these have com-

pletely coalesced — as they have in "Sea-change" in Ariel's song from
The Tempest.

A literary symbol may be *conventional* or *created,* and, in either
case, the tie between A-term and B-term may range from *arbitrary* to
correlative. Each of these aspects must be discussed if we are to understand how symbols function in poetry.

A conventional symbol is one that brings its metaphorical meaning into the poem from somewhere else. A created symbol is one
that achieves a metaphorical meaning within an individual poem or,
as frequently happens, within the work of an individual poet. A
conventional symbol is a traditional metaphor, such that the word
itself, through past usage, carries a symbolic denotation in addition to
its original denotation. The cross, the elephant, and the donkey are
all conventional symbols, though only the first has played any sizable
role in poetry: in each of them the word *denotes* a symbolic meaning
as well as denoting an object. In Housman's poem "To an Athlete
Dying Young," quoted in the last chapter, the lines "And early though
the laurel grows / It withers quicker than the rose" depend for their
full meaning upon the reader's recognition of two conventional symbols, "laurel" and "rose." Here the words denote not only growing
plants but victory, athletic honor (laurel), and feminine beauty (rose).
Not only these two lines but the poem itself depends upon the reader's
understanding the conventional symbols, for, without mentioning the
rose, the final stanza returns to the contrast between them:

> And round that early-laurelled head
> Will flock to gaze the strengthless dead,
> And find unwithered on its curls
> The garland briefer than a girl's.

The final line is surprising: the athlete's unwithered laurel garland is
"briefer than a girl's [garland]." One may wonder what the girl's garland is, and why it should receive the final emphasis in the poem. The
athlete's garland, his laurel wreath, is his glory, his time of triumph,
that which would wither were he to remain alive. But what is the
girl's garland? In contrast with laurel, it would appear to be a garland
of roses, but the symbol runs into the difficulty that a garland of
laurel in fact remains intact longer than a garland of roses, while
these lines would appear to be saying instead that the young athlete's
time of glory is briefer than a girl's time of glory. We are thus left

with a symbolic paradox, since the A- and B-terms of the two symbols appear to have been switched.

May not this paradox be related to the central irony of the poem as we read it earlier? We may note that the final emphasis upon "girl's" has an additional effect, working through connotations rather than symbols. This athlete had been no brutish fullback; Housman has not given us the broad-shouldered muscle-man, but a young runner, swift, slight, almost feminine, and here, in the final emphasis, he reinforces that concept — not literally, grammatically, but in terms of the connotations that spread beyond the syntax. The pathos Housman wants, the pathos which both creates and is heightened by his irony, is that of death before maturity, and he achieves it by evoking the boy not yet a man, the grace that is as much feminine as masculine.

In other words the original contrast of conventional symbols develops into a paradoxical contrast of particular meanings which are central to this poem. Interpretation may lead us still further: we may see the poem as implying that maturity, responsibility, mature sexuality, are terrible burdens of which the dead boy is well rid. Whether or not he is willing to accept this idea, however, an alert reader should be aware of the poem as creating a complex experience of a possible, though surprising, response to death. But the main point to be made here is that merely substituting the conventional symbolic denotations for the words "laurel" and "rose" is not enough; one must respond to both literal and symbolic denotations and must, further, be alert to their developing interactions with the rest of the poem.

Occasionally a conventional symbol functions also as an allusion (see Chapter II). This is what happens whenever the word not only carries a symbolic denotation but reminds us of a specific instance of its earlier occurrence — usually the occasion of its origin. In addition to its meaning as a symbol, the word, as an allusion, conveys a context for that meaning. In Richard Wilbur's poem "Mind" (pp. 208–9), for example, after the "caverns" have been established as the bat's environment — the reality, in the simile, against which the mind manages not to "conclude" — Wilbur moves, in the final line, to the word "cave." Our experience of the poem is enriched by our realization that this is a traditional symbol for limited human understanding, the darkness in which we grope, but it is enriched much further to the extent that we are familiar with the best known instance of that symbol, Plato's simile of the cave in *The Republic*. Remembering this, we especially appreciate Wilbur's new twist on the idea in "A graceful error may correct the cave." Wilbur can assume that the passage in Plato is so well known to his prospective readers that he is able to allude to it without calling attention to what he is doing. His problem has, in fact, been one of preventing his readers from jumping too quickly to the tradition — which he does by avoiding the word "cave" at first — in order to bring them to a fresh reconsideration of the aptness of the simile. The distinctions cannot be drawn rigidly, but we may say that, in Wilbur's poem, an explanatory image, the bat, becomes a created symbol, while the environment in which it moves, the caverns, another created symbol, is then equated with a traditional symbol, the cave, which also alludes to Plato.

The poet who uses a conventional symbol counts upon his readers' having sufficient background to recognize it. Naturally the assumption is not always safe, but, when the meaning of a symbol is in fact traditional, the responsibility for understanding it lies with the reader. He needs to learn traditional symbolic denotations just as he needs to learn any other denotations. Though a regular dictionary will provide many symbolic denotations, there is no substitute for wide-ranging and attentive reading.

When, however, a poet uses a new symbol, one with no tradition behind it, the primary responsibility for establishing its symbolic meaning lies with him. This is not to say that he must label his symbol with its additional meaning the first time he uses it; he must in some way or other provide a sufficient key. The key need not be blatant or obvious, but it must be available if he wishes the symbol to convey more than an aura of mystery.

In fact, we usually come to understand a symbol through precisely the same process by which, without recourse to a dictionary, we come to understand any word — through encountering it in a number of contexts. The symbol may not disclose its full significance, or even the fact that it is a symbol, when it is first encountered, but that significance gradually comes clear as it reappears in the poem or in the work of an individual poet. In T. S. Eliot's *Four Quartets,* for example, the rose achieves a most complex symbolic meaning which is derived not only from the traditional association with feminine beauty, but from other literary or historical associations (the English Wars of the Roses, Dante's ultimate vision in the *Paradiso*), from earlier uses in

Eliot's own poetry ("The Hollow Men," "Ash Wednesday"), and, especially, from accumulated associations as the concept reappears within the quartets themselves.

In "Burnt Norton," the first of the *Four Quartets,* after ten lines of entirely abstract language, "Time present and time past . . ." (which we have already quoted as an example of poetry without images), Eliot offers the first images in his poem:

> Footfalls echo in the memory
> Down the passage which we did not take
> Towards the door we never opened
> Into the rose-garden. My words echo
> Thus, in your mind.
> > But to what purpose
> Disturbing the dust on a bowl of rose-leaves
> I do not know.

The images are serving primarily to clarify the meaning of the preceding abstractions, to bring the senses into play and thus give body to the intellectual concepts. The reader therefore may not be aware, upon first acquaintance, that these roses are symbolic, but the sensitive reader will suspect that they probably are. Why? For a number of reasons. First, he will know the traditional symbolic denotations of "rose," and they will be hovering over this image in his mind, awaiting confirmation. Thus he will be wondering whether the image of the rose-garden not entered is one of feminine beauty not enjoyed, while that of the bowl of rose-leaves will suggest beauty remembered. Meanwhile, insofar as he knows Eliot's earlier poetry, these possibilities will be both confirmed and modified. The garden not entered may remind him of Prufrock, thus confirming the idea of sensual experience avoided, but at the same time, if he remembers Eliot's use of the rose in "Ash Wednesday," he may balance this possibility against another, the image may be a symbol for a religious experience. He will not need to be told that the psychological experiences of — as well as the terms for — love for another human being and love for God have always been closely interwoven.

In other words, the reader's previous experience with the image and with the poet will suggest to him that the word "rose" is symbolic in this passage. (In fact, because a conventional symbol is a word with a symbolic denotation, the symbolic meaning is present and may appear whether wanted or not. It is difficult to rid certain words of their symbolic denotations: any poet would find it difficult, for example, to avoid entirely the symbolic overtones of eating an apple if he wanted to treat this action as a subject in a poem.) In addition, the word "rose" will seem symbolic in Eliot's lines because any image to which one's attention is strongly directed, either through repetition or through other emphasis (syntactical, rhythmical, etc.), will tend to push toward symbolism in the reader's mind.

It is surely emphasis which first suggests to us that the tiger in Blake's poem is a symbol:

> Tyger Tyger burning bright,
> In the forests of the night:
> What immortal hand or eye
> Could frame thy fearful symmetry?
>
> In what distant deeps or skies   5
> Burnt the fire of thine eyes?
> On what wings dare he aspire?
> What the hand dare seize the fire?
>
> And what shoulder, and what art,
> Could twist the sinews of thy heart?   10
> And when thy heart began to beat,
> What dread hand? and what dread feet?
>
> What the hammer? what the chain?
> In what furnace was thy brain?
> What the anvil? what dread grasp   15
> Dare its deadly terrors clasp?
>
> When the stars threw down their spears
> And water'd heaven with their tears:
> Did he smile his work to see?
> Did he who made the Lamb make thee?   20
>
> Tyger Tyger burning bright,
> In the forests of the night:
> What immortal hand or eye
> Dare frame thy fearful symmetry?

Given this emphasis, and given the surprising questions, we are quickly aware that we are facing more than a jungle cat. The connotations push us toward symbolism, but we have no tradition to explain the symbol directly. "Tyger" is not a word with a conventional symbolic denotation.

This is a created symbol, and we might ask ourselves, therefore, how it achieves the meaning which it undoubtedly has. That is, after the prominence of the image has suggested that it may be a symbol, how do we decide what concept will help us to understand the poem? We keep our attention on the image, allowing the descriptions and questions to develop certain of its connotations until the symbolic meaning gradually emerges. Then we note that, as though to confirm our judgment, Blake, in his penultimate question, has brought his created symbol in direct contrast with a conventional symbol, the Lamb. What then is this Tiger, blazing with terrifying beauty in the innermost depth of the darkness? (Any attempts to paraphrase such simple-sounding phrases as "fearful symmetry" and "burning bright, / In the forests of the night" are inevitably unsatisfactory.) This Tiger attracts and it repels. It has been created, forged on an anvil like a lifeless artifact, but it lives. Its eyes burn; the sinews of its heart have been twisted. The stars wept when it was fashioned. Even before we reach the Lamb, we realize, or at least suspect, that the Tiger in this poem is a symbol of evil. Capitalized, "the Lamb" may denote not only innocence, but Christ himself; thus the Tiger may symbolize not only evil, but Satan. However, though Christ is more complex than innocence, Satan is no more complex than evil, so the additional symbolic possibility hardly affects the meaning of the poem.

This Tiger is a supremely successful symbol of evil: of its power, of its capacity simultaneously to fascinate and to destroy, of the unequivocal fact of its existence. But, having discovered this, too many readers are content to stop, to think of the symbol as the point of the poem rather than recognizing that Blake is using it for a larger purpose. The symbol is not an end, but a means. Blake is not primarily engaged in creating a symbol of evil; he is engaged in the bolder enterprise of questioning the nature of God.

In the process of creating a symbol, Blake's poem takes for granted the existence of the force symbolized. The Tiger *is* — evil exists — with such and such characteristics. This is not questioned. Instead the

Tiger is asked: what, given your nature and your power, must be the nature and power of the God who created you? The questions may seem at first to focus upon how powerful must be the God that could create so frightfully beautiful, so compelling, so potent a creature as the Tiger. But the concept of a powerful God is not unusual, and it is much less terrifying than the concept Blake ultimately suggests. A God with the power to "twist the sinews of the heart" is less terrifying than a God with the willingness, or even desire, to twist them. What do we mean by *God* in a universe containing this Tiger? In lines 11 to 16 the questions are incomplete, spasmodic, as though they flooded in upon the speaker too rapidly for formulation. What? What? What? What is implied by the Tiger? Then in the next stanza, the fifth, the full horror is formulated: Is God so detached from human beings that he could smile upon that which caused the very stars to weep? Could the same God create both the Lamb and the Tiger? (Where, then, is the Christian concept of the loving Father?) Is God so remote from concern for man? Is he malicious? or just disinterested? In the final stanza, note how the alteration of a single word deepens the question with which the poem began. What must a God be like who would *dare* to forge so indomitable a Tiger? The poem provides no answers, but the implications of the questions it asks are terrifying. Blake is not creating a theological position to which one may respond with a counter-argument; he is creating an experience of fundamental theologic awe. The reader should not be content merely to ticket the symbol; he should respond to the full poem of which the symbol is a part.

Whether conventional or created, a symbol may be seen to fall somewhere along an axis from arbitrary to correlative.* A correlative symbol is one in which there is a fitness between the terms, one in which the connotations of the B-term all serve to enrich the A-term. A completely arbitrary symbol would be one in which the meaning of the A-term had no apparent relevance to the meaning of the B-term to which it had been added. Completely arbitrary symbols, though logically possible, are in fact very rare in poetry. Mathematical signs are arbitrary symbols, there being no reason in the nature of the sign

---

* The distinction we make here is sometimes discussed as one between "arbitary" and "true" symbols. We prefer "correlative," which describes, to "true," which evaluates.

why + should not stand for *minus* or — for *plus:* the meanings have been arbitrarily assigned, just as letters are arbitrary representations of sounds. A poet might also assign a symbolic meaning arbitrarily, perhaps, but the very fact that the B-term to which he assigns it will have potential connotations, in addition to its denotation, means that certain of those connotations are apt to be strengthened by the symbol-making and to move toward relevance.

In Yeats's "Sailing to Byzantium," to take an extreme example, wise men of the past are called upon to "Come from the holy fire, perne in a gyre." The reader's primary difficulty here is with the unusual words: a "pern," the dictionary tells him, is a Honey Buzzard, a European bird related to the larger American hawks; a "gyre" is a circular or spiral motion. He then may paraphrase tentatively: Come from the holy fire like a hawk soaring in a circle. As he hears more about Yeats, he will learn that this poet developed a whole "system" of symbols which he both used in his poems and discussed at length apart from the poems. He may come across a note to another poem, "Shepherd and Goatherd," in which Yeats speaks of "pern" as a local word for "spool" (which does not explain why he chose to put an "e" on the word here). The spool becomes more meaningful in "Sailing to Byzantium" through its use also in the related poem "Byzantium," but it does not eliminate the image of the hawk. The reader will discover that, in Yeats's system, the "gyre" has a particular meaning as a historical movement or a movement of an individual soul, and relates to a complex presentation of the meaning of life in terms of a metaphysics of symbolic "cones" and "husks" and "masks." Insofar as "gyre" in "Sailing to Byzantium" refers to this complex system of ideas, it would seem to be a completely arbitrary symbol. One would not suspect the existence either of the system or of the individual symbol from the presence of the image in this poem. But, although it is to some degree arbitrary, bringing its symbolic meaning into the poem through our knowledge of Yeats's uses of it — and his direct discussion of it — elsewhere, we must admit that the connotations of the image do move toward relevance in this poem. Not only is the "gyre" correlative as a symbol within the system (there being a natural fitness between an expanding or contracting spiral motion and the ideas of individual or historical development or decline), but the image of the spiral soaring of a hawk in this poem conveys connotations (distance, watchfulness, indirection, etc.) appropriate to the approach of a "sage" coming from "God's holy fire." *

Poetic symbols may be more or less arbitrary or correlative; the degree will be relative, not absolute.

One group of correlative symbols may be called *universal* because the A- and B-terms are so congenial that the relationship between them appears to be basic to human experience. Such symbols are of course conventional, but they are more than that: they depend for their effect not so much upon a myth or a literary tradition as upon a natural and profound fitness. They are dependent either upon the fact that there are certain experiences which, as human beings, we all share or, according to the theories of some psychologists, upon a pre-disposition born in us. Examples of such universal symbols would be the seasons of the year or the times of the day as symbols for the stages of a man's life, or the river as a symbol for the passing of time. Universal symbols will be natural phenomena that have an inescap-able metaphorical relevance to human experience — and they also tend to be related to concepts of time, the most insistent of human experiences. The symbolic denotations of these words are very strong indeed. It would be almost impossible to write a poem about autumn that avoided any symbolic overtones of the human decline from full vigor to old age.

In calling a symbol a particularly compact metaphor, we may seem to be contradicting something we said in the preceding chapter. When a metaphor is extended for a number of lines, we said there, it will usually turn into the special kind of metaphor called a symbol. The contradiction between "compact" and "extended" in these two state-ments is more apparent than real: the extended image (a term we had not yet introduced) moves towards symbolism simply because con-tinuing attention opens our minds to additional understanding. The symbolic B-term, however, remains a single object — a rose, a game of chess, a steam engine — though the continuing attention to its details may serve to display some of the complexity of the A-term.

For example, Robert Bridges' poem "London Snow" is almost

* Yeats's greatness as a poet is not dependent upon the ingenuity of his occult sys-tem; it is dependent upon the success with which he has written his poems. Though the serious student of Yeats must eventually study the system, the fact is that the finest poems communicate abundantly quite apart from it. If they did not do so, they would be cryptograms rather than poems.

purely descriptive. As we consider the extended image we realize
that each of the words in the title is becoming symbolic. (Titles frequently point to images that are to be considered symbolically.) The
symbols are compact — "London" and "Snow" — but the details
of the poem both establish them as symbols and define them through
their interaction with each other. (As with the "smokeless air" of
Wordsworth's London sonnet, we are reminded that this city is noisy
by being told of the silence of the snow.) The ugly "city brown"
(either word may be the adjective, either the noun) has been transformed by the "large white flakes." It is a fresh world in which boys
can revel, a world they greet with astonishment. Then the "trains
of somber men, past tale of number" begin the process of restoring
the city's ugliness, treading "long brown paths, as towards their toil
they go." But even the men are briefly kept from their routine
thoughts by the sight of the beauty which they themselves destroy.
"Snow" thus becomes a symbol of transforming natural beauty, and
"London" a symbol of man-made ugliness with such ramifications as
are suggested by the details:

London Snow

When men were all asleep the snow came flying,
In large white flakes falling on the city brown,
Stealthily and perpetually settling and loosely lying.
    Hushing the latest traffic of the drowsy town;
Deadening, muffling, stifling its murmurs failing;   5
Lazily and incessantly floating down and down;
    Silently sifting and veiling road, roof and railing;
Hiding difference, making unevenness even,
Into angles and crevices softly drifting and sailing.
    All night it fell, and when full inches seven   10
It lay in the depth of its uncompacted lightness,
The clouds blew off from a high and frosty heaven;
    And all woke earlier for the unaccustomed brightness
Of the winter dawning, the strange unheavenly glare:
The eye marvelled — marvelled at the dazzling whiteness;   15
    The ear hearkened to the stillness of the solemn air;
No sound of wheel rumbling nor of foot falling,

And the busy morning cries came thin and spare.
    Then boys I heard, as they went to school, calling,
They gathered up the crystal manna to freeze   20
Their tongues with tasting, their hands with snowballing;
    Or rioted in a drift, plunging up to the knees;
Or peering up from under the white-mossed wonder,
'O look at the trees!' they cried, 'O look at the trees!'
    With lessened load a few carts creak and blunder,   25
Following along the white deserted way,
A country company long dispersed asunder:
    When now already the sun, in pale display
Standing by Paul's high dome, spread forth below
His sparkling beams, and awoke the stir of the day.   30
    For now doors open, and war is waged with the snow;
And trains of sombre men, past tale of number,
Tread long brown paths, as toward their toil they go:
    But even for them awhile no cares encumber
Their minds diverted; the daily word is unspoken,   35
The daily thoughts of labour and sorrow slumber
At the sight of the beauty that greets them, for the charm they have
    broken.

Much poetry of natural description is similarly involved in turning an image into a symbolic statement. If a poem of this kind were to deal with a tiger (which it is unlikely to do, Blake having usurped the field), there would be no anvils nor immortal hands; there would be no such initial emphasis on the image; there would be instead a natural description of a possible tiger, either in its jungle habitat or misplaced, perhaps, in a circus or a zoo. We would gradually realize that the image was symbolic because our attention would be directed toward a sufficient number of selected details for us to recognize the additional meaning toward which they were tending.

However, Blake's "Tyger" also is finally confirmed as symbolic by the way all the details of the poem compel such an understanding. The two kinds of poem depend ultimately upon the same process. The difference is that the tiger poem we are imagining would, as it were, steal upon its symbolic meaning without having issued Blake's warnings. This quiet transformation of image into symbol is the aim of much

nature poetry, but may equally occur in poems dealing with inanimate objects — skyscrapers, shoes, or helicopters. Looking back at
Stevens' "A Postcard from the Volcano" (pp. 204–5), you can perhaps
see now that the "mansion-house" in that poem is transformed into
a symbol of the many-chambered physical world of the present,
"shattered" in the future time of the "Children picking up our bones"
— but, even then, "Smeared with the gold of the opulent sun."

Such poetry appeals to, expresses and sustains the human propensity
for finding meaning throughout the universe. It can easily become
sentimental, either because the symbolic weight is out of proportion
to the image or because the image is distorted through a one-sided
choice of details. But it need not be sentimental if the balance is kept.
Blake's "Tyger" is not sentimental: the choice of details, though indeed one-sided, leads to a symbolic question so overwhelming that
the reader feels there has been no exaggeration. "London Snow" is
not sentimental: its symbolism is rather an invitation than a demand;
the reader is apt to feel that he has discovered the additional meaning for himself — that it is inherent in the image — and not that the
poet has forced it upon him. Nothing in Bridges' poem destroys
the sense of actual snow on an actual London. The symbolism lies in
the overtones.

In fact, "symbol" tends to be a dangerous word to use in discussing
this kind of poem, for, once they have learned the word, unfledged
critics tend to take advantage of it, forgetting that the symbol is also
an image and that the two are not entirely separable. The reader who
leaps to a simple symbolic equation — satisfied, say, that "snow"
stands for "beauty" and that he may therefore translate the poem into
an abstract generalization — is apt to miss the whole complex experience that Bridges presents. "Snow" does not cease to stand for
snow. Once again we must insist that the symbol is not an end in
itself, but a means, an instrument for the fuller communication of
simultaneous experience and meaning.

In order to demonstrate the difference between a sentimental and
an unsentimental symbolic handling of an image from nature, let
us consider two poems in which birds are used to symbolize visions
of joy. The first is by Thomas Wentworth Higginson and the second
by William Wordsworth:

The Baltimore Oriole

A winged sunbeam flashes through the trees
    And whistles thrice, as if the air took voice
    And all the embodied springtime cried, "Rejoice!"
The jocund notes enchant the morning breeze,
Now here, now there, still shifting as they please, —   5
    "O fear not! all is well since I am here."
    The blind, the imprisoned, know that cry of cheer,
And grief must yield to joy's blithe litanies.

A myriad blossoms cluster round his feet,
    And all the air is full of heaven-sent things.   10
    Hark! once again the jubilant treble rings,
Swift as that hurrying flight, though wild and sweet.
What room is left for meanness or deceit
    Or fear, in planets where the oriole sings?

To the Cuckoo

O blithe New-comer! I have heard,
I hear thee and rejoice.
O Cuckoo! shall I call thee Bird,
Or but a wandering Voice?

While I am lying on the grass   5
Thy twofold shout I hear,
From hill to hill it seems to pass,
At once far off and near.

Though babbling only to the Vale,
Of sunshine and of flowers,   10
Thou bringest unto me a tale
Of visionary hours.

Thrice welcome, darling of the Spring!
Even yet thou art to me
No bird, but an invisible thing,   15
A voice, a mystery;

The same whom in my school-boy days
I listened to; that Cry
Which made me look a thousand ways
In bush, and tree, and sky.   20

To seek thee did I often rove
Through woods and on the green;
And thou wert still a hope, a love;
Still longed for, never seen.

And I can listen to thee yet;   25
Can lie upon the plain
And listen, till I do beget
That golden time again.

O blessèd Bird! the earth we pace
Again appears to be   30
An unsubstantial, faery place;
That is fit home for Thee!

At first reading these poems appear to resemble each other quite closely. Each moves through a description of the bird to a generalization about the nature of the world ("planets where the oriole sings," "the earth we pace"). Certainly the diction is similar: they share the words "blithe," "rejoice," "cry," and "voice," and Higginson's "sunbeam," "blossoms," "springtime," and "things" are balanced by Wordsworth's "sunshine," "flowers," "Spring," and "thing." Of the two, Wordsworth's diction might at first appear the more sentimentally weighted: "babbling," "darling," "invisible," "mystery," "school-boy days," "golden time," "blessèd," "faery," and the archaic second-person singular pronoun and verb forms ("thou wert") outweighing Higginson's "jocund," "enchant," "litanies," "jubilant," and "sweet."

But the sentimentality, or lack of it, does not lie in the diction alone; it lies in the conception symbolized or, more precisely, in the relation of the natural image to that conception. Wordsworth's poem is carefully guarded against the sentimentality into which Higginson's falls. Higginson tells us what his "winged sunbeam" says — "O fear not! all is well since I am here" — and he tells us that "grief must yield" to the bird, even, apparently, the grief of the blind and the imprisoned.

His final, rhetorical question implies that the oriole's song leaves no room in the world for "meanness or deceit / Or fear." These are large claims to make and the slightest thought tempts us to deny them. The oriole is a beautiful bird with a lovely song, but it is not strong enough to carry the symbolic weight that Higginson has loaded upon it.

Wordsworth avoids the quicksands into which Higginson sinks by writing a basically different poem. He does not make statements about the meaning of the bird; he makes statements about the experience of hearing it. Such statements, reporting experience, do not so readily invite denial. In fact, Wordsworth keeps us aware of an actual bird which differs from his experience of it:

> Though babbling only to the Vale,
> Of sunshine and of flowers,   10
> Thou bringest unto me a tale
> Of visionary hours.
>
> Thrice welcome, darling of the Spring!
> Even yet thou art to me
> No bird, but an invisible thing,   15
> A voice, a mystery.

The "Even yet" is important to the complexity of the experience with which Wordsworth deals. The speaker knows, now, that it is a bird but — aided immensely here by the correlative fitness of a bird heard more often than seen — he asserts the effect the song had upon him in the past, an experience that hearing it now still recalls to him. The poem is built upon the two tenses established in the first two lines: "I have heard, / I hear thee . . . ." Mingled with the present experience of hearing the bird are memories of hearing it "in my school-boy days." It was then, when he was a child, that the speaker, unable to locate the singer, developed the notions of a disembodied "wandering Voice" expressing "a hope, a love," which was "Still longed for, never seen." Now, as an adult, he is wiser; he knows that such meaning as the bird seems to express is, in fact, "babbling," incoherent prattle. Nevertheless, "Even yet," the sound of the bird can lead him to rejoice. But there has been a profound change. The tense of "Thou wert still a hope, a love" informs us that the bird song has lost its earlier meaning. The "golden time" which he now "begets" under the influence of the song is not the future once "longed for"; it is the past, the time of his youth, the time when he was still able to experience that hope. The bird is blessed now because it carries him back in memory to the happy time in his childhood, and once again the earth "appears" to be "An unsubstantial, faery place." The symbol is kept from sentimentality by the implied knowledge that the earth is not, in fact, such as, under the influence of the bird's song, it "appears to be." Nostalgia for the past has replaced hope for the future.

Wordsworth's poem is not better than Higginson's simply because it is more complicated: it is better because it is more precise. For example, even the vague word "thing" in Wordsworth's "an invisible thing, / A voice, a mystery" directly evokes the sense of an unknown oracle behind the bird's "twofold shout." But what in the world are the "heaven-sent things" that fill the air around Higginson's oriole? And what is the reason for the "though" in Higginson's twelfth line? (Are "wild and sweet" in fact opposed to "Swift"?) And what is the point, in the final line, of suggesting the possibility of other "planets where the oriole sings"? If we are to assume that there are no such other planets, the flourish is irrelevant; if we are to assume that such others may exist, the idea is presumably intended to extend Higginson's general benevolence further into the universe. But we can't be sure: it is too isolated and too vague. Note, in contrast, Wordsworth's use, at this point in his poem, of "the earth we pace," which undergirds "appears" by insisting upon an actual earth traversed by slow (and distracted?) steps, in contrast to the "unsubstantial, faery place" the voice suggests. And note the semicolon after "place;" this transforms the final line from a subordinate, merely restrictive clause to a final, emotionally intricate tribute to the bird.

Higginson has written a vague poem that loads his image with more one-sided, unbalanced, and therefore sentimental, symbolic meaning than it can bear; Wordsworth has written an exact poem in which his symbolic meaning is submitted to the interaction of several perspectives, each of which is faithful to the natural image. Higginson imprecisely symbolizes a proposition that invites disagreement; Wordsworth precisely creates an experience of complex symbolic understanding.

However, even Wordsworth's poem is apt to strike many modern readers as sentimental, in part because of the diction of direct ad-

dress — "O blithe New-comer . . . Thou bringest unto me a tale" —
diction which must be seen in historical perspective, but largely because they distrust any assigning of human meaning to natural phenomena. A poet writing today knows that his readers are unlikely to
accept "Birds in their little nests" as an adequate symbol for children,
or "the meanest flower" as worthy of "Thoughts that do often lie too
deep for tears." He knows in addition that many in his audience will
find fault not only with particular symbols but with the very assumptions upon which symbolization is based. What is sentimental,
they feel, is the whole idea that objects may be interpreted as having
secondary meanings for mankind: the falling snow and the voice of
the cuckoo are natural events following their own rigid laws and not
proclamations in a man-centered universe.

   Though this change in conviction keeps some fine poets from using
symbolic nature images, the human propensity for finding experience
meaningful has not atrophied, and other fine poets continue to cater
to it. They realize that men continue to experience and to interpret
the universe as though it were man-centered, whether or not they are
justified in doing so. However, the sensitive poet writing such a poem
today is apt to be cautious and make no large claims; he is apt, in fact,
to be much less explicit than was once possible, seeming to leave his
symbol for the reader's own interpretation. His poem will center upon
a creative image that releases symbolic overtones. Consider, for example, John Ciardi's description of an old Italian woman, and the
small symbolic joy with which it concludes:

>   Nona Domenica Garnaro sits in the sun
>   on the step of her house in Calabria.
>   There are seven men and four women in the village
>   who call her *Mama,* and the orange trees
>   fountain their blooms down all the hill and valley.   5
>   No one can see more memory from this step
>
>   than Nona Domenica. When she folds her hands
>   in her lap they fall together
>   like two Christs fallen from a driftwood shrine.
>   All their weathers are twisted into them.   10
>   There is that art in them that will not be carved
>   but can only be waited for. These hands are not

sad nor happy nor tired nor strong. They are simply
complete. They lie still in her lap
and she sits waiting quietly in the sun   15
for what will happen, as for example, a petal
may blow down on the wind and lie across
both of her thumbs, and she look down at it.

It is, once again, restraint that makes this poem so effective. Instead of saying ,"No one anywhere has more memories," it says only, "No one can see more memory *from this step.*" In the first stanza her children and the orange trees are linked with a simple conjunction and both are related to the memory she "can see." Then our attention is focused primarily upon her hands, with a simile and direct interpretation (both negative and positive) to define their effect. The final symbolic interaction is one between these ancient, weathered hands and the single petal from the orange trees which may fall to lie across their thumbs. We join Nona Domenica in contemplating the petal, but our perspective is not the same as hers, for we contemplate her as she contemplates. Ciardi's poem, like many others written in our time, gains its effectiveness through restrained use of a natural image with symbolic overtones. An actual petal is presumed to fall upon actual thumbs but, in the context of the poem, this event enlarges our perception not only of the old woman's life, but of our own.

THE CONSORT OF IMAGES

Our desire in this chapter to isolate varieties of images and analogies has frequently led to emphasis on one aspect of the imagery in a poem in which it has several aspects. In order to illustrate the varieties interacting in a single poem, let us consider, by way of summary, the images in this poem by Yeats:

Lapis Lazuli

(For Harry Clifton)

I have heard that hysterical women say
They are sick of the palette and fiddle-bow,

Of poets that are always gay,
For everybody knows or else should know
That if nothing drastic is done   5
Aeroplane and Zeppelin will come out,
Pitch like King Billy bomb-balls in
Until the town lie beaten flat.

All perform their tragic play,
There struts Hamlet, there is Lear,   10
That's Ophelia, that Cordelia;
Yet they, should the last scene be there,
The great stage curtain about to drop,
If worthy their prominent part in the play,
Do not break up their lines to weep.   15
They know that Hamlet and Lear are gay;
Gaiety transfiguring all that dread.
All men have aimed at, found and lost;
Black out; Heaven blazing into the head:
Tragedy wrought to its uttermost.   20
Though Hamlet rambles and Lear rages,
And all the drop-scenes drop at once
Upon a hundred thousand stages,
It cannot grow by an inch or an ounce.

On their own feet they came, or on shipboard,   25
Camel-back, horse-back, ass-back, mule-back,
Old civilisations put to the sword.
Then they and their wisdom went to rack:
No handiwork of Callimachus,
Who handled marble as if it were bronze,   30
Made draperies that seemed to rise
When sea-wind swept the corner, stands;
His long lamp-chimney shaped like the stem
Of a slender palm, stood but a day;
All things fall and are built again,   35
And those that build them again are gay.

Two Chinamen, behind them a third,
Are carved in lapis lazuli,
Over them flies a long-legged bird,

A symbol of longevity;   40
The third, doubtless a serving man,
Carries a musical instrument.

Every discoloration of the stone,
Every accidental crack or dent,
Seems a water-course or an avalanche,   45
Or lofty slope where it still snows
Though doubtless plum or cherry-branch
Sweetens the little half-way house
Those Chinamen climb towards, and I
Delight to imagine them seated there;   50
There, on the mountain and the sky,
On all the tragic scene they stare.
One asks for mournful melodies;
Accomplished fingers begin to play.
Their eyes mid many wrinkles, their eyes,   55
Their ancient, glittering eyes, are gay.*

Yeats might be said to be defining the word "gay" in this poem, correcting the superficial sense of that word with which the poem begins until he arrives, through images that illustrate, clarify, and create, at the profound conception with which the poem closes. Redefinition of the word is hardly his primary purpose, however; he is defending art against shallow misunderstanding. Let us discuss his procedure, giving our main attention to the varying ways in which his images are used.

To call the women "hysterical" is to reject their opinion even before we have heard what it is. Yeats warns us at once that there is a basic superficiality in the view that considers art irrelevant, even in the face of threatened annihilation. "Palette" and "fiddle-bow" are illustrative images, making the women's meaning palpable to the senses; technically, they are metonymic, the tools of the artist standing for the art itself — palette for painting, fiddle-bow for music. The diction of this first verse-paragraph partakes of the superficiality, or the hysteria, of the women. "Fiddle-bow" is clearly a disparaging image for

* l. 7 *King Billy:* Kaiser Wilhelm, Emperor of Germany during World War I
l. 29 *Callimachus:* Greek sculptor in the fifth century B.C.
l. 38 *lapis lazuli:* an azure-blue stone, often carved like jade

music just as "poets that are always gay" is a shallow conception of poetry. "Palette" is less obviously derogatory, but, paired with "fiddle-bow," it is also reductive: the image is one of unrelated blobs of color rather than of a finished painting. Similarly, "Pitch like King Billy bomb-balls in" suggests (more through the alliteration and stress than through the image) the stridency of the women.

However, in spite of his choice of diction and image to create an effect of hysteria, and in spite of the fact that he is using World War I images ("Zeppelin," "King Billy") in this poem written not long before World War II, Yeats is not dealing with an isolated issue. We need hardly be reminded of the increased threat of destruction in our time, or of the many today who feel that art is irrelevant because it is not "drastic" enough to accomplish what needs to be done. We may, in fact, hold that Yeats has loaded this paragraph unfairly in making the women hysterical.

The second paragraph, with its imagery from the theater and its specific allusions to *Hamlet* and *King Lear*, adds another art form to the three already mentioned, but seems at first to have no other obvious tie to the preceding statement. The relation between them is logical, however, though not explicit. Against the assertion that whole-sale disaster impends, Yeats sets the counter-assertion that every individual ("All") is in any case the leading actor in his own tragedy. "There" and "That's" point not only to the characters in Shakespeare's tragedies but to individuals around us who may be undergoing experiences equally tragic. The continuing explanation demands this double focus: the "they" who are appearing on the stage are not merely the actors playing Shakespeare's roles, they are all of us, all the Hamlets and Cordelias who must play out our own tragedies, who must "strut" unsubdued. The images in this paragraph are primarily explanatory, developing the metaphor of life as a "tragic play."

Not all the images in the paragraph are confined to this single function, however. The idea of the "last scene" and the image of "The great stage curtain about to drop," for example, take on obvious symbolic overtones within the metaphor (which might even be said to be tending briefly here in the direction of allegory).

That "Hamlet and Lear are gay" is a fact that may be checked easily by reference to their plays, but this is joy of a very different quality from that ascribed to the "poets" by the "hysterical women."

A "Gaiety transfiguring all that dread" is a much profounder emotion than a trivial gaiety which is simply unaware of the horror.

But Yeats is not ready to concentrate upon the gaiety and he continues with the idea of personal tragedy. His third sentence in this paragraph uses two powerful illustrative images to clarify the experience of loss:

> All men have aimed at, found and lost;
> Black out; Heaven blazing into the head:
> Tragedy wrought to its uttermost.   20

After the summary statement of the abstract pattern underlying every life (however the details may vary), come two complex images, one of darkness and one of light. "Black out" is, first, a technical theatrical term for the sudden extinguishing of all the stage lights, usually at some climax in the action; it is, secondly, an image of sudden unconsciousness; and, reverting to the imagery of war in the first paragraph, it is an image for the darkened town expecting attack from the air. By inserting this image devoid of explicit syntax, Yeats is able to call upon all three of these areas of reference, and all three serve to intensify the emotional experience. The next image, "Heaven blazing into the head," can be seen to function also in all three areas, combining the ideas of revelation and destruction — whether as the experience of insight after an overwhelming theatrical performance, as the return to a fuller consciousness, or as the arrival of destruction from the sky. This whole complex of emotions illustrates the experience of individual loss.

Tragedy has not, indeed, been "wrought to its uttermost" unless there is this sense of revelation at the moment of loss, unless men have "found" what they are losing. Given the universality of eventual extinction, neither the loss of gaiety nor the occurrence of simultaneous destruction can add "an inch or an ounce" to what is already complete. The image of "all the drop scenes drop[ping] at once" is one of chaotic collapse in mid-drama, in contrast to the image of "The great stage curtain about to drop" at the close of a completed "last scene." Even if this were to occur simultaneously "Upon a hundred thousand stages," the disaster for any given individual could be no greater.

Again there is a logical but not explicit transition from one paragraph to the next. From the idea of the wholesale destruction of our civilization, Yeats moves to an illustrative image of civilizations following upon each other as though in a procession, the regularity of the rhythm — "Camel-back, horse-back, ass-back, mule-back" — adding to the sense of a repetitive process. Each of these civilizations has been destroyed and how utterly is shown by the example of an artist, this time a sculptor, known only by his reputation: "No handiwork of Callimachus . . . stands." The statement is interrupted by two general illustrative images (he "handled marble as if it were [as malleable as] bronze" and "made draperies" so realistic they seemed to move in the breeze) and followed by a specific illustrative image ("His long lamp chimney") which is, in turn, explained by a simile ("shaped like the stem / Of a slender palm"). What, one may well wonder, was the use of Callimachus' effort? Yeats summarizes this sombre conclusion ("All things fall") and then moves on to the affirmative corollary of a cyclical view of civilization ("and are built again"). "And those that build them again are gay." We have returned to the thematic quality, which is now affirmed, not as an imperceptive triviality, nor even as a transfiguring emotion, but as the natural concomitant of creativity. Whatever the ultimate fate of Callimachus' handiwork, there was joy in creating it. And this joy needs no apology.

The fourth paragraph describes, so briefly that we might almost say it merely lists, the figures carved on a piece of lapis lazuli, a brooch, perhaps, or the lid of a box — the item is unspecified. Introduced thus without comment, the image is not illustrative nor explanatory but creative; the remainder of the poem develops from contemplation of it. The logic of the transition is again implicit rather than explicit: having spoken of art objects that have not survived, Yeats turns to contemplate a small carving that does, in fact, exist. ("In fact" refers only to the implication of the poem; it makes no difference whether Yeats is describing an actual object or an imagined one.) This carving, like so many others or like an anonymous poem, has no known creator — no Callimachus — and must speak entirely for itself, unrelated to any known period or artist. In addition to the three human figures, one of whom he surmises to be "a serving man," it bears "a long-legged bird," a traditional Chinese "symbol of longevity." Thus, though he does not say so, Yeats implies that the stone itself is old and, in contrast to the "handiwork of Callimachus," has endured from the past. The idea of persistence is reinforced also by these being "Chinamen," for China is considered one of the most ancient of civilizations and connotes a venerable philosophic serenity. (These are the relevant connotations, however history has altered them since the poem was written; more than likely, they were not ever pertinent to the lives of average Chinese, but the connotations existed nevertheless.)

The bird and the three figures, one with a musical instrument, are all that is carved on the stone. But, like Keats contemplating the Grecian urn, Yeats finds much more there, and he finds it through the same process of imaginative comprehension. First, the color variations and incidental flaws in the stone add a suggestion of background to the figures. Lapis lazuli is a naturally mottled and frequently flawed stone, but Yeats, in developing this creative image is heightening symbolic overtones; therefore he uses the words "discoloration" and "accidental," suggesting not so much the nature of the material as changes which have occurred in its passage through time. Similarly, the "water-course," the "avalanche," and the "lofty slope" are not merely landscape details but carry symbolic overtones. Flowing water is a universal symbol for the passing of time; an avalanche is here at least a correlative symbol for a disaster; a mountain is a traditional, perhaps universal, symbol for an object of aspiration, which leads Yeats to infer that the men are climbing. To overstress the symbolic point by making a statement of an implication, we may say that small modulations in the universe ("discoloration") can often seem major disasters or challenges to an individual.

With the phrase "Though doubtless," Yeats leaves the carved stone entirely in an overt act of the imagination ("overt" because the whole poem is itself of course an act of the imagination) to create a natural image with correlative symbolic overtones implying his additional meaning. Though there is a "lofty slope where it still snows" (we think of the mountain peak as the ultimate, or most ambitious destination), they "climb towards" only a "little half-way house" sweetened by "plum or cherry-branch." And he "Delight[s] to imagine them" as having reached their unpretentious, immediate goal. We all dream of reaching, sometime, a point in life when we can relax our efforts, rest, though it will still be spring, and arrive at a larger understanding of where we have been and where we are going.

> There, on the mountain and the sky,
> On all the tragic scene they stare.

This is a moment for facing the reality of the "tragic scene" (a vista on the whole of life, or, recalling the theatrical metaphor of the second paragraph, as much as one knows at a given time of the whole "tragic play"), a moment for coming to as full as possible an understanding of it. And this is where art comes in:

> One asks for mournful melodies;
> Accomplished fingers begin to play.

Not the superficiality of trivial distractions, but an art which encompasses the tragedy by increasing our emotional comprehension of it — this is the relevance of art for a civilization, or an individual, threatened, as all are, with destruction. Though not "drastic" enough to remove the threat, art is an effective instrument for creating a capacity to face it.

Yeats's final image, his superb final image, is a created, correlative symbol for the quality of this deepest understanding. The word for it, the word with which he concludes, is "gay." But this is the same word used in the third line by the "hysterical women." It is not the word itself, but the eyes, the symbol created in the poem, which convey the profound quality Yeats shows it to be:

> Their eyes mid many wrinkles, their eyes,
> Their ancient, glittering eyes, are gay.

The repetition, as in Burns's "red, red rose," forces our attention to the image. "Their eyes mid many wrinkles," eyes in faces that have weathered time and eventualities; "their eyes," the most living element of a man; "Their ancient, glittering eyes," wisdom and zest, experience and light —"Their ancient, glittering eyes, are gay." This ingrained joy, not the superficial gaiety that sickens, is the quality of the builder, the artist, and of the sage, the comprehender; this — encompassing, not evading, tragedy — is the true gaiety of art.

VI
Pattern and Form

A poem is, in addition to all that we have discussed so far, a pattern of sounds. We have left until last this aspect of poetry, though it would strike many as the obvious place to begin. We have done so not only in order to proceed from prose statement to poetic interaction, but also in order to emphasize the relation of sound to meaning. To begin discussing poetry by listing various meters or classifying various phonetic effects tends to suggest that sound patterns are molds into which meanings are poured. Like a symbol, a particular meter — say iambic pentameter, for the most obvious example — is not an end in itself. Similarly, just as a symbol is not an interchangeable segment but an integral component of a total poetic meaning, so a particular meter is not a mere vehicle for the poet's thoughts but an integral component of the ultimate effect, and thus helps determine the ultimate meaning of his poem. The sound of a poem is not merely something to be scanned and catalogued, but the medium in which, moment by moment, the poem exists. Though we certainly would not suggest that the prudent reader could simply ignore the vocabulary describing poetic sound patterns, we do insist that he must remain alert to the reasons for, or the effect of, those patterns — and variations from them — in a particular poem.

Once again it must be pointed out that patterned sound is not an exclusive prerogative of poetry: prose also has rhythms. The sound patterns of poetry differ from those of prose not in the kind but in the degree of regularity and repetition.

RHYME

Before dealing with rhythm, it would perhaps be helpful to look at some less complex instances of sound patterning. The most obvious of these is rhyme. Consider first the effect of an isolated rhyme in a context of unrhymed poetry. These are the final lines of Shakespeare's *King John*:

> This England never did, nor never shall
> Lye at the proud foote of a Conqueror,
> But when it first did helpe to wound itselfe.
> Now, these her Princes are come home againe,
> Come the three corners of the world in Armes,
> And we shall shocke them: Naught shall make us rue,
> If England to itselfe do rest but true.

The repetition of the vowel sound at the ends of two rhythmic units (two lines) calls attention to itself, standing out from the passage, providing an emphasis and a sense of conclusion. (Note that it is not merely the repetition of sound, but rhythmic placement that creates the effect here: "to" and "do" in the final line also rhyme with "rue," but this is likely to pass unnoticed unless one's attention is called to it.) The poetry need not have concluded at this point; that is to say, the speech could have been continued if the playwright had wished. Had he done so, there would have been less emphasis provided, no doubt: the very fact that the rhyme comes at the end of the speech — here, at the end of the play — provides additional emphasis; the silence following the line allows its effect to remain unimpeded in the mind. But there would still have been a heightening: the sound, unexpectedly calling attention to itself through repetition at the point of usual rhythmic pause, adds an emphasis which, though it has nothing to do with the meaning of the individual words, affects the ultimate meaning of the poetic statement by stressing particular words. "True," as it happens, relates to a central theme in *King John,* the difficulty of maintaining personal integrity in a world of power politics, and the fact that the word receives the emphasis of final rhyme helps to leave it ringing in the hearer's consciousness. In addition to this emphasis on particular words, the final rhyme also emphasizes form. Shakespeare, like other authors of poetic drama, frequently uses a rhyme at the end of an otherwise unrhymed scene to provide an appropriate formal conclusion. The repeated sound "rounds off" the passage by providing a sense of completed pattern.

If an unexpected or isolated rhyme provides emphasis, what is the effect of repeated rhyme? Consider a few lines from Whittier's once perhaps over-rated, but now surely under-rated, poem "Snow-Bound":

> Unwarmed by any sunset light
> The gray day darkened into night,
> A night made hoary with the swarm
> And whirl-dance of the blinding storm,
> As zig-zag, wavering to and fro,   5
> Crossed and recrossed the wingéd snow:
> And ere the early bedtime came
> The white drift piled the window-frame,
> And through the glass the clothes-line posts
> Looked in like tall and sheeted ghosts.   10

This rhyme also provides emphasis, but not to the extent of the isolated rhyme in the passage from *King John*. Instead of an element of surprise, there is here a repeated expectation. After the first rhyming pair, we expect others, and the rhyme comes rather as a satisfaction than as a surprise. The first line of each pair sets up a demand which the second line meets. The rhyme primarily emphasizes the form of the poem by serving to keep us aware of the lines as units at the same time that it groups them in pairs. There is a definite sense of pattern and a pleasure (slight but distinguishable) which comes from having our expectations fulfilled. This pleasure should not be thought of as merely "emotional," nor the pattern as "ornamental," but as rhetorically functional. When we say that a statement has neither "rhyme nor reason," we are not disparaging rhyme as incapable of appealing to rational man, but, perhaps unconsciously, admitting that rhyme — or poetry — is like reason in carrying conviction. Like reason, rhyme reduces chaos to order, and orderliness, to the human mind, is powerfully convincing. Pattern, and the pleasure it creates, is thus a highly persuasive force; a patterned statement — whether the pattern is that of structure, as in the epigram, or sound, as in rhyme — is more readily acceptable to the reader than an unpatterned one.

Here is a slightly more complex example of repeated rhyme, a speech spoken by a chorus of priests in Fulke Greville's play *Mustapha:*

> Oh wearisome Condition of Humanity!
> Borne under one Law, to another bound:
> Vainely begot, and yet forbidden vanity,
> Created sicke, commanded to be sound:
> What meaneth Nature by these diverse Lawes?   5
> Passion and Reason, selfe-division cause:
> Is it the marke or majesty of Power
> To make offences that it may forgive?
> Nature herselfe, doth her owne selfe defloure,
> To hate those errors she her selfe doth give.   10
> For how should man thinke that he may not doe
> If Nature did not faile and punish too?
> Tyrant to others, to herselfe unjust,
> Onely commands things difficult and hard.
> Forbids us all things, which it knowes is lust,   15
> Makes easie paines, unpossible reward.
> If Nature did not take delight in blood,
> She would have made more easie wayes to good.
> We that are bound by vowes, and by Promotion,
> With pompe of holy Sacrifice and rites   20
> To teach beleefe in good and still devotion,
> To preach of Heaven's wonders and delights:
> Yet when each of us, in his own heart lookes,
> He findes the God there farre unlike his Bookes.

Both expectation and surprise function as we read this passage. The appearance at the end of the third line of the word "vanity," rhyming with "humanity" in the first line, causes us to expect at the end of the fourth line a word to rhyme with "bound." That is to say, the third line, in repeating a sound from the first, creates not only a pattern but a sense that the pattern is partial: it creates a demand. The fourth line satisfies the demand and completes the pattern. (It need not have done so; the demand might have been frustrated, temporarily or entirely.) This small completed pattern gives a moment of rest, and we may note that Greville's sentences and rhyme patterns end together, thus allowing an interacting emphasis.

Once a pattern has been set up, and the poem continues, we tend to expect that pattern to be repeated. Thus "cause" in the sixth line comes as a slight surprise, completing a two-line pattern where we had been expecting the second line of a four-line pattern, a word that would not rhyme with "laws." This completion is therefore a surprise rather than the satisfaction of an expectation. (These effects are naturally much slighter in fact than they appear when spelled out this way.) Surprise and satisfaction offer psychologically distinguishable emphases: the rhyme that falls into an expected place gratifies; the unexpected rhyme impresses; each is a source of pleasure, emphasis, and proportioning. Had Greville set up his chorus in six-line stanzas, we would have seen in advance that the four-line pattern could not be repeated. The two-line pattern would have been less of a surprise, but it would have gained in a feeling of inevitability. As it is, of course, the surprise operates only upon first reading, and then only for the first six lines. Soon the pattern is established and we read in six-line groups with expectation. The net effect, besides fulfilling expectation, is the proportioning of the verse, and the rhyme-groups act almost as a form of intensive paragraphing with the added dimension of what we might call "sound parallelism"— as in syntactical parallel structure, we tend to consider these groups of lines as comparable, even more or less equal, units of thought.

Next we should look at the effect of rhyme when it follows no regular order. This is Matthew Arnold's best-known poem:

Dover Beach

The sea is calm to-night.
The tide is full, the moon lies fair
Upon the straits; — on the French coast the light
Gleams and is gone; the cliffs of England stand,
Glimmering and vast, out in the tranquil bay.   5
Come to the window, sweet is the night-air!
Only, from the long line of spray
Where the sea meets the moon-blanch'd land,
Listen! you hear the grating roar
Of pebbles which the waves draw back, and fling,   10
At their return, up the high strand,

Begin, and cease, and then again begin,
With tremulous cadence slow, and bring
The eternal note of sadness in.

Sophocles long ago   15
Heard it on the Ægæan, and it brought
Into his mind the turbid ebb and flow
Of human misery; we
Find also in the sound a thought,
Hearing it by this distant northern sea.   20

The Sea of Faith
Was once, too, at the full, and round earth's shore
Lay like the folds of a bright girdle furl'd.
But now I only hear
Its melancholy, long, withdrawing roar,   25
Retreating, to the breath
Of the night-wind, down the vast edges drear
And naked shingles of the world.

Ah, love, let us be true
To one another! for the world, which seems   30
To lie before us like a land of dreams,
So various, so beautiful, so new,
Hath really neither joy, nor love, nor light,
Nor certitude, nor peace, nor help for pain;
And we are here as on a darkling plain   35
Swept with confused alarms of struggle and flight,
Where ignorant armies clash by night.

If we follow the conventional method of describing rhyme patterns
by using letters, each letter to represent the sound-ending of a line, a
repeated letter thus indicating rhyme — so that the pattern of Greville's chorus would be described as *ababcc* — the first fourteen lines of
"Dover Beach" would have to be described as *abacdbdcefcgfg*. Although the initial *aba* might lead to an expectation that the fourth
line will end with a *b*-rhyme, it does not do so and, in fact, because of
the irregular lengths of the lines, that expectation will probably not
have been strong. At any rate, such expectations of regularity as are
formed are frustrated, and yet, with one exception each line either
begins, completes, or repeats a rhyme pattern. The only exception

to this is "roar" in line 9, indicated in the description with an *e,* which has no exactly rhyming counterpart in this fourteen-line unit. (It is picked up some thirteen lines later with "shore," but that is probably too far away for the sound to have remained in the mind awaiting repetition. "Shore" is echoed three lines later when "roar" appears again.) Though not an exact rhyme, "roar" in the ninth line is sufficiently close to "air," in the sixth, to be called a *near-rhyme,* and therefore might have been indicated in the description with a *b'* (b-prime) instead of an *e.* Near-rhyme occurs again in the third section of the poem when the sound of "Faith," in line 21, is echoed only with the near-rhyme of "breath," in line 26. We will discuss varieties of near-rhyme in a moment.

These two near-rhymes excepted, the lines of the poem all rhyme exactly, but the rhymes occur in no patterned order. Though one might argue that both expectation (of some rhyme, if not of a particular rhyme) and surprise are functioning here, they would not seem to be the best words to describe the effect of rhyme in a poem like this. The repeated sounds might better be described as adding to the *cohesion* of the poem. We choose that word in preference to "coherence" because we are speaking not of the logic of the statements but of the sense that the lines "belong together." Of course, rhymes in a patterned order also create a strong effect of cohesion, but that can be more precisely described as the repeated fulfillment of expectation. Occurring in an irregular order, rhymes integrate the poem without calling so much attention to themselves. Since both rhyme pattern and metrical pattern here are loose, the effect may be thought of as giving the illusion of speech, while the presence of rhyme and meter, however irregular, gives the intensity, emphasis, and cohesion of poetic form.

Though rhyme in general has the effect of proportioning, heightening, and unifying a statement, and perhaps making it more acceptable, what one wants to note about the rhymes in any particular poem is the way they interact with the total meaning — how they relate to the syntax, whether or not they emphasize the more important words, whether they are ostentatious or unobtrusive. In "Dover Beach," for example, one might notice how the rhymes move toward a regular pattern as the poem draws to a close. In the third portion of the poem, where the reason for despair is most explicit in the fine image of Faith withdrawing from the world like a tide, the chaos of feelings is mirrored in the scattering of the rhymes (*abcdba'dc*). In the final portion, however, where he makes his small affirmation of individual love as a refuge against the terrifying impersonality of the world, he makes use finally of a regular pattern of rhymes (*abbacddcc*). The new regularity both creates an effect of order found after disorder and allows the concluding emphasis of pairs of rhyming lines. Which is not to say that this rhyme scheme *means* "disorder reduced to order" no matter what words may be used, any more than a parallel syntactical structure *means* what its words say without the words; it is simply an appropriate interaction of meaning and structure, each emphasizing the relevant aspect of the other, just as a well-designed building will not only "fit" its surroundings but will also call attention to certain aspects of them, while the surroundings will call attention to certain features of the building.

In general, rhyme in serious poetry should function as a natural, integral part of statement rather than as a separate or separable element in itself. For an example of what may be called a disparate or obtrusive rhyme, consider the first eight lines of Poe's poem "The Sleeper." The rhythm is so mechanically regular and the rhymes are so exact that we are forced to mispronounce the rhyme-word in the seventh line, with an unfortunately humorous effect:

> At midnight, in the month of June,
> I stand beneath the mystic moon.
> An opiate vapor, dewy, dim,
> Exhales from out her golden rim,
> And, softly dripping, drop by drop,
> Upon the quiet mountain top,
> Steals drowsily and musically
> Into the universal valley.

The humorous effect here is unfortunate because it is not functional: the violation of sense in the enforced pronunciation makes us lose confidence, as it were, in the sense of the statement, almost as if this were a bit of faulty reasoning. We have here been made conscious of rhyme and statement as separate "pieces" which do not "fit."

The inexact or forced rhyme can, of course, be used for deliberately comic effect, the pleasure coming from the unusual, or even preposterous rhyme. The poet best known for his exploitation of such humor is Ogden Nash, whose effects depend, of course, not only upon his unusual rhymes but, among other things, upon his irregular lines, so that the rhyme comes sometimes with a swift impact and is sometimes withheld while your expectation increases. Consider this poem of his:

This Is Going to Hurt Just a Little Bit

One thing I like less than most things is sitting in a dentist chair
    with my mouth wide open,
And that I will never have to do it again is a hope that I am against
    hope hopen.
Because some tortures are physical and some are mental,
But the one that is both is dental.
It is hard to be self-possessed   5
With your jaw digging into your chest,
So hard to retain your calm
When your fingernails are making serious alterations in your life
    line or love line or some other important line in your palm;
So hard to give your usual effect of cheery benignity
When you know your position is one of the two or three in life most
    lacking in dignity.   10
And your mouth is like a section of road that is being worked on,
And it is all cluttered up with stone crushers and concrete mixers
    and drills and steam rollers and there isn't a nerve in your head
    that you aren't being irked on.
Oh, some people are unfortunate enough to be strung up by thumbs,
And others have things done to their gums,
And your teeth are supposed to be being polished,   15
But you have reason to believe they are being demolished,
And the circumstance that adds most to your terror
Is that it's all done with a mirror,
Because the dentist may be a bear, or as the Romans used to say,
    only they were referring to a feminine bear when they said it,
    an ursa,
But all the same how can you be sure when he takes his crowbar in
    one hand and mirror in the other he won't get mixed up, the

way you do when you try to tie a bow tie with the aid of a
mirror, and forget that left is right and vice versa?   20
And then at last he says That will be all; but it isn't because he then
coats your mouth from cellar to roof
With something that I suspect is generally used to put a shine on a
horse's hoof,
And you totter to your feet and think, Well it's all over now and
after all it was only this once,
And he says come back in three monce.
And this, O Fate, is I think the most vicious circle that thou ever
sentest,   25
That Man has to go continually to the dentist to keep his teeth in
good condition when the chief reason he wants his teeth in good
condition is so that he won't have to go to the dentist.

We have been taking the word "rhyme" for granted, but before
leaving the subject we should establish some definitions. One single-
syllable word rhymes with another when it repeats the vowel sound
and, if there is one, the sound of the concluding consonant. Vowel
rhymes: *too — true, high — pie, grey — day.* Vowel-consonant
rhymes: *hot — blot, oath — growth, turn — earn.* Note that we are
dealing with the *sound* of the words, not necessarily with the spelling.
Such single-syllable rhymes are called *masculine rhymes* because they
are relatively forceful. (These terms were, of course, invented by men.)
Multi-syllable words also constitute masculine rhymes when the
rhyme occurs in an accented final syllable: *apply — decry, bassoon —
lagoon, dominate — hesitate, suppose — foreclose.* (Such a pair as
suppose — impose is not rhyme at all, but simple repetition of the
relevant syllable.) When the accented rhyming syllables precede the
final ones and the final syllables are identical, we have what is known
as *feminine rhyme* because it is relatively less forceful: *berry —
merry, groping — hoping, madly — gladly.* Feminine rhymes are usually *double,* like those just quoted, but may be *triple,* such as
glorious — victorious, opportunity — community or *carefully —
prayerfully.* This is about as far forward as the accented syllable can
be placed, and even the triple rhyme is rarely used except for humorous effect as, for example, in the first and second, and sixth and
seventh lines of each stanza of Guy Wetmore Carryl's delightful
retelling of the Bluebeard story —"How the Helpmate of Blue-

Beard Made Free with a Door." We have room here, unfortunately, for only the first of the ten stanzas:

> A maiden from the Bosphorous,
> With eyes as bright as phosphorous,
> Once wed the wealthy bailiff
> Of the caliph
> Of Kelat. 5
> Though diligent and zealous, he
> Became a slave to jealousy.
> (Considering her beauty,
> 'Twas his duty
> To be that!) * 10

Since rhyme is a question of sound, it is not surprising that, because of changes in pronunciation, contemporary reading of older poems distorts the original effects, just as changes in the meaning of words, as we have seen, can distort the original statements of older poems. This is one of the reasons why, if one is to read Chaucer, for example, with anything approaching full appreciation, one must make the effort to learn Chaucerian pronunciation. Something is obviously lost, in rhyme and rhythm, if one reads

> She was a worthy womman al hir lyve,
> Housbondes at chirche-dore she hadde fyve

as though it were

> She was a worthy woman all her life,
> Husbands at church-door she had five.

Certain rhymes were used so often in older poems that they are occasionally repeated in modern poems, in spite of the fact that pronunciation has changed. Thus you will sometimes find a modern poet rhyming *again* with *rain,* or a cold *wind* with *find.* These are now

---

* You will note that the humor here is dependent upon a procedure almost the opposite of Nash's: here we delight in the dexterity and profusion of rhyme within a regular pattern; there we delight in the almost frantic distortion of pattern and the apparently wild irrelevance of statement (the lines in your palm, the female bear) for the sake of a frequently preposterous rhyme.

merely *eye rhymes,* that is, the similar spellings make the words look
as if they ought to rhyme, and they continue to appear in exactly
rhymed poems only because of a literary tradition from a time when
they rhymed in fact.

In addition to *end rhyme,* rhyme occurring at the ends of lines,
which we have been considering so far, there may also be *internal
rhyme,* rhyme occurring within lines. Here, for example, are the opening lines of Shelley's "The Cloud":

> I bring fresh showers for the thirsting flowers
>> From the seas and the streams;
> I bear light shade for the leaves when laid
>> In their noonday dreams.
> From my wings are shaken the dews that waken   5
>> The sweet buds every one,
> When rocked to rest on their mother's breast,
>> As she dances about the sun.
> I wield the flail of the lashing hail,
>> And whiten the green plains under,   10
> And then again I dissolve it in rain,
>> And laugh as I pass in thunder.

Sustained in this way — and Shelley's poem goes on for some seventy
additional lines — the regularly spaced internal rhymes tend to break
the lines in half, creating pauses in the reading just as though they
were end rhymes. It is almost impossible to avoid reading the poem
as though it were written:

> I bring fresh showers
> for the thirsting flowers
> From the seas and the streams;
> I bear light shade
> For the leaves when laid
> In their noonday dreams. . . .

Such short rhyming lines create a pattern that tends to fall into a
metrical jingle apt to destroy any serious meaning. However, internal
rhyme need not be handled so mechanically. Like any other rhyme,
it can be used unexpectedly to add emphasis and cohesion. Consider
the internal rhyme in the fourth line of Shakespeare's "Sonnet 86":

> Was it the proud full saile of his great verse,
> Bound for the prize of (all too precious) you,
> That did my ripe thoughts in my braine inhearce,
> Making their tombe the wombe wherein they grew? . . .

Here the rhyme is a kind of pun, as "tomb" is made into "womb" both in the metaphorical statement and in the shift of a single letter. The rhyme ties the two words together, emphasizing them as the important concepts in the statement.

It is more difficult to describe the effect of the two internal rhymes in these lines from T. S. Eliot's "The Dry Salvages":

> Also pray for those who were in ships, and
> Ended their voyage on the sand, in the sea's lips
> Or in the dark throat which will not reject them . . .

Internal rhyme need not be confined to a single line. As with all sound-patterns in poetry, the test is whether or not the effect can be heard. In these lines, there is no question but that the words "ships, and" in the first line are echoed in reverse order — and that we hear the echo — in "sand, . . . lips" in the second. (Each of these four words receives the additional emphasis of a slight pause following it, either syntactical, as indicated by the commas, or formal, as indicated by the line endings.) The verbal music of this fourth portion of "The Dry Salvages" involves much more than a few internal rhymes, and perhaps it is enough here to suggest once again that the sound-echoes both add emphasis to particular words and add cohesion to the passage.

As a summary of the effects of rhyme — and perhaps as an antidote to such of our examples as may have suggested that rhyme is primarily comic — consider this fine poem by Louis MacNeice, written in the late 1930's under the shadow of the impending war. Here the conventional method of describing the stanza rhyme-scheme (*abcbba*) is scarcely adequate, for, in addition to this end-rhyme pattern, there is an unusual pattern of internal rhymes in which the second line *begins* with the *a*-rhyme and the fourth with the *c*-rhyme. Unlike most internal rhyme, which breaks across the line pattern, the regularity of this pattern tends to strengthen the line pattern. This immediate rhyming is in no danger of creating a jingle, however; the effect of the unexpected emphasis is closer to syncopation. Like Arnold and many other poets of the past century, MacNeice makes his limited but compelling affirmation in the face of chaos. Whatever lies ahead, the past has been good. The very achievement of pattern is itself a kind of affirmation in the face of chaos.

The Sunlight on the Garden

The sunlight on the garden
Hardens and grows cold,
We cannot cage the minute
Within its nets of gold,
When all is told   5
We cannot beg for pardon.

Our freedom as free lances
Advances towards its end;
The earth compels, upon it
Sonnets and birds descend;   10
And soon, my friend,
We shall have no time for dances.

The sky was good for flying
Defying the church bells
And every evil iron   15
Siren and what it tells:
The earth compels,
We are dying, Egypt, dying

And not expecting pardon,
Hardened in heart anew,   20
But glad to have sat under
Thunder and rain with you,
And grateful too
For sunlight on the garden.*

* l. 7 *free lances:* writers not employed by a particular periodical or publisher, but selling their work wherever they can. Behind this modern meaning of the term, the military origin of the metaphor also functions in the poem: the "free lance" was that of the mercenary who sold his services to some country other than his own; the

REPETITION AND REFRAIN

If rhyme, which is repetition of terminal sounds, adds to the cohesion of a poem, one would expect that repetition of whole words might do so to an even greater degree. This may or may not be true, but such cohesion as is engendered by repetition proceeds more from idea and statement than from sound and was therefore properly discussed in Chapter III. Although the repetition that occurs, for example, in the sestina — in which seven stanzas repeat the same six terminal words — is naturally a sound pattern, the monotony which is the sestina's primary danger is rather a monotony of meaning than of sound. In spite of the variation Kipling may bring to his use of the word "all," we are apt to feel we have been kept on a treadmill by his enforced worrying of six repeated words. (And his sestina is neither much better nor much worse than most in English.) The problem of the poet who would write a sestina, in other words, is that of creating variation within his rigid repetition.

Rhyme, in contrast, already includes variation, of both sound and meaning, with its repetition: both the initial sounds and, consequently, the senses of the words being rhymed are necessarily *un*like. Thus rhyme is in less danger of simple monotony than is repetition of words, phrases, or lines, and has the added advantage of relating dissimilarities. Repetition is most successful in poetry, then, when it is the direct servant of meaning, as in the passages quoted in Chapter III from *Richard III* and from "Let me not to the marriage of true mindes," or when it includes variation or increment of meaning, as in the shifting concept of Cummings' "etcetera" or Yeats's "gay."

Though capable of such increments of meaning as develop in "Edward," refrain probably had its origin as a pattern of meaning-

---

speaker and his friend can expect that the impending war will bring about their conscription.

l. 18 *We are dying, Egypt, dying:* Shortly before his death in the fourth act of Shakespeare's play, Antony says to Cleopatra, "I am dying, Egypt, dying." By shifting the pronoun, MacNeice reminds us that — as Antony did not know — both of the lovers died in the same general catastrophe; he makes the statement less self-centered. By alluding here to Shakespeare's play, he brings upon the impending war the focus of both personal tragedy and the destruction of empires. That is to say, the allusion brings into this poem, for those who know Shakespeare's play, a flood of relevant emotions.

less sounds, as a purely musical device of nonsense syllables used to
fill the melodic intervals between statements. One well-known example would be this secular Christmas carol:

> Deck the halls with boughs of holly,
> Fa la la la la la la la la;
> 'Tis the season to be jolly,
> Fa la la la la la la la la;
> Don we now our gay apparel,
> Fa la la la la la la la la;
> Troll the ancient Yuletide carol,
> Fa la la la la la la la la.

(Though the alternate lines look identical on the page, anyone knowing the melody will in fact read the third quite differently from the
others, as though they were punctuated, "Fa la la la la, la la, la, la,"
and it, "Fa la la, la la la, la, la, la.") English poetry includes many
lyrics with such refrains of *fa la la's* or *hey nonny no's*. They keep the
emphasis on the music and, indeed, in the absence of the melody,
songs that are charming when sung are apt to appear repetitive and
dull on a page.

From the nonsense refrain, it is only a step to the refrain which
involves a simple repetition of a part or all of the line, as in this stanza
from Burns's "O Wert Thou in the Cauld Blast":

> Or were I in the wildest waste,
>   Sae black and bare, sae black and bare,
> The desert were a Paradise,
>   If thou wert there, if thou wert there;
> Or were I Monarch o' the globe,
>   Wi' thee to reign, wi' thee to reign,
> The brightest jewel in my crown
>   Wad be my Queen, wad be my Queen.

Such repetition suggests a soloist and a chorus, which is indeed just
the way it is often used, as for example by Gilbert and Sullivan in *The
Pirates of Penzance* when the chorus of deadpan policemen absurdly
repeat the latter part of each line in the Sergeant's solo, come sense or
nonsense, thereby making fun of the form itself:

> When a felon's not engaged in his employment —
>   His employment,

Or maturing his felonious little plans —
     Little plans,
His capacity for innocent enjoyment —
      'Cent enjoyment
Is just as great as any honest man's —
      Honest man's. . . .

These uses of the refrain are all primarily musical, involving an immediate repetition of a sound pattern for melodic effect. With the refrain that involves the repetition of a whole line, usually at somewhat wider intervals, as at the end of each stanza, the musical effect may remain strong, but we are more aware of reiterated meaning. The following anonymous Jacobean lyric, set to music several times, perhaps most beautifully by Edward Purcell, is, without its melody, a bit static on the page. There is little increment of meaning in the refrain — on its last appearance it means little more than it did on its first, though it may be more convincing — and therefore it becomes something of a dead note, a passage at which, as with the *fa la la's,* one's attention relaxes while awaiting the next move forward:

There is a Lady sweet and kind,
Was never face so pleasde my mind,
I did but see her passing by,
And yet I love her till I die.

Her gesture, motion and her smiles,   5
Her wit, her voyce, my hart beguiles,
Beguiles my hart, I know not why,
And yet I love her till I die.

Her free behaviour winning lookes,
Will make a Lawyer burne his bookes;   10
I toucht her not, alas not I,
And yet I love her till I die.

Had I her fast betwixt my armes,
Judge you that thinke such sports were harmes,
Wert any harm? no, no, fie, fie,   15
For I will love her till I die.

Should I remaine confinëd there,
So long as Phebus in his spher,

I to request shee to denie,
Yet would I love her till I die.   **20**

Cupid is wingëd and doth range,
Her countrie so my love doth change,
But change she earth, or change she skie,
Yet will I love her till I die.

Anyone who knows Purcell's lovely melody is apt to resent our treatment of this poem; also an argument could be made for more incremental meaning in the refrain than we have admitted, an argument based upon the same common pun that closes "I serve a Mistres whiter than the snowe," quoted early in Chapter V. But the fact remains that the purely musical use of refrain palls quickly when apart from the music. In any form demanding much repetition — the sestina, the villanelle, the ballad, any poem with a refrain — it is the variation introduced within the repetition that creates fullness of meaning.

NEAR-RHYME AND ALLITERATION

If we think of the sound of the usual one-syllable word as consisting of consonant-vowel-consonant (CVC) — though it may, of course, vary as CV, VC, or simply V — we may then represent the pattern of rhyme as xVC, meaning by this that rhyme repeats the vowel and the final consonant, with x representing the element that must change. On the basis of this model, we may use the following chart to define the various partial repetitions available to poetry:

NAME	PATTERN	EXAMPLES
Rhyme	xVC, xV	send — bend, cart — heart, go — beau
Alliteration	Cxx, Cx, (Vx)	fat — fish, knight — now, why — which, (eel — ear)
Assonance	xVx, Vx	hope — boat, fat — ham, fake — tale, eel — ear
Consonance	CxC, xC	hope — hip, fat — fate, green — grain, it — at
Half-Rhyme	xV'C, xV', V'C	have — grave, again — rain, truth — mouth, he — gay, at — ate

Note again that we are dealing with sound, not spelling. "Sugar" and "sound" are not strictly alliterative because of the *sh* sound in "sugar." "Why" and "who" begin with differing sounds. "Truth" and "cool" are assonant in spite of appearances, while "swan" and "bad" are not. Other possible variations are usually considered to be species of those named above. CV*x*, for example, combines both alliteration and assonance but has no name of its own. Only with difficulty can *xx*C be distinguished strictly from *x*V′C, half-rhyme. The latter, sometimes called slant-rhyme or off-rhyme, involves very slight shifts of vowel sound, but even such a shift as is involved between, say, "growth" and "heath" has sometimes been called a half-rhyme. Thus the *x*C form of consonance ("it" — "at") might also be considered half-rhyme (V′C). What is known as eye-rhyme is a variant of half-rhyme, but, occurring in a pattern of exact rhymes, eye-rhyme tends to enforce a similar pronunciation of the vowels for the sake of consistency while half-rhyme depends upon the vowels being pronounced differently.

Our examples have all been monosyllabic words. Though it is not customary to speak of masculine or feminine assonance or consonance, any of these sound qualities may, like rhyme, be present in words of more than one syllable as long as the relevant syllable is stressed. One may, indeed, distinguish between the feminine assonance of stressed syllables followed by identical syllables ("saving" — "grating") and double assonance in which the unstressed syllables are also assonant rather than identical ("sulpher" — "ductile"). Similarly, alliteration is a matter of stressed syllables and not merely of initial syllables, so that the *s*'s alliterate in the phrase "consider the sun." For most purposes of discussion, assonance, consonance, and half-rhyme may be grouped together under the general heading of near-rhyme, though there are naturally times when greater precision of nomenclature is required.

Knowledge of this technical vocabulary has little value in itself. Not simply categorizing sound patterns, but rather developing an ability to perceive and the means to describe the effects created in a particular poem, is the aim of this discussion.

Half-rhyme can be used like rhyme to establish a pattern unifying a poem, but it can be subtler than rhyme, achieving its unifying effect while calling less attention to itself. Here, for example, is a poem by Emily Dickinson in which the second and fourth lines of each stanza are tied by a half-rhyme pattern closer to *xx*C than to *x*V′C:

The Spider holds a Silver Ball
In unperceived Hands —
And dancing softly as He knits
His Coil — of Pearl — expends —

He plies from Nought to Nought —   5
In unsubstantial Trade —
Supplants our Tapestries with His —
In half the period —

An Hour to rear supreme
His Theories of Light —   10
Then perish by the Housewife's Broom —
His Sophistries — forgot — *

Assonance and consonance are rarely used now as consistent line-end patterns, though they are often used for occasional effects, substituting for rhyme or half-rhyme. Here, however, is a poem by Louis MacNeice that does use assonance (and, in the first two lines, consonance) to achieve an effect of wry discord in his comment on a world madly lost.

Bagpipe Music

It's no go the merrygoround, it's no go the rickshaw,
All we want is a limousine and a ticket for the peepshow.

---

* As you will recall, Dickinson usually punctuated with dashes, which served as commas, as periods, or simply as pauses for particular emphasis.

The editor of *The Complete Poems of Emily Dickinson* has chosen to reprint only the poet's first drafts, ignoring the changes she made on her manuscripts. What any poet would think of this procedure can easily be imagined. The present copyright holders are perpetuating the editor's choice through using their legal power to insist that his versions be reprinted unchanged. They have graciously agreed to make an exception in this case, however, allowing us to reprint the poet's revisions in our text as long as we indicate here how they differ from the first draft. The poet's changes and the words with which she was dissatisfied are as follows:

> l. 3 *as He knits:* to Himself
> l. 4 *Coil* — : Yarn
>   *expends* — : unwinds —
> l. 10 *Theories:* Continents
> l. 11 *perish by:* dangle from
> l. 12 *Sophistries* — : Boundaries —

Each change in this poem improved the first draft. There is, incidentally, still another manuscript version of the fourth line: "Pursues his pearly strands — ."

Their knickers are made of crepe-de-chine, their shoes are made of
    python,
Their halls are lined with tiger rugs and their walls with heads of
    bison.

John MacDonald found a corpse, put it under the sofa,   5
Waited till it came to life and hit it with a poker,
Sold its eyes for souvenirs, sold its blood for whiskey,
Kept its bones for dumb-bells to use when he was fifty.

It's no go the Yogi-Man, it's no go Blavatsky,
All we want is a bank balance and a bit of skirt in a taxi.   10

Annie MacDougall went to milk, caught her foot in the heather,
Woke to hear a dance record playing of Old Vienna.
It's no go your maidenheads, it's no go your culture,
All we want is a Dunlop tyre and the devil mend the puncture.

The Laird o'Phelps spent Hogmannay declaring he was sober;   15
Counted his feet to prove the fact and found he had one foot over.
Mrs. Carmichael had her fifth, looked at the job with repulsion,
Said to the midwife 'Take it away; I'm through with overproduc-
    tion.'

It's no go the gossip column, it's no go the Ceilidh,
All we want is a mother's help and a sugar stick for the baby.   20

Willie Murray cut his thumb, couldn't count the damage,
Took the hide of an Ayrshire cow and used it for a bandage.
His brother caught three hundred cran when the seas were lavish,
Threw the bleeders back in the sea and went upon the parish.

It's no go the Herring Board, it's no go the Bible,   25
All we want is a packet of fags when our hands are idle.

It's no go the picture palace, it's no go the stadium,
It's no go the country cot with a pot of pink geraniums.
It's no go the Government grants, it's no go the elections,
Sit on your arse for fifty years and hang your hat on a pension.   30

It's no go my honey love, it's no go my poppet;
Work your hands from day to day, the winds will blow the profit.

The glass is falling hour by hour, the glass will fall forever,
But if you break the bloody glass you won't hold up the weather.*

Notice that MacNeice is here exploiting the strident (bagpipe) effect
of assonance, aiming at cacophony rather than melody, so that the
effect here, unlike the subtle unifying effect of Emily Dickinson's use
of half-rhyme, is to call attention to the imperfection of the rhyme,
and thus to the cacophony. He is creating a world — or reporting a
world — that does not harmonize neatly. The effect is aided by the
fact that the assonance all occurs in multi-syllable words (sometimes
"feminine," sometimes double assonance) which, rather than round-
ing off the pairs of lines, makes the discord seem to trail away. And,
of course, there is discord in the meaning too, a clash between the
frequently funny details and the impending doom. It is this discord
in meaning that, interacting with the assonance, brings forth that
aspect of the sound pattern — just as context will call forth one or
another connotation of a richly potential word. Assonance does not
abstractly *mean* "discord," though this is a potential effect of which
MacNeice has here made full use.

Assonance and consonance, like rhyme, can be used to establish a
pattern by relating lines to each other, but, unlike rhyme, they simultaneously strain against the relationship they have established. Though
they thus may have a subtle unifying effect, they may at other times
emphasize dissonance as opposed to melody.

* l. 1 *It's no go:* It's useless; it doesn't work. This is a poem about futile attempts
to escape boredom and to find meaning in modern life.
l. 9 *Yogi-Man:* Teacher of Yogi as a faddish religious discipline. MacNeice presumably wanted the echo of "Bogy-man" here.
 Blavatsky: Mme. Elena Petrovna Blavatsky (1831–91), a spiritualist and theo-
sophist who attained great notoriety with what her followers considered miracles
l. 15 *Hogmannay:* New Year's Eve (Scottish)
l. 19 *Ceilidh:* (Pronounced kay' lee.) The Scottish word means a friendly visit or a
private conversation. It came to stand for an evening's musical entertainment also.
Capitalized, it probably refers to a club organized for music and/or conversation.
l. 23 *cran:* a measure for fresh herring; one cran is equal to about 45 gallons.
l. 24 *bleeders:* a variant on *bloody* (l. 34) which, in the British Isles, has been considered an extremely vulgar expletive
l. 26 *fags:* cigarettes (British slang)

Alliteration, naturally an internal rather than an end-line pattern,* also has a distinct unifying effect. In fact, it probably preceded rhyme as a unifying device in English poetry, for most of the poetry in Anglo-Saxon, or what is called Old English, was composed in a four-beat, alliterative line taken over from earlier Germanic languages. Rather than quoting from "Beowulf" or from one of the Old English lyrics, where the original would be more difficult to follow, we will quote from a much later poem, "The Vision of Piers Plowman," which, being written in what is called Middle English, is more easily comprehended by modern readers:

> And ich bowede my body and bihelde al aboute,
> And seih Þe sonne and Þe see and Þe sand after,
> Wher Þat briddles and bestes by here makes ʒeden,
> Wilde wormes in wodes and wonderful foules
> With fleckede fetheres and of fele colours;
> Man and hus make ich myghte see boÞe,
> Pouerte and plente bothe pees and werre,
> Blisse and biter bale bothe ich seih at ones,
> And how that men mede token and mercy refuseden.†

By the time of "Piers Plowman," this alliterative line was already somewhat old-fashioned, and Chaucer turned his back on it, choosing to write in rhyme instead. Regularly used this way, alliteration tends to emphasize the rhythmic beat of the line. Of all the sound effects available to poetry, it probably calls attention to itself most insistently, and it is dangerously easy. Used properly, it emphasizes important words; used too frequently with less important words, it

* Alliteration need not be confined to a single line but may carry over into succeeding lines or may occur between emphasized words rather more widely separated. There is thus no way to define it mechanically; the only test is the ear.

† And I bowed my body and looked all around,
And saw the sun and the sea and, afterwards, the land
Upon which [where that] birds and beasts went with their mates,
Wild serpents in the woods and wonderful birds
With flecked feathers and of many colors;
Man and his mate, I could see both,
Poverty and plenty, both peace and war,
Bliss and bitter evil, I saw both at once,
And how men took bribes and refused mercy.

loses its effect and is not available to the poet when needed, just as exclamation points, italics or such intensives as *terrible, awful, very, beautiful* lose their effectiveness if indiscriminately wasted on relatively weak occasions. Shakespeare makes fun of alliteration in the Pyramus and Thisbe play performed by Bottom and his companions in *A Midsummer Night's Dream*:

> Whereat, with blade, with bloody blamefull blade,
> He bravely broacht his boiling bloudy breast . . .

However, Shakespeare also uses it frequently and with great success for incidental effects:

> Let me not to the marriage of true mindes
> Admit impediments. . . .

The alliteration here is under the control of the rhythm and contributes to the sense. Introduced with the unstressed word "me," it adds to the stress on the key words "marriage" and "mindes," reappears in and stresses "Admit," and then echoes, though not alliteratively, in "impediments." All this leads up to the repetitions we have already discussed.

A coincidence showing that it is not only the words themselves but the words in their context that determine the effect, is the fact that two of the key words in the Pyramus and Thisbe parody turn up forcefully and seriously in the third line of Shakespeare's "Sonnet 129":

> Th'expense of Spirit in a waste of shame
> Is lust in action, and till action, lust
> Is perjurd, murdrous, bloudy, full of blame,
> Savage, extreame, rude, cruell, not to trust . . .

Admittedly, the sonnet suffers if one is reminded of the parody it echoes.

Though alliteration discreetly used may add emphasis or assist in unifying a passage, it is rarely sustained at any length by contemporary poets, both because it so easily becomes blatant and thus ineffective as a means of emphasis and because it has more or less been supplanted by rhyme as the primary unifying device. Often it seems alliteration is most effective where it is most needed: in poems with numerous run-on lines which muffle the rhyme or stanza-structure or with distorted syntax that blurs the emphasis of the statement.

This is notably true, for example, in the poetry of Gerard Manley Hopkins, as this sonnet may illustrate:

Spring

Nothing is so beautiful as spring —
    When weeds, in wheels, shoot long and lovely and lush;
    Thrush's eggs look little low heavens, and thrush
Through the echoing timber does so rinse and wring
The ear, it strikes like lightnings to hear him sing;   5
    The glassy peartree leaves and blooms, they brush
    The descending blue; that blue is all in a rush
With richness; the racing lambs too have fair their fling.

What is all this juice and all this joy?
    A strain of the earth's sweet being in the beginning   10
In Eden garden. — Have, get, before it cloy,
    Before it cloud, Christ, lord, and sour with sinning,
Innocent mind and Mayday in girl and boy,
    Most, O maid's child, thy choice and worthy the winning.

When rhythm, rhyme, and syntax are more or less regular, frequent alliteration tends to be obtrusive and to seem forced, mechanical, or merely decorative, as in this stanza from Swinburne's "When hounds of spring" (a chorus from *Atalanta in Calydon*):

    The full streams feed on flower of rushes,
        Ripe grasses trammel a travelling foot
    The faint fresh flame of the young year flushes
        From leaf to flower and flower to fruit;
    And fruit and leaf are as gold and fire,
    And the oat is heard above the lyre,
    And the hoofèd heel of a satyr crushes
        The chestnut-husk at the chestnut-root.

Rhyme, which ties whole lines and even stanzas together, seems to answer the needs of English poetry better than does alliteration, which can bind only word to word. Auden, who has tried his hand — often with brilliant success — at most available sound patterns, has produced a lengthy alliterative poem entitled *The Age of Anxiety*, but he cannot be said to have redeemed the form.

CONSONANT AND VOWEL RHYTHMS

The vocabulary for forms of verbal repetition is useful primarily in isolating and naming — thus enabling one to perceive — effects which can create the sound of poetry only when they are all working together. Perhaps the most effective verbal music comes not from exact repetition, however, but from *modulations,* slight shifts of vowel or consonant sounds for which there is no precise vocabulary. Therefore, we shall attempt here to describe, or simply point to, the related sounds in several poems or parts of poems. We call these *rhythms* because repetitions and modulations are necessarily rhythmical, even when they are brief and irregular; we call them *consonant and vowel rhythms,* or *verbal rhythms,* to indicate that we are not yet discussing stress or accent.

The materials available to verbal rhythms go beyond simple repetition because there are certain natural groupings of kinds of sounds. Vowels may be short or long (or somewhere between),* and a preponderance of one type will have a noticeable effect upon the tempo of a line. Compare, for example, the effects of the vowel sounds in these two pairs of lines written by the same poet (Keats) in the same meter:

> Hedge-crickets sing; and now with treble soft
> The red-breast whistles from a garden croft . . .

> No, no, go not to Lethe, neither twist
> Wolf's bane, tight-rooted, for its poisonous wine . . .

The only vowels that could possibly be read as long in the first pair of lines are the unstressed articles, "The" and "a," and these are more easily read as short also. A preponderance of the vowels in the second pair are long, and even more striking is the effect of the three uninterrupted long-*o*'s with which the lines begin.

* Short vowels: *fat, met, bit, hop, wood, cut.*
  Long vowels: *fate, meet, bite, hope, food, cute.*
  Intermediate (examples only, not a complete list): *care, arm, orb, urn.*

Consonants also have distinct family relationships,* and a brief cluster from one group may create subtler effects than those tied to the repetition of an individual sound. Notice, for example, the effect of the plosives in "tight-rooted," in the line quoted above, or how, in the second line of "Lapis Lazuli," the plosives require a precision of enunciation that helps to create an effect of feminine overemphasis:

> I have heard that hysterical women say
> They are sick of the palette and fiddle-bow . . .

Or, in the final lines of the same poem, notice how the balance shifts from nasals to plosives at the same time that the poem is building from a moment of relative relaxation to its climactic image:

> One asks for mournful melodies;
> Accomplished fingers begin to play.
> Their eyes mid many wrinkles, their eyes,
> Their ancient, glittering eyes, are gay.

These isolated sound-elements do not contain meaning in themselves nor create it by themselves, of course, but, in context, they interact with the statement most appropriately to create the ultimate meaning.

Like an overdose of alliteration, an overdose of a particular sound-family can be too insistent, not only calling attention to itself but making too many passages of the poem seem of undifferentiated importance. The sibilants are especially dangerous in this regard, being both common in English and particularly offensive to many ears, as, for example, in this line by Hopkins:

> This was the prized, the desirable sight, unsought, presented so
> easily . . .

No precise division can be indicated between what is effective and what is not; one can only develop his sensitivity and decide for himself in particular circumstances.

Let us look now at the verbal rhythms in a short dirge from John Webster's play *The White Devil:*

---

* The most important in English are perhaps the *plosives* (*b, p, d, t, k,* hard *g*), the *fricatives* (*f, v, h,* both *th*'s), the *sibilants* (*s, sh, z, zh*), and the *nasals* (*m, n, ng*). Soft *g* and *ch* begin by stopping the breath, like plosives, but end as sibilants.

Call for the Robin-Red-breast and the wren,
Since ore shadie groves they hover,
And with leaves and flowres doe cover
The friendlesse bodies of unburied men.
Call unto his funerall Dole   5
The Ante, the field-mouse, and the mole
To reare him hillockes, that shall keepe him warme,
And (when gay tombs are robb'd) sustaine no harme, —
But keepe the wolfe far thence, that's foe to men,
For with his nailes hee'l dig them up agen.   10

We have sometimes asked our students to devise for themselves a
method of marking, with different colored pencils or with circles,
squares, and triangles, the repeated sounds in a poem such as this.
They are often surprised at what they find. First, a reader will usually
notice the rhyme pattern (*abbaccddaa*), and then the alliteration
("*R*obin-*R*ed breast . . . *wr*en," "*b*odies of un*b*uried," "*m*ouse . . .
*m*ole," "*h*im *h*illockes . . . *h*im" and the pair in "*f*ar *th*ence, *th*at's
*f*oe"). But these are only the most obvious repetitions and he will soon
begin to notice others: the additional, unalliterative *r*'s in the first
line, and its assonant short-*e*'s in "*R*ed-br*ea*st . . . wr*e*n"; the *v*'s and
the assonance of "sh*a*die" and "th*e*y" in the second; the *n*'s and *d*'s
in the fourth, which are continued and framed by *l*'s in the fifth. He
may then notice that six of the seven *n*'s in lines 4, 5, and 6 are preceded by three pairs of short vowels: "fri*en*dlesse . . . *un*buried
m*en* . . . *un*to . . . A*n*te . . . a*n*d." Of the vowels preceding *n*'s
only the long-*u* of "f*u*nerall" is unrepeated. The *en*-sound is repeated
again in "th*en*ce" and "m*en*" in line 9, and is the rhyme-sound in
lines 9 and 10 as it was in 1 and 4. Then there are the *r*'s and *m*'s of
lines 7 and 8, with the repetition in "*are*" and "h*arme*," and the assonance of "g*ay*" and "sust*ai*ne." "Thence," in line 9, not only echoes
the frequent *en*-sound and alliterates with "that's," but ends with the
ts-sound also immediately repeated by "that's." "Thence" and "that's"
begin and end with the same sounds but are not exactly consonant
(do not have consonance) because of the dissimilar *n*-consonant in
"Thence." The *s*-termination is repeated in "hi*s* naile*s*" in line 10,
which also contains the assonant short-*i*'s of "w*i*th h*i*s . . . d*i*g" and
repeated *n*'s, *l*'s, and *g*'s.

So much for direct repetitions. Of subtler but perhaps more directly musical effect in a poem are the modulations and combinations, the rhythms of changing vowels, the clusters or alternations of related consonants. For example, in the second line here — "Since ore shadie groves they hover" — the repeated sounds, *s*'s, *v*'s, *r*'s and assonant long-*a*'s, hardly begin to tell the whole story of sound patterning. Even without moving on to meter or stress, while still thinking of verbal rhythm alone, one should notice the modulation of vowels through "ore . . . groves . . . hover," words that account also for all the *v*'s and *r*'s. We would have to make use of a phonetic alphabet to represent the pattern exactly, but we can perhaps indicate it roughly thus, with slant lines dividing the eight syllables:

$$\text{s-s / or / sha\={} / / rovs / a\={} / huv / r}$$

Only the fourth syllable is not involved directly in this verbal rhythm, and its long-*e* is echoed in the third syllable of the next line. When we add to our perception the fact that there are alternate metrical accents (which here coincide with the stresses demanded by the meaning of the words, a distinction we will be discussing soon), we might represent the effect thus:

$$\text{s-\'s / or / sh\'a\={} / / r\'ovs / a\={} / h\'uv / r}$$

Then we can see that the stressed syllables carry the primary verbal rhythms too, and that a fuller description of the sound pattern would require recognition of such subtleties as the unstressed-stressed-unstressed rhythm of the *r*-sound, the modulation from stressed to unstressed of the long-*a*, the *r-v, v-r* interchange.

Some students are fascinated by such patterns, and it is difficult to curb their ingenuity in pursuing them. Others, priding themselves on their common sense, will object, "So what? There are only so many sounds. You can't write without repeating them, so why all the fuss?" (Occasionally they will say that there are only twenty-six sounds, confusing them with the letters used to represent the approximately thirty-eight meaningfully different sounds of standard American English.*) There is sufficient truth in this objection to make it seem persuasive. What then is the relevance of such verbal rhythms as we have been indicating?

* A respectable international phonetic alphabet — one with a character for each vocal sound actually distinguished meaningfully in some language or dialect — requires about one hundred and twenty characters.

It is perfectly true that it would be impossible to write a sustained passage in English free of any repetitions of verbal sounds. But this is beside the point. We are dealing with repetitions within quite limited groups of words, rarely extending beyond three lines of a poem. And we are dealing with effects that — even if they were unavoidable — account for much of our pleasure in the sound of poetry. The poem, as E. M. Forster said of another art-form, "hangs together because it is stitched internally, because it contains rhythms." * Though we may be unconscious of most of these internal stitches and, indeed, probably cannot make ourselves conscious of them all, the more sensitive we are as readers, the more we will be aware of their existence. A full account of the verbal rhythms of any poem would require mentioning every sound-relationship in every line, plus such as relate adjacent lines and any that reappear with sufficient prominence to unite separated passages — a process of cataloguing as useless for most purposes as it would be dull. (We perhaps approached it too closely for comfort in discussing Webster's second line.) Some verbal rhythms are naturally more effective than others. Even then it is difficult to do more than point, so that the best comment on the verbal rhythm is, ultimately, a sensitive reading of the poem.

Another frequent objection to such close attention to the sound of a poem is the refusal to believe that poets could possibly pay attention to such details in writing their poems. "The poet was just trying to *say* something. He couldn't pay that much attention to the sound. He probably doesn't even know these things are in his poem."

There are two answers which must be given. The first is that, even if these assertions were true, the fact of verbal rhythms would remain, with their partial responsibility for a poem's effect and thus its meaning. The second is that the assertions are not generally true.

Naturally it is possible that a poem might contain some verbal rhythms of which the poet remained unconscious, and that he might express surprise upon having them pointed out to him. We cannot here go into the problems of conscious and unconscious creation, or of what may be involved in what is called inspiration; we can say, however, that an artist is increasingly successful (as an artist — we are not talking of finance) to the extent that he has control, conscious or unconscious, over an increasing number of the elements that constitute his work of art. A poet is working with meaningful *sounds*

---

* *Aspects of the Novel* (New York, 1927), p. 236

and — however his lines may have been inspired originally — he has to decide whether to discard them, change them, or leave them alone. In making such choices, in choosing among synonyms or between alternate possibilities, he must deal with everything at once: meter, stress, verbal rhythm, statement. No one doubts that a poet is responsible for end-rhyme; such a pattern is not unavoidable in English and must be arranged. The better the poet, the more he will be arranging all his details, not only his rhymes. Sometimes English will not provide him with a word that will fit into the complex demands of both statement and sound. Then he must rearrange the whole, or compromise, or invent, or abandon his attempt. The effort to achieve a seemingly effortless control of all these details so that the result has the appearance of wholeness, inevitability, and "rightness," is precisely the "difficult labor" of writing poetry, precisely why, of the many who write verse, so few manage to become poets.

The objections that verbal rhythms are inevitable or that poets may not be conscious of them do not, either of them, stand up against the fact of effective verbal rhythms in particular poems. A sounder objection to looking for them is the fact that, having found them, there is so little we can say. We can only point to one source of the infinite richness of a good poem. Our enjoyment of that richness increases as we discover more of its sources, and one way of developing our sensitivity is through attempting to discover as many verbal rhythms as possible in a few poems, even at the expense of over-ingenuity. Having found them, a reader can then try to distinguish the more from the less effective and important. In considering further poems, he will find that the patterns demanding his attention are those which most directly interact with statement to mold the meaning. One should remember Shakespeare's "bloody blamefull blade" and realize that verbal rhythms must be consistent with — if they are not to be destructive of — meaning; self-centered distractions can only harm a poem. (Shakespeare's outrageous alliteration is, of course, precisely creative of the total meaning desired, for the aim is ludicrous parody.) Nor is any effect fine enough to avoid monotony and the loss of the very emphasis for which it strives, if it is insisted upon too often.

Let us turn now to another poem, not in order to catalogue every detail of the verbal rhythm, but to attempt a description of such details as seem most directly creative of the poem's meaning. Tennyson's

In Memoriam is a long loosely-related series of short elegies on the death of his friend Arthur Hallam. It is one of these, the fifteenth, that we shall examine:

> To-night the winds begin to rise
> > And roar from yonder dropping day;
> > The last red leaf is whirl'd away,
> The rooks are blown about the skies;
>
> The forest crack'd, the waters curl'd,   5
> > The cattle huddled on the lea;
> > And wildly dash'd on tower and tree,
> The sunbeam strikes along the world:
>
> And but for fancies, which aver
> > That all thy motions gently pass   10
> > Athwart a plane of molten glass,
> I scarce could brook the strain and stir
>
> That makes the barren branches loud;
> > And but for fear it is not so,
> > The wild unrest that lives in woe   15
> Would dote and pore on yonder cloud
>
> That rises upward always higher,
> > And onward drags a laboring breast,
> > And topples round the dreary west,
> A looming bastion fringed with fire.   20

This is a description of a windstorm and a cloud at sunset, interacting with thoughts of the ship returning with Hallam's body.* The details create so intense an experience, however, that the result is an almost eschatological sunset; emotionally, it is as though this were the end of the world. Nothing else gives literal meaning to the statement that the "forest" is "crack'd." One may think of this vaguely as the sound of falling branches, or as a curious effect of light, but the statement is plain. Taken literally it adds immensely to the red leaf's finality, the rooks' loss of control, and the cattle's terror. All the details move in this direction. "Gold" would be equally autumnal and

---

* Hallam died in Vienna. His body was returned to England via boat from Trieste, then an Austrian port.

monosyllabic for describing the leaf, but it is not the color of blood. "Molten glass" is not only smooth, as required, but white hot, searing. The cloud "topples"; the bastion "looms"; everything is either threatening, or being threatened with, destruction. The ominous apocalyptic warning in the first line of the poem grows steadily in intensity to its climax in "fire." The curling of the water, in this context, suggests the Red Sea, not so much parting for the Israelites as about to descend upon the Egyptians. The sunbeam, with the verb "strikes," suggests a final spark, the final destructive thunderbolt.

But the poem remains a literal description, and the emotional exaggeration is also under the control of the poet's awareness of his being simultaneously repelled from ("I scarce could brook") and attracted to ("The wild unrest . . . Would dote") the destructiveness of the storm and the emotion. His "fancies" and his "fear" in thinking of his returning friend — much as though Hallam were still alive — restrain him from abandoning himself to his emotion, keeping both repulsion and attraction conditional ("but for"). In other words, his very consciousness of his loss prevents his abandoning himself to it, which is a piercing insight into the self-centered psychology of loss.

With such control over his details, the poet would presumably exert equal control over his verbal rhythms, and, indeed, they interact with the other details, thought, and emotion, to create the meaning. The ominous quality of the first line comes not only from the statement it makes, or from the image, but from the sound: the modulation of the *i* from long to short and then back from short to long, the plosives setting off the first word, the nasals and sibilants letting the rest of the line flow as the stressed syllables are extended. Many of the verbs are onomatopoeic: "roar," "whirl'd," "blown," etc. In fact, in the second stanza, whole lines could be said to fulfill the action of their verbs. The harsh double plosive (*kt*) at the end of "crack'd" in the second stanza's first line breaks it with an insistent pause, while the softer *rl* between the plosives of "curl'd" makes that word, and the end of the line, much less abrupt. The movement of the second line is quite unlike that of the first, but the two are held together by the alliteration ("crack'd . . . curl'd . . . cattle") and by the repeated combination of plosive and *l* in the second line which combine the primary effects of the separate verbs in the first. Because they contain no other plosives, the rest of the words tend to elide and the second line seems to draw in upon "cattle huddled." The spaced plosives in the third line are the very impediments against which the sound dashes itself, while the last line, though it continues to have some of the same effect in "strikes," is slowed by the lingering sonority of its nasals to a more dignified pace, in keeping with the vastly increased perspective.

Admittedly analysis like this is dangerously neat. Is the suggestion that the *sound does* what the *words say* not both too easy and too far-fetched? Would the sound have this effect upon someone who did not know the meaning? Probably not — though it is difficult to be sure. The statements in the poem are undoubtedly the primary determinants here, but, while making every effort to distinguish between the two, one can only say that the verbal rhythms contribute strongly to the statements. That the sound of the first line is "crack'd," or that the next line "huddles" are not entirely nonsensical assertions, though sounds, like words themselves, are complex structures of potential meanings which are selected from and realized by the whole context. The effect is not often so striking, nor is it repeated in any other stanza of this poem, but perhaps we have said enough to demonstrate the potentialities of verbal rhythms in interacting with statements to create effective meanings.

METER

Verbal rhythms in English poetry, however important to the effect, are necessarily brief and irregular. Most English poetry — and here it is distinguished from prose — sustains another kind of rhythm, a regular pattern which, through repetition, unifies a whole poem. Whatever it is that constitutes this regular rhythmic pattern is called *meter*. There is probably no element of poetry about which critics are in less agreement — though to read some of the handbooks which lay the subject out dogmatically, one would never suspect that to be the situation.

We may start then by agreeing that some kind of rhythmic reguuarity exists in many poems, for we are aware of something's having gone wrong when it is broken. Here, for example, is a well-known pattern, the limerick:

> There was an Old Person of Tring
> Who, when somebody asked her to sing,
>> Replied, "Ain't it odd?
>> I can never tell 'God
> Save the Weasel' from 'Pop Goes the King.' "

With that pattern in our minds — and the vast store of bawdy limericks has perhaps helped to establish it — we readily note its breakdown in this apt example:

> A decrepit old gasman named Peter,
> While hunting around for the meter,
>> Touched a leak with his light;
>> He rose out of sight —
> And, as everyone who knows anything about poetry can
>> tell you, he also ruined the meter.

Regularity of metrical pattern can exist. The disagreement arises over attempts to explain what it is that constitutes that regularity.

We still describe English metrical patterns with Greek words, like *iambic hexameter* or *trochaic tetrameter,* which referred originally to particular combinations of long and short vowels. Greek meter was a form of regularly repeated verbal rhythm. If anything is clear, it is that vowel length is not the basis of metrical patterns in English.* We apply the Greek words, like metaphors, to something else entirely. But to what?

In spoken English, the sense depends upon the stressing of some syllables more than others, and one plausible suggestion has been that the metrical rhythm in an English poem is a regular pattern of stressed and unstressed syllables. For example:

> to-NIGHT / the WINDS / beGIN / to RISE
>> and ROAR / from YON / der DROP / ping DAY . . .

or

> i SPRANG / to the STIR / rup, and JOR / is and HE;
> i GAL / loped, dirck GAL / loped, we GAL / loped all THREE.

* A number of English poets, notably Robert Bridges, have experimented with "quantitative" verse in which there is a regular pattern of short and long vowels, but the difficulties are very great, since the other, more dominant, rhythms of English tend to intervene, subordinating the vowel rhythm.

We should note that, in the stressed syllables of the first of these lines, two of the *i*'s are short and two are long. As a candidate for the basis of English meter, stress seems more likely than vowel length. And yet — if by stress we refer to that emphasis which sense normally requires on certain syllables — it turns out that meter, as a regular pattern, cannot be entirely dependent upon it. The stress pattern in a poem rarely continues for more than a few lines without irregularity. There is no regular alteration of stressed and unstressed syllables, for example, if we read the following lines according to normal English prose emphasis:

> when MEN were all aSLEEP the SNOW came FLYing,
> in LARGE WHITE FLAKES FALLing on the CITy BROWN
> STEALTHily and perPETually SETtling and LOOSEly LYing.
> HUSHing the latest TRAFfic of the DROWSy TOWN . . .

There is, then, some regularity of pattern — which we call meter — that must be distinguished from stress. In addition to the stress pattern of

> my LUVE is like a RED, RED ROSE

there is a metrical pattern:

> my LUVE is LIKE a RED, red ROSE.

We shall therefore distinguish the word *stress,* meaning emphasis according to the prose sense of the words, from the word *accent,* meaning emphasis according to the metrical pattern. Thus we may say that the word "Luve," in this line, receives the emphasis of both stress and accent; "like" is accented but unstressed, while the second "red" is stressed but unaccented. This sounds like nonsense, and the obvious question is that of how one can simultaneously accent without stressing or stress without accenting. One cannot. What we are describing is not a performance of the line, but rather the two sources of emphasis, which may sometimes work together and sometimes work against each other. One may read the line aloud either in accordance with the stress pattern or in accordance with the accent pattern, or one may attempt a series of compromises between them. (Even here we are simplifying the discussion by omitting *pitch,* or the rise and fall of the voice, another kind of emphasis and sound pattern.)

Clearly, if we insist upon reading a poem in strict accordance with
its accentual pattern, the result will be monotonous at best — and
often absurd. Any poem is debased if we try to read it as though we
were metronomes; rigid pattern becomes destructive of meaning:

> let ME / not TO / the MAR / riage OF / true MINDES
> adMIT / imPED / iMENTS / love IS / not LOVE
> which AL / ters WHEN / it AL / terA / tion FINDES
> or BENDS / with THE / reMOV / er TO / reMOVE . . .

On the other hand, prose stress alone can be almost as subversive
(though never as absurd); meaning becomes destructive of pattern:

> let me NOT
> to the MARriage
> of TRUE
> MINDES
> admit imPEDiments.
> LOVE
> is NOT love
> which ALters
> when it alterAtion findes,
> or BENDS
> with the reMOVer
> to reMOVE . . .

As a matter of fact, it is impossible to represent prose stress accurately by any system that admits of only two degrees: its presence
or its absence. There are many degrees of stress, with infinite shad-
ings from performer to performer, and even from performance to
performance. But it takes a delicate electronic instrument to register
the slight differences, and those the human ear can distinguish may
be recorded by systems with ranges from three to probably no more
than six degrees. Let us, for the moment, adopt a three-degree system
in which ^{1} indicates minimum stress (still some, on the assumption
that stress cannot be entirely absent if a syllable is sounded at all), ^{2}
indicates intermediate stress, and ^{3} heavy stress. Then we might annotate one possible performance (there are others) of the lines read
as prose as follows:

> Let^2 me^1 not^3 // to^1 the^1 mar^{3}riage^2 / of^1 true^3 mindes^3 /
> Ad^{1}mit^3 im^{1}ped^{3}i^{1}ments^2, // love^3 / is^1 not^3 love^2 /

Which^1 al^{3}ters^2 / when^1 it^1 al^{2}ter^{1}a^{3}tion^1 findes^1, //
Or^1 bends^3 / with^1 the^1 re^{1}mov^{3}er^1 // to^2 re^{1}move^3 . . .*

The same lines, and the same performance, might be annotated on the basis of a four-, five-, or six-degree system — or even more, with the aid of recording instruments — in an attempt to describe either an actual performance or someone's conception of an ideal performance. Modern descriptive linguistics has tended to find most satisfactory a system recognizing four degrees of stress, but three are sufficient for the purposes of this discussion.

Though there are obviously varying degrees of stress, there are only two degrees of metrical accent — accented and unaccented (′ and ×) — and many of the disagreements over the subject of meter seem to us to stem from mistaken attempts to merge stress with accent. The two concepts must be kept separate. A metrical analysis of a poem does not describe a performance, real or ideal, but rather an underlying pattern, a rhythmical skeleton, as it were, upon which the stress rhythms (and the verbal rhythms) are the flesh. The word *analysis* is proper here, for the meter usually has to be found, while a stress pattern — some irregular stress pattern or other — will be present in any reading of a poem, however clumsy. Hence it is proper to speak of *metrical analysis,* but the words *stress analysis* may be left to engineering. In discussing a poem, we do not so much analyze the stresses as point them out. There are, however, two important types of stress pattern, differing to a greater or lesser extent, which should be distinguished: that which occurs if the words are read as though they were prose, and that which occurs when the words are read as poetry (prose stress under the influence of meter). When the context does not otherwise make clear which we are discussing, we may call them *prose stress* and *performance stress.*

The best performance of "Let me not to the marriage of true mindes" — perhaps not a vocal performance but one "heard" in the imagination of a sensitive reader — attends both to the metrical pattern and to the demands of the prose syntax. Such a performance may be *described* by a system of differentiated degrees of stress, but it is *determined* by both the meter and the prose sense, sometimes co-operating and sometimes straining against each other. The ideal performance will keep us aware of the underlying meter without ever being so dominated by it that the result sounds mechanical.

* In describing a performance, the slant lines indicate pauses, with // a longer pause than /.

But how can meter be found? What is it? Can it be said to exist at all when, in fact, a so-called accented word may or may not be stressed?

Meter is found by reading the poem, stressing as the apparent meaning requires, with an ear alert for the occurrence in any line or lines of some regularity of pattern in the spacing of emphases. The very fact that we are reading *lines* is a large step in the direction of regularity — since the line will be a rhythmical entity — but we are looking now for smaller rhythmic units which will be repeated within lines, or from line to line. *The meter of a poem may be inferred from such regularity as may be found in the occurrence of the prose stresses.* For example, reading Burns's lines according to the prose stresses marked on a three-degree scale, we might have:

$$\text{My}^1 \text{ Luve}^3 \text{ // is}^1 \text{ like}^1 \text{ a}^1 \text{ red}^3, \text{ red}^3 \text{ rose}^3, /$$
$$\text{That's}^1 \text{ new}^3 \text{ly}^1 \text{ sprung}^3 / \text{ in}^1 \text{ June}^3: //$$
$$\text{My}^1 \text{ Luve}^3 \text{ // is}^1 \text{ like}^1 \text{ a}^1 \text{ mel}^3 \text{o}^1 \text{dy}^2 /$$
$$\text{That's}^1 \text{ sweet}^3 \text{ly}^1 \text{ play'd}^3 \text{ in}^1 \text{ tune}^3. //$$

The alert ear quickly picks up the fact that, with a few exceptions (four out of fourteen possibilities), we have an alternation of minimum stress with maximum stress. In one of these exceptions, the last two syllables of "melody," there is in fact intermediate stress following minimum stress, and thus, on the two-degree scale of meter, there may still be said to be accent which is sounded. The other three exceptions are, twice, the word "like" which has minimum stress where an accent would be, and the second "red," which has maximum stress where no accent would be. The metrical pattern, then, may be said to be one in which two syllables, an unaccented followed by an accented, form the unit (called a *foot*); the first and third lines have four of these feet, while the second and fourth have three. The meter, in other words, is a norm that may be indicated like this:

$$\overset{x}{\text{My}} \overset{\prime}{\text{Luve}} / \overset{x}{\text{is}} \overset{\prime}{\text{like}} / \overset{x}{\text{a}} \overset{\prime}{\text{red}}, / \overset{x}{\text{red}} \overset{\prime}{\text{rose}},$$
$$\overset{x}{\text{That's}} \overset{\prime}{\text{new}} / \overset{x}{\text{ly}} \overset{\prime}{\text{sprung}} / \overset{x}{\text{in}} \overset{\prime}{\text{June}}:$$
$$\overset{x}{\text{My}} \overset{\prime}{\text{Luve}} / \overset{x}{\text{is}} \overset{\prime}{\text{like}} / \overset{x}{\text{a}} \overset{\prime}{\text{mel}} / \overset{x}{\text{o}} \overset{\prime}{\text{dy}}$$
$$\overset{x}{\text{That's}} \overset{\prime}{\text{sweet}} / \overset{x}{\text{ly}} \overset{\prime}{\text{play'd}} / \overset{x}{\text{in}} \overset{\prime}{\text{tune}}.*$$

* In metrical analysis, the slant lines are simply used to divide feet; they have no value of their own. Because they are dividers, they are not needed at the ends of lines, which provide automatic divisions.

What is this metrical pattern? It is the rhythmical skeleton that underlies the poem; it is a normative pattern unifying the poem.

If we are right that the proper reading is determined by a sensitivity to both the meter and the prose sense, what happens in performance at those places where the two contradict each other? We suggest that a kind of compromise is often reached, so that the first line may be read:

$$My^1 \ Luve^3 \ // \ is^1 \ like^2 \ a^1 \ red^3, \ red^2 \ rose^3, \ /$$

Accent is relative: as far as the three-degree scale is concerned, 1-2, 1-3, and 2-3 all fulfill the condition of an accented syllable following an unaccented syllable. Thus accent may be sounded in this stanza by a reading that modifies the prose stress on only three syllables out of twenty-eight. Even if the reader prefers not to make these compromises, the meter remains recognizable in the near-regularity of the stress pattern.

This has been an oversimplified account, ignoring everything except prose stress, substituting three degrees for the voice's full range, but perhaps even this caricature can suggest the kinds of adjustments that a sensitive reader is constantly making in the amount of emphasis he gives to syllables as he approaches them with the potentialities of meter and prose stress hovering in his mind. At times he may compromise between the two, as we have just suggested; at times one and at times the other will win out, depending upon their relative strengths at that point. We have all been aware of lines in which the metrical demand is strong enough to force the mispronunciation of a word. In Poe's lines, quoted earlier, we are forced by the insistent metrical accent to mispronounce "musically"; the subsequent rhyme merely confirms the mispronunciation:

> And, softly dripping, drop by drop,
> Upon the quiet mountain top,
> Steals drowsily and musically
> Into the universal valley.

In other circumstances the demands of meaning may, just as easily, override those of meter. To return to Shakespeare's "Sonnet 116," written in the same two-syllable metrical foot, an unaccented followed by an accented, there is no acceptable compromise that will convert the second foot in the first line into one in which the accented second syllable, "to," is in fact stressed more than the unaccented "not." The metrical pattern is this:

$$\overset{x}{\text{Let}} \overset{\prime}{\text{me}} / \overset{x}{\text{not}} \overset{\prime}{\text{to}} / \overset{x}{\text{the}} \overset{\prime}{\text{mar}} / \overset{x}{\text{riage}} \overset{\prime}{\text{of}} / \overset{x}{\text{true}} \overset{\prime}{\text{mindes}}$$

Though there are various ways it might be read, a performance is surely going to be much closer to the prose-stress pattern than it is to anything approaching the accent pattern. It will be read something like this:

$$\text{Let}^2 \text{ me}^1 \text{ not}^3 \text{ // to}^1 \text{ the}^1 \text{ mar}^3\text{riage}^2 / \text{of}^1 \text{ true}^3 \text{ mindes}^3 /$$

In other words, compromise is not inevitable; it is simply one of the possibilities.

With such a divergence between accent and stress as we have in Shakespeare's line, however, one may well ask how we can be sure of the metrical foot. We can actually take it for granted in advance, since we know the poem to be a sonnet: by definition, all sonnets (properly so-called) are composed in that foot. Shakespeare may depart as far from the norm as he does in this line just because he need not establish his norm but may assume it. However, setting aside this *a priori* knowledge, let us analyze the meter as we did for Burns's stanza. Considering the prose stress, which we annotated a few pages back, the hypothetical reader (who somehow knows what he is looking for though he has never heard of a sonnet) might begin by seeing, in the first line, an accentual pattern which goes:

$$\overset{x}{\text{Let}} \overset{x}{\text{me}} \overset{\prime}{\text{not}} / \overset{x}{\text{to}} \overset{x}{\text{the}} \overset{\prime}{\text{mar}} / \overset{x}{\text{riage}} \overset{x}{\text{of}} \overset{\prime}{\text{true}} / \overset{?}{\text{mindes}}$$

Even though he ignored the problem of the last syllable, he would find that this pattern does not repeat itself in any two consecutive feet in the following lines. Setting aside the first line as metrically misleading, he might then notice that the next phrase is quite regular in another pattern:

$$\overset{x}{\text{Ad}} \overset{\prime}{\text{mit}} / \overset{x}{\text{imped}} \overset{\prime}{} / \overset{x}{\text{iments.}} \overset{\prime}{}$$

This pattern is no sooner suggested than it is broken by "love^3 / is^1 not^3 love^2 /". It recurs, however, in eight of the ten feet in the next two lines, and thus, by the end of the fourth line, is established as the metrical foot in spite of exceptions.

Metrical accent is found, in other words, in such regularity of prose stress as does occur. This regularity may then be seen as the norm upon which the poem is based, so that those places at which it does not occur may be considered exceptions. Without these exceptions, the poem's rhythm would be monotonous; there would be no emphasizing of key words, so that every accented syllable would be on a footing of dead-level equality with every other and, given the irregularity of stress in English, there would be strong evidence that the poet was sacrificing everything else in his language to guarantee this metronomic regularity. But where these exceptions occur, the meter exerts a pull toward regularity while the prose stress exerts a pull away from it.

Critics have often referred to a "tension" occuring between these two pulls; we referred earlier to the reader's making constant adjustments in emphasis as the potentialities of meter and prose stress hover in his mind. Here is yet another way, then, in which poetry both requires and creates an intensity of awareness in the reader, for these adjustments of emphasis involve adjustments of meaning. For example, in spite of the apparent metrical confusion of the first line of the sonnet we have been considering, it is the meter, the traditional sonnet meter, which determines the fact that we are not talking of "true^3 mindes^1 " as opposed to false ones. The accent exerts its pull toward emphasis on "mindes" and clarifies a meaning that might be uncertain in printed prose. Similarly, in the second line, though the prose stress might well be as we have indicated — "love^3 / is^1 not^3 love^2 " — the accent exerts its pull on the last word and the absence of accent exerts its contrary pull on "not" to create in performance, most likely, "love^3 / is^1 not^2 love^3 " or, possibly, "love^3 / is^1 not^3 love^3." These three potential emphases involve three differing shades of meaning, and the mind hovering to select among them is brought to increased awareness both of the meaning selected (or, more nearly, imposed) and those which hover about it as potential meanings. The emphasis given these four words by the meter has its counterpart in the dramatic paradox of the statement (how can "love" *not* be "love"?), a fine example of the interaction of meter and statement to create ultimate meaning. Nor is this emphasis arbitrary: the entire poem is, in fact, a definition of (real) love as opposed to what is sometimes considered and called love.

To speak of composition rather than performance and analysis, the poet's task — one of his tasks — is that of controlling his meter, using it, neither losing it nor letting it dominate the poem. The meter will dominate if the stress too regularly falls upon the accented syllables, and thus fails to differentiate the relative importance of words within the poem, as, for example, in this passage from Addison's "A Poem to His Majesty" (King William III, "Our Nassau" in this excerpt):

> But see, at length, the British ships appear!
> Our Nassau comes! and, as his fleet draws near,
> The rising masts advance, the sails grow white,
> And all his pompous navy floats in sight.
> Come, mighty prince, desired of Britain come!   5
> May heaven's propitious gales attend thee home!
> Come, and let longing crowds behold that look
> Which such confusion and amazement strook
> Through Gallic hosts: but, oh! let us descry
> Mirth in thy brow, and pleasure in thy eye;   10
> Let nothing dreadful in thy face be found;
> But for a while forget the trumpet's sound;
> Well-pleased, thy people's loyalty approve,
> Accept their duty, and enjoy their love.
> For as, when lately moved with fierce delight,   15
> You plunged amidst the tumult of the fight,
> Whole heaps of dead encompassed you around,
> And steeds o'erturned lay foaming on the ground:
> So crowned with laurels now, where'er you go,
> Around you blooming joys and peaceful blessings flow.*   20

The eighteenth century, especially, produced among a few masters numerous poets who turned out this kind of thing by the volume. It is not bad enough to be funny; it is just dull and undifferentiated — the poet has not evaluated his language and details. One may, of course, object to more than the dominating meter: that final request that "blooming joys and peaceful blessings" flow around him as he was earlier surrounded by "heaps of dead" and "steeds o'erturned," is rather vulgar, for example. But the problem is largely one of too

---

* l. 8 *strook*: struck, a now-obsolete form of the verb

Note the extra foot in the final line. The addition of a sixth foot to a five-foot line is a traditional way of achieving an effect of finality, especially when the poem is already in rhymed couplets and the final couplet thus has no other way of achieving a distinctive effect.

constant and indiscriminate reinforcement of metrical accent by prose stress.

Even in so inferior a passage as this, however, there are forces working for variety. One of these is the fact that syntactical pauses occur at different points in otherwise similarly stressed lines, thus varying the rhythm. For example:

> The^1 ris^{3}ing^1 masts^3 / ad^{1}vance^3, // the^1 sails^3 / grow^1 white^3, //
> And^1 all^2 his^1 pomp^{3}ous^1 na^{3}vy^1 // floats^3 / in^1 sight^3. //

Traditional metrics calls the longest of these pauses within each line the *caesura*,* to which we shall return in a moment.

Another force working for variety is the two-syllable word with its stress on the first syllable, which will not fit into a single foot of this unaccented-accented pattern. The word "advance" in the first line strongly reinforces the meter, but the words "rising," "pompous," and "navy," even though they all fit the meter exactly, work against it, imposing stressed-unstressed word units on top of a pattern of un-accented-accented feet. Addison also uses five three-syllable words in this passage, though none of more. In spite of these, and some other, instances of variety, his lines are decidedly monotonous.

Lest we appear to be blackening all eighteenth-century poetry, however, let us reproduce some admirable rhymed couplets in the same meter. In *The Dunciad*, Alexander Pope portrays certain of his contemporary poets as worshiping the goddess Dulness. "Bays," the poet laureate (Colley Cibber), raises an altar of books and thus addresses her:

> Then he: "Great Tamer of all human art!
> First in my care, and ever at my heart;
> Dulness! whose good old cause I yet defend,
> With whom my Muse began, with whom shall end.
>
> .   .   .   .
>
> O thou! of Bus'ness the directing soul!   5
> To this our head like byass to the bowl,

---

* The caesura may be marked with two upright lines, which may or may not substitute for the slant line dividing feet, that is, which may or may not occur at the end of a foot. Thus these lines would be annotated metrically:

> x   /   x   /   x   /   x   /   x   /
> The ris / ing masts / advance,|| the sails / grow white,
> x   /   x   /   x   /   x   /   x   /
> And all / his pomp / ous na / vy || floats / in sight.

Which, as more pond'rous, made its aim more true,
Obliquely wadling to the mark in view:
O! ever gracious to perplex'd mankind,
Still spread a healing mist before the mind;   10
And, lest we err by Wit's wild dancing light,
Secure us kindly in our native night.
Or, if to Wit a coxcomb make pretence,
Guard the sure barrier between that and Sense;
Or quite unravel all the reas'ning thread,   15
And hang some curious cobweb in its stead!
As, forc'd from wind-guns, lead itself can fly,
And pond'rous slugs cut swiftly thro the sky;
As clocks to weight their nimble motion owe,
The wheels above urg'd by the load below: 20
Me Emptiness, and Dulness could inspire,
And were my Elasticity and Fire.
Some Dæmon stole my pen (forgive th' offence)
And once betray'd me into common sense:
Else all my Prose and Verse were much the same;   25
This, prose on stilts, that, poetry fall'n lame.*

Pope's lines are satiric and thus already have an advantage in complexity of interest over Addison's straight eulogy. It is not unfitting
that our example of successful couplets in this meter should be
satiric, however, for — though they are called "heroic couplets" because they had their first important use in epic poems and dramas
presenting heroic deeds — they are in fact at their best when the
rhymes give emphasis to an epigram or some terse and cleverly ex-

* l. 6 *like byass to the bowl:* the bowling ball ("bowl") of the period, like the ball
used in lawn-bowling today, was weighted on one side so that its path was curved.
Both the weight and the arc were called the bowl's "bias," and this bias had to be considered in aiming at a target. Pope's simile treats the bias as an aid rather than a hin-
drance: with Dulness the bias of their heads, her worshipers need not worry about
missing their aim, however obliquely their verses waddle.

l. 11 *Wit's wild dancing light:* to a worshiper of Dulness, Wit is a false God

l. 14. *the sure barrier between that and Sense:* if a dullard should attempt to reach
Wit, let him at least be preserved from the greater heresy of making sense.

l. 17 *wind-guns:* air guns, guns which discharge through the release of compressed air

ll. 23–4 *Some Dæmon . . . common sense:* this is a confession of sin, an alibi,
and a request for forgiveness.

pressed aspersion. Though called heroic, such couplets are often delightfully antiheroic.

But we are primarily interested here in the variety Pope attains within this often abused meter. In addition to the kinds of variation pointed out in Addison's lines, and in addition to the five-syllable word he uses in one line, Pope brings variety into this meter through several other means. For one thing, he uses a number of two-syllable words in which both syllables must be stressed: "coxcomb," "cob-web," "wind-guns." * Thus he imposes an additional two-syllable word unit involving adjacent stresses on top of the metrical foot. Also, he uses two words — "barrier" and "curious" — which, though actually three-syllabled, are placed where the meter allows them only two. This introduces a kind of syncopation into the rhythm, since the middle, consonantless syllable must be sounded, even though slighted or slurred:

$$\overset{x}{\text{And}} \overset{\prime}{\text{hang}} / \overset{x}{\text{some}} \overset{\prime}{\text{cu}} / \overset{\overset{x}{\frown}}{\text{rious}} \overset{\prime}{\text{cob}} / \text{web} \parallel \overset{x}{\text{in}} / \overset{x}{\text{its}} \overset{\prime}{\text{stead}}! \dagger$$

But perhaps the major antidote against monotony in these lines is Pope's placement of the longest syntactical pause, or caesura. In Addison's lines only four of these pauses occur in the middle of feet; the other sixteen occur following the second, fourth, or sixth syllables, thus emphasizing the metrical beat. In Pope's last twenty lines — to take a segment of the same length as Addison's — eleven of these pauses occur in the middle of feet, thus cutting across the metrical beat. Within his traditional metrical form, and in a century when this meter often tramped roughshod through poetry, Pope, with his fine wit and his finer ear, kept monotony to a minimum.

The meter, then, may be too dominant if the stress regularly falls on the accented syllables. The other extreme is not the successful

---

* Though Addison's "Well-pleased" might seem an example, it reaches the ear as two words, an adverb and an adjective, which the compound noun "wind-guns" does not.

† Note that we are still defining meter as the normative pattern underlying the stress pattern. The fourth foot is not, in fact, performed "$\overset{x}{\text{web}} \parallel \overset{\prime}{\text{in}}$", but "web [3] // in [1]."

poem which avoids monotony within an accentual pattern, but the poem in which the meter may be lost — or cannot in fact be said to have existed — because no pattern of accent can be found at all among the syllables receiving prose stress. However, two concepts should be kept distinct in theory, though there may be borderline cases that are difficult to distinguish in fact: the concept of poems that attempt meter, and fail to establish it; and the concept of poems that are not accentual at all but, quite successfully, something else.

The "something else" is often called *free verse,* meaning verse free of the restraint of meter, but there are such various non-accentual forms, some of which are not in the least "free," that the term is more misleading than useful. Though the Old and Middle English alliterative line, for example, cannot be measured in accentual feet, this is the only sense in which it is free. Look again at the passage we quoted from "The Vision of Piers Plowman." It is not accentual at all, but depends for its pattern upon the presence in each line of four irregularly spaced, maximum stresses, three of which alliterate. (Four stresses to a line is a kind of measure, and therefore may, strictly speaking, be called a meter, but it is probably less confusing to confine the word *meter* to accentual measures only.) Modern English poets have experimented with similar lines, with or without the alliteration. They usually hope to write poems approximating the rhythms of speech more closely than they feel accentual lines allow, perhaps fearing that the requirements of form might force them to distort the "truth" of their statements. Their problem, of course, is that of achieving some substitute for the heightened impact of the pervasive pattern furnished by accentual meter and the evaluation and emphasis — ultimately, meaning — which pattern can create. In poems based upon the Old English line, this substitute will usually be a certain number of maximum-stress syllables per line; with an indeterminate number of minimum-stress syllables and no regularity of alternation.

A few poets have experimented with *isochronous* lines — lines of equal length, not in the sense of having the same number of metrical feet but in the literal sense of taking (supposedly) the same amount of time to voice. Other languages, notably French, have meters based simply upon the number of syllables in a line, and some poets have attempted this in English also. Marianne Moore, for example, has written many poems in lines with neither accents nor stresses nor isochronism as the measure, but instead an arbitrary number of syllables. In "The Mind Is an Enchanting Thing," quoted in our last chapter, she sets up a stanza in which the first line has six syllables; the second, five; the third, four; the fourth, six; the fifth, seven; and the last, nine. This pattern she repeats, with only one exception, in the following five stanzas. One cannot criticize such a pattern *because* it is arbitrary: metrical patterns are also arbitrary (as are, in fact, syntactical patterns). Though much more could be said about Miss Moore's poetry, the only point now is that it is neither accentual, nor isochronous, nor dependent upon a certain number of stresses per line, and yet it is not free and unrestricted but achieves a pattern through the simple counting of syllables in which any syllable, stressed or unstressed, its vowel long or short, is equal to any other.

The haiku, which translates so effectively into English, combines this strict counting of syllables with a particular vividness or suggestiveness of imagery. Perhaps the only form of non-accentual verse that should be called free verse is that which, without the syllable-counting of the haiku, depends for its primary effect upon the impact of a vivid image, like Williams' "The Red Wheelbarrow." We earlier suggested a roughly algebraic balance in the total interaction which creates poetry such that strengthening one powerful poetic element will permit weakening of another: increasing vividness of imagery will sustain decreasing regularity of sound pattern by creating all the emphasis and precision forfeited by the absence of pattern, so that the result is clearly poetry and not chopped-up prose.

The vast majority of poems in English are accentual, however, and it is of these that we are now speaking. We have, perhaps with some inconvenience, withheld the usual vocabulary of metrics because we have been trying to help the reader consider what that vocabulary covers, and we have found in the past that readers are frequently willing to substitute memorizing terms for attempting to understand them. But the time has now come for supplying the vocabulary, the Greek words which are still used to name English feet. This can perhaps be done most simply through charts.

Using our definition of meter as a normative pattern underlying the stress pattern in a poem, there are four feet that account for most accentual poetry in English:

Accent Pattern	Name (Noun)	(Adj.)	Example
x /	iamb (or iambus)	iambic	The wound / ed sur / geon plies / the steel
x x /	anapest	anapestic	I have sought / thee in splen / dor and dress
/ x	trochee	trochaic	Why so / pale and / wan, fond / lover?
/ x x	dactyl	dactylic	Take her up / tenderly

Lines written in iambs or anapests are said to be written in a rising rhythm, since the feet move toward emphasis; trochees or dactyls yield a falling rhythm, since the feet move away from emphasis.

There are a number of other named feet which cannot be used as the basis of extended passages in English and thus are not metrical feet (in English) according to our definition. Traditional metrists often use these words to describe the effect of prose stresses in performance, speaking of one of these feet as having been *substituted* for the normative foot. Therefore it is worth learning the names of the four most common substitute feet:

/ /	spondee	spondaic	The last / *red leaf* / is whirled / away
x x	pyrrhic	pyrrhic	Secure / us kind / *ly in* / our na / tive night
/ x /	cretic	cretic	Not as with / sundering / *of the* earth
x / x	rocking foot		Like to / the lark / at break / of day / *arising*

Of course one of the common metric feet may be substituted for another also: performance of the last line quoted demands a trochee in place of the first iamb. Note that a rocking foot * will occur any time an otherwise iambic line ends with an extra syllable in a feminine

---

* So-called because it rises and then falls. This name is now more common than the old one: "amphibrach" (adjective: "amphibrachic").

rhyme. In performance, a pyrrhic is frequently the result of a caesura
in the middle of an iamb: "Secure / us kind / ly || in / our na / tive
night." The very concept of the caesura, like that of a substitute foot, is
a move toward description of performance and away from the concept of meter as a normative pattern. In other words, we are not
describing the *meter* of Pope's line, in the strict sense of the normative
measure, if we include the caesura or the pyrrhic; we are describing
the way the line is performed. The metrical vocabulary is a great con-
venience in making such descriptions: a rocking foot (or even an
amphibrach) is a simpler term than a 1-3-1 which might be a 1-2-1
or a 2-3-2. Use of this vocabulary for performance has been, however,
the greatest stumbling block in distinguishing among meter, prose
stress, and performance. Hidden behind our illustration of a cretic
foot, for example, is the fact that it is the result, in performance, of
a compromise between the dactylic accentual pattern and the 1-1-3
(or anapestic) prose stress.

The same vocabulary may be used in variant ways to describe the
same performance. Because of the effect of the caesura, it would be a
somewhat more adequate description of the *individual line* to say that
"Secure us kindly in our native night" consists of four feet: a rocking
foot, a trochee, an anapest, and an iamb. We do not describe it that
way because to do so is to lose all sense of meter: it is not merely an
individual line but a line in an iambic poem. The normative line
pattern is one of five iambic feet and we tailor our description to that
normative pattern.

In addition to the names of feet, we need the traditional and useful
vocabulary for the number of feet to a line. Counting from one to
ten, it goes: *monometer, dimeter, trimeter, tetrameter, pentameter,
hexameter, heptameter, octameter, enneameter,* and *decameter.*

Some of these words are much less common than the others: enneameter, for example, or monometer. We are not likely to find a
poem written in monometric lines, but the word remains useful when
describing stanzas. The fifth and seventh lines of each stanza in Herrick's "To Daffadills" are instances of monometric lines. There is little
need for words to describe lines of more than ten feet (*hendecameter,
dodecameter,* etc.), since such lines would tend to break into shorter
segments, however they might be set on the page. And this may
happen with lines of less than ten feet also. The line is a rhythmic
entity, not merely a visual entity. Thus, though Housman put "The

Land of Biscay" on the page as octameter, it reaches the ear — thanks to the regularity of the caesura — as tetrameter:

> Sons of landsmen, sons of seamen, hear the tale of grief and me,
> Looking from the land of Biscay on the waters of the sea. . . .

Lines are described as *catalectic* when one or more syllables are missing from the final foot. Thus, to translate our point here into traditional terminology, we are saying that Housman sets his poem on the page as catalectic trochaic octameter in rhyming couplets, but that it reaches the ear as trochaic tetrameter in quatrains rhyming *abcb* with the rhyming lines catalectic.

The concept of catalectic feet allows us to describe such a line as Swinburne's "Maiden most beautiful, mother most bountiful, lady of lands." This is a catalectic dactylic hexameter: "Maiden most / beautiful, / mother most / bountiful, / lady of / lands." (Note how the words "beautiful" and "bountiful" reinforce the metric pattern.) Similarly, it allows us to describe Housman's "Hell Gate" as catalectic trochaic tetrameter. We quote only a few of its hundred lines:

> Onward led the road again
> Through the sad uncolored plain
> Under twilight brooding dim,
> And along the utmost rim
> Wall and rampart risen to sight
> Cast a shadow not of night,
> And beyond them seemed to glow
> Bonfires lighted long ago.

One might wonder why, if some foot is lacking a syllable, it would not be just as adequate to call this iambic tetrameter in which the first foot, not the last, is truncated. Although one might point to the iambic two-syllable words, "again," "along," and "ago," as reinforcing an iambic pattern, they are in fact overbalanced by the preponderance of trochaic two-syllable words. There is no reason in this poem, therefore, to abandon the traditional concept that only final feet are catalectic.

But look what happens if we consider Blake's "Tyger Tyger" in this way:

> Tyger Tyger burning bright,
> In the forests of the night:

> What immortal hand or eye
> Could frame thy fearful symmetry? . . .

After three lines of what would traditionally have to be considered catalectic trochaic tetrameter, strongly reinforced by the trochaic words "Tyger," "burning," and "forests," we find a line of straight iambic tetrameter. There are no lines in the poem in which the eighth syllable of the tetrameter creates a trochee at the end of the line; there are seven lines, out of the twenty-four, in which the eight-syllable tetrameter is iambic. Therefore Blake's poem is more adequately described as iambic tetrameter than as trochaic, even though there is no traditional way to describe truncation of the first foot.

And *description* — whether of accentual pattern or of performance — remains the primary usefulness of this, at first baffling, vocabulary. It provides a means, not merely of classifying the poem, but of discussing rhythmic details, of discriminating among various shades of emphasis in their effects upon meaning. Whether we call Blake's lines trochaic or iambic, what is worth describing — and thus bringing to consciousness — is not the mechanical measure but the uses to which the measure has been put: the way the catalectic lines juxtapose a final stress in one line with an opening stress in the next, thus insisting upon the pause between lines and making the line-entity more pronounced, with an effect, especially when the lines are broken by a strong caesura, that is almost spasmodic; or the subtlety of the shift in emphasis on the identical opening words in the third and fourth lines of the fifth stanza, the accent shifting with the foot and creating a precise shade of meaning in the questions:

> When the stars threw down their spears
> And water'd heaven with their tears:
> Did he smile his work to see?
> Did he who made the Lamb make thee?

Attention may be called to this subtlety by saying that the accent falls on "Did" in the third, catalectic line and on "he" in the fourth line. But even this is not enough to indicate the full effect of the shift, for the heavy emphasis in the third line is on "smile" — "Did^2 he^1 smile^3 // his^1 work^2 to^1 see^2? /" This smile is the horror we are asked to contemplate, and our horror, our contemplation, is assumed in the emphasis upon the pronouns in the next line: "Did^1 he^3 / who^1 made^2 the^1 Lamb^3 // make^1 thee^3? /" Such effects are created by the inter-

actions of prose stress with meter and we need to learn the metrical
vocabulary if we are to discuss those patterns of rhythmic regularity
which, however modified in performance, constitute the accentual
basis for recognizing that the words performed are poetry.

For practice, the reader might now turn to a number of the poems
we have discussed in past chapters and attempt to find and name the
underlying metrical patterns. Then, remaining within the traditional
terminology, he might name any feet in which performance stress
varies from accent. (Readers ought to agree on meter, but they may
well disagree on performance stress. Without the metrical terminology, their disagreements would be more difficult to discuss.) When
he has had some practice in naming metrical feet and substitute feet,
his next step is the attempt to distinguish what determines performance stress in each situation and to discover what effects these potential emphases would have upon the meaning of the poem. He
should thus discover what we mean by the statement that some of the
meaning of a poem results from the fact that prose stress has been
brought under the influence of meter.

STANZAS

In poems other than those in which metrically identical, unrhymed
lines follow uninterruptedly — as in, for example, *Paradise Lost* —
one is soon aware of a unit of rhythmic pattern larger than either the
foot or the line. This is the stanza. Stanzas may be created by a pattern
of rhyme or near-rhyme at the ends of metrically identical lines, by
a pattern of variation in the number or kind of feet in succeeding
lines, or by a pattern combining both metrical variation and rhyme.
Any repeated pattern involving two or more lines is stanzaic. Thus
rhymed couplets, as in the passage recently quoted from Pope, are in
effect short stanzas, even though they are rarely separated from each
other on the page. At the end of each couplet a two-line pattern, a
stanza, has been completed. However, the word is usually reserved
for patterns involving more than two lines. There are many short
stanza-forms in which metrically identical lines are arranged in units
with a particular pattern of rhymes. Four-line patterns, for example,
may rhyme *abcb, abab, aaba,* or *abba.* Tennyson's *In Memoriam,*
from which we quoted "To-night the winds begin to rise," is an

illustration of the last of these, being composed entirely in quatrains
of iambic tetrameter rhyming *abba.*

Occasionally one finds quatrains rhyming *aabb:* "There is a Lady
sweet and kind," or Housman's "To an Athlete Dying Young" are
examples. By our definition, these couplets should constitute two
stanzas rather than one, and so in a sense they do. However, if the
poet is not merely being arbitrary about his arrangement, one will find
some reason for it. Each of the quatrains of the poems mentioned constitutes a single sentence: the stanzaic pattern is not only one of meter
and rhyme but of a grammatical unit. These stanzas are, quite
literally, units of thought as well as of rhythmic pattern. It is perhaps
not pushing too far to say that in these poems thought is itself
rhythmic.

Certain stanza forms are common enough to have individual names.
"My Luve is like a red, red rose" is written in an *abcb* quatrain in
which tetrameter alternates with trimeter. Though Burns's poem is
not a ballad, this is the *ballad stanza,* so called because it has been
used for the majority of ballads from before "Sir Patrick Spens" to
after "The Ancient Mariner." One can even discern the ballad stanza
under all the repetitions in "Edward."

Terza rima is a three-line stanza best known through its use by
Dante in the *Divine Comedy* but often tried, though with less success, in English. In this pattern, the rhymes interlock from stanza to
stanza: *aba, bcb, cdc,* and so forth. Shelley's "Ode to the West Wind"
is perhaps the best-known example in English. "London Snow" also
uses this pattern, though Bridges indented rather than separated his
stanzas.

Rhyme royal, so named because James I used it, is a seven-line
stanza of iambic pentameter rhyming *ababbcc.* James was not its
originator, however, for it was used first in English, as far as we know,
by Chaucer in his "Compleynte unto Pite," and subsequently, with
great skill, in his *Troilus and Criseyde.* Here, by way of an example
that avoids the problems of pronouncing and translating Middle English, is a stanza from Shakespeare's *The Rape of Lucrece:*

> For men have marble, women waxen mindes,
> And therefore are they form'd as marble will,
> The weake opprest, th' impression of strange kindes
> Is form'd in them by force, by fraud, or skill.

> Then call them not the Authors of their ill,
>   No more than waxe shall be accounted evill
>   Wherein is stampt the semblance of a devill.

One may note how the stanza comes to a brief moment of rhythmic completion after the first four lines. The fifth line does not so much form a couplet with the fourth — which has completed the quatrain pattern — as suggest the beginning of a new, interlocking pattern, a suggestion denied by the firmly concluding final couplet. In the best uses of a stanza such as this, the rhythm of the thought will coincide with the rhythm of the stanza, as the puctuation itself will frequently indicate.

Ottava rima is an eight-line pattern, adding, as it were, one additional rhyme to the pattern of rhyme royal: *ababbcc*. Here, though there may be a turn in the thought after the first quatrain, the major turn is apt to come most naturally between the sestet and the couplet, a fact which frequently invites a witty summary or reversal of the thought at the end of the stanza. Our example comes from Byron's *Don Juan:*

> What are the hopes of man? Old Egypt's King
>   Cheops erected the first pyramid
> And largest, thinking it was just the thing
>   To keep his memory whole and mummy hid;
> But somebody or other rummaging,
>   Burglariously broke his coffin's lid:
> Let not a monument give you or me hopes,
> Since not a pinch of dust remains of Cheops.

Then there is the *Spenserian stanza,* a nine-line pattern, *ababbcbcc,* in which the last line adds a sixth foot to the iambic pentameter norm. (This iambic hexameter line is called an *Alexandrine* because of one or the other of the early romances on the subject of Alexander the Great, both of which were written in hexameters, one in French, the other in Castilian.) The Spenserian stanza gets its name, of course, from its inventor, who used it in *The Faerie Queene.* The effect of this stanza is that of two interlocking quatrains, with the last line, which might otherwise suggest the beginning of a third quatrain, achieving a sense of finality through its extra length and additional rhyme. The withholding of the rhyme for an extra two syllables, after the preceding regularity, is enough to slow and then stop the movement. Here is an example from James Thomson's "The Castle of Indolence":

> A bard here dwelt, more fat than bard beseems;
> Who, void of envy, guile, and lust of gain,
> On virtue still, and nature's pleasing themes,
> Poured forth his unpremeditated strain:
> The world forsaking with a calm disdain,
> Here laughed he careless in his easy seat;
> Here quaffed, encircled with the joyous train;
> Oft moralizing sage! his ditty sweet
> He loathèd much to write, ne carèd to repeat.

In all of these stanzas the same iambic pentameter line is used (with the exception of the Alexandrine at the end of the Spenserian stanza) and the stanzaic form appears to be primarily a matter of a particular pattern of rhymes. It is, in fact, much more than this, for, as we have several times indicated, the well-written stanza is one in which there is coherence between the rhythm of the form and the rhythm of the thought. The best stanzas are not those in which the pattern appears to have been imposed upon the material, but those in which they enhance each other.

A poet need not write in stanzas, of course. "The Waltzer in the House," "Dover Beach," and "Lapis Lazuli" are poems we have already discussed in which, in place of the uniformity of stanzas, the poet has preferred the freedom of verse-paragraphs, their individual lengths determined entirely by the logic of his statements. In " 'Not Marble nor the Gilded Monuments,' " MacLeish, though writing in four-line stanzas, has been willing to break his pattern, for the sake of his logic, to the extent of adding as a fifth line to the fifth stanza what might have been conceived as the first line of his sixth.

A poet adopts the additional restrictions of writing his narrative poem in stanzas not merely for the delight of running an obstacle course (though such delight may well be present), but because heightened awareness of the multiple details of form helps to create and sustain the heightened awareness of experience that poetry demands. The stanza, as a unit of pattern in a lengthy narrative, provides a larger rhythm than foot or line — a larger rhythm of expectations pushing one ahead and fulfillments allowing for rest, even as the narrative continues. This rhythm, when it is sustained without obvious verbal dislocation, can add immeasurably to our sense of the fitness, our acceptance of the inevitability of the poet's words. It serves, at the same time, as a repeated reminder of the control implicit behind that effect of inevitability. We respond with more attention than we would be likely to pay to the details of the same narrative if it were written in prose.

Two of the longest stanza forms to have been used effectively are those that Spenser invented for his marriage poems, "Epithalamion" and "Prothalamion." In the first of these poems, the normative stanza has nineteen lines, iambic pentameter except for lines 6, 11, and 17, which are trimetric, and line 19, which is a hexameter. The rhyme scheme (with roman type for the trimetric lines) goes: *ababccdcdeef-gg*f*hh*i*i*. The final couplet is a varying refrain, which of course adds considerably to the sense of completion at the end of each stanza. (Though the first line of the couplet differs widely from stanza to stanza, it ends consistently with the word "sing," while the final line, with varying verbs and pronouns, always includes the words "woods . . . answere . . . eccho ring.") Of the twenty-four stanzas, only eleven follow this normative pattern exactly, but the others, except for the concluding seven-line stanza, vary only slightly from the norm. For example, there are five eighteen-line stanzas that, in effect, drop line 16 of the norm, repeating the *f*-rhyme for the trimetric line, thus ending: *f*gg*f*t*hh*. One seventeen-line stanza is just like the norm with lines 10 and 11 omitted.

Here is a single stanza of this poem written in honor of Spenser's own bride:

> Open the temple gates unto my love,
> Open them wide that she may enter in,
> And all the posts adorne as doth behove,
> And all the pillours deck with girlands trim,
> For to recyve this Saynt with honour due,   5
> That commeth in to you:
> With trembling steps and humble reverence,
> She commeth in, before th' almightie's vew.
> Of her ye virgins learne obedience,
> When so ye come into those holy places   10
> To humble your proud faces:
> Bring her up to th' high altar, that she may

The sacred ceremonies there partake,
The which do endlesse matrimony make,
And let the roring Organs loudly play   15
The praises of the Lord in lively notes,
The whiles with hollow throates,
The Choristers the joyous Antheme sing,
That all the woods may answere, and their eccho ring.

The success of this poem was such that Spenser was commissioned
to write another for the double wedding of the daughters of the Earl
of Worcester. For the "Prothalamion," he settled upon an eighteen-
line stanza, again iambic pentameter, with four trimetric lines, rhyming *abbaacdcd*deefeff*gg*. Here there are two final couplets, one of
trimetric lines and the other of pentameter. The last couplet is again
a refrain, with its first line varying prepositions, pronouns, and verbs,
while its second is unchanging through the ten stanzas:

> Against their Brydale day, which is not long:
>   Sweete *Themmes:* runne softly, till I end my song.*

The only variations from this pattern are in the first three stanzas,
in which Spenser carried the *b*-rhyme of the first quintain over into
the second quintain, yielding, in the first and third stanzas, *bcbcc,* and
in the second, *cbcb*b. Presumably Spenser found this repetitive rhyme
too limiting to sustain and he moved, in the fourth stanza, to the pattern he then maintained through the rest of his lovely poem.

Narrative stanzas, just because they are going to be repeated again
and again, must be relatively "open"; they cannot be too ingenious
or complex without interfering with the progress of the narrative.
The demands they make must be such that they can be met without
undue strain or monotony. This is why the lines in narrative stanzas
tend to be tetrameter or longer; shorter lines keep attention too constantly upon the pattern. The trimetric lines in the stanzas of Spenser's
marriage poems are appropriate, however, just because those poems
are closer to lyric than to narrative.

In a lyric, the form may be most complex, varying line length and
scrambling rhymes in ingenious ways. Such stanzas can be most
effective, but would not be likely to remain so if they were repeated
too often. Herrick's "To Daffadills," for example, which we discussed

* *Themmes:* the River Thames

in relation to creative images in Chapter V, is written in a stanza with
ten iambic lines, beginning like a ballad stanza (four lines of alternate
tetrameter and trimeter, rhyming *abcb*), then adding four lines that
alternate monometer with trimeter before returning, in its last two
lines, to the tetrameter-trimeter alternation. Meanwhile the last six
lines supply, in addition to two new rhymes, words to rhyme with
the unrhymed *a* and *c* of the first quatrain. The whole pattern, indicating numbers of feet and rhymes, looks like this:

$$4 - a$$
$$3 - b$$
$$4 - c$$
$$3 - b$$
$$1 - d$$
$$3 - d$$
$$1 - c$$
$$3 - e$$
$$4 - a$$
$$3 - e$$

Herrick's poem has, you will remember, only two stanzas. Sense
and form cohere perfectly. After the quatrain — a unit of thought as
well as of rhythm — the first monometric line is, in performance, a
spondee where stress and brevity join for particular emphasis: "Stay,
stay," in the first stanza; "We die," in the second. The second monometric line, iambic in stress as well as accent, receives much less emphasis, since it does not stand alone as the first does but, in each
stanza, completes the sense of the preceding trimetric line and leads
directly into the next:

> Until the hasting day
> Has run
> But to the Even-song; . . .
> . . . and drie
> Away
> Like to the Summer's raine . . . .

Herrick's control in this poem would appear to be total. One could
hardly expect even the best poet to sustain so complex a stanza through
anything longer than a short lyric.

One may wonder whether a rhyming word appearing nine lines after the word with which it rhymes, as with the *a*-rhyme in Herrick's stanza, can be effective for the ear. Is it a functional — or functioning — part of the pattern? There is no single answer. A reader very likely does not notice it in his first time through the poem, but that does not necessarily mean that the echo has not affected, subconsciously, his sense of the poem's coherence. And once he has discovered this detail of the pattern, we know from experience that it can affect his conscious pleasure in the poem.

Certain ingenuities of pattern, however, may well lead to a kind of abstract admiration without actually being available to the reader's experience. Such, for example, is the pattern Dylan Thomas adopted for the "Author's Prologue" he wrote for his *Collected Poems*. This is not actually a stanza pattern, for Thomas did not repeat it, but it is germane to the present point. Halfway through his poem of 102 non-accentual lines (four to eight syllables and two to five stresses), Thomas begins a pattern of rhymes in reverse. Line 52 rhymes with line 51, line 53 with line 50, line 54 with line 49 — and on through the pattern until the one-hundred-and-second line rhymes with the first. In fact, for the last three lines, he not only rhymes with but repeats the actual final words of lines 3, 2 and 1, presumably as a way of being somewhat more insistent upon his pattern. This is ingenious, and one can admire Thomas's skill in carrying it out, but — even when aware that the pattern is there — one can hardly experience it as a part of the poem. One can trace it and assure oneself that it exists; when reading the poem, however, it is almost impossible at, say, line 78 to retain any expectation of what the rhyme ought to be. Without expectation there can be no sense of fulfillment, nor can the rhyme occur as an unexpected echo. The original sound is simply too far away to be remembered. Since, however, we argue that individuals can train themselves for increased awareness and sensitivity, perhaps we should be willing to admit the remote possibility of readers developing sufficient sensitivity to experience even so lengthy a pattern as Thomas's.

As a poet who took especial delight in inventing stanza forms, George Herbert deserves mention in this discussion. Of the 169 poems in his volume, *The Temple,* 116 are in differing stanza forms not repeated outside their individual poems. In only fifty-three poems does he repeat stanza forms he has used elsewhere. Occasionally one of these many forms may appear arbitrary — as when, in "The Altar" (which we quoted in Chapter III) and in "Easter Wings," he uses the stanza to make a design on the page — but more often the shape of the stanza is an integral part of the rhythm of the experience. And even "Easter Wings," in which the iambic lines move down from pentameter to monometer, dropping a foot at a time, and then build up to pentameter again, making wings on the page, the thought is beautifully consistent with the form. The node, the point to which the stanza draws in, is "Most poor" in the first and "Most thin" in the second. And the movement out again begins, in both stanzas, with a turn away from the self, with the words "With thee," and ends with reference to flight.

Herbert's poems are all lyrics of personal religious experience and they are some of the finest in the language. Since we have quoted so many segments of poems in our recent discussions, it will be good to quote the whole of the following that you may consider the interactions of rhymes and verbal rhythms with meter and stanza, and all of these with the rhythms of thought:

The Flower

How fresh, O Lord, how sweet and clean
Are thy returns! ev'n as the flowers in spring;
   To which, besides their own demean,
The late-past frosts tributes of pleasure bring.
      Grief melts away   5
      Like snow in May,
   As if there were no such cold thing.

Who would have thought my shrivel'd heart
Could have recover'd greennesse? It was gone
   Quite under ground; as flowers depart   10
To see their mother-root, when they have blown;
      Where they together
      All the hard weather,
   Dead to the world, keep house unknown.

These are thy wonders, Lord of power,   15
Killing and quickning, bringing down to hell

And up to heaven in an houre;
Making a chiming of a passing-bell.
            We say amisse
            This or that is: 20
Thy word is all, if we could spell.

Oh, that I once past changing were,
Fast in thy Paradise, where no flower can wither!
    Many a spring I shoot up fair,
Offring at heav'n, growing and groning thither: 25
            Nor doth my flower
            Want a spring-showre,
My sinnes and I joining together.

But while I grow in a straight line,
Still upwards bent, as if heav'n were mine own,   30
    Thy anger comes, and I decline:
What frost to that? what pole is not the zone,
            Where all things burn,
            When thou dost turn,
And the least frown of thine is shown?   35

And now in age I bud again,
After so many deaths I live and write;
    I once more smell the dew and rain,
And relish versing: O my onely light,
            It cannot be   40
            That I am he
On whom thy tempests fell all night.

These are thy wonders, Lord of love,
To make us see we are but flowers that glide:
    Which when we once can finde and prove,   45
Thou hast a garden for us, where to bide.
            Who would be more,
            Swelling through store,
Forfeit their Paradise by their pride.*

* l. 3 *demean:* behavior, demeanor
l. 18 *Making a chiming of a passing-bell:* turning into harmony or concord a bell
denoting death (passing)
l. 28 *My sinnes and I joining together* [to weep]
l. 48 *Swelling through store:* becoming greater through accumulated wealth

SONNETS

Having defined the stanza as a pattern of two or more lines repeated within a poem, we need to pause briefly to consider a few patterns that are repeated, not within single poems, but from one poem to another. The distinction between stanzas, as parts of poems, and whole poems cannot be insisted upon too severely here, however, for there is no reason why a poet should not write an eight-line poem corresponding to a stanza of ottava rima and, if he does so, there is no reason for withholding that traditional stanza name. Nevertheless, a discussion of patterns in poetry must also acknowledge those instances in which a whole poem, stanzaic or not, repeats the pattern of another.

We are speaking primarily of traditional forms, but we should point out that such repetitions need not be traditional. One poet may take over and repeat a pattern he finds in the work of another, as Henry Vaughan repeated many of the stanzas (and ideas) he found in Herbert, or a poet may invent a form which he himself uses more than once. T. S. Eliot, for example, in each of his *Four Quartets* follows a general pattern that he had originally invented for *The Waste Land:* there are five sections, the first, third, and fifth of which are rather more colloquial and less intense than the other two. The fourth is a brief lyric, metrically regular, and the second is divided between a more lyrical and regular first half and a more relaxed second half. There are some exceptions within these five poems, but the fact is clear: having invented a pattern, Eliot consciously repeated it.

Of the named forms that poets have copied from each other, we have already discussed several, and need only mention them here: the sestina, the villanelle, and, more recently in English, the haiku. Though the first two of these are commonly set up with individual stanzas of their own, the point here is that the total form is prescribed — the number of lines and the rhyme scheme not only of the stanzas but of the whole poem. By all odds the commonest of such traditional forms is the sonnet.

Actually there are a number of varieties of sonnets, the Petrarchan or Italian, the Shakespearean or English, and several sub-species. They all have in common the basic requirement of fourteen lines of iambic pentameter; * they differ in the arrangement of their rhymes, and

* However, the word "sonnet" originally meant simply "little song," and thus was

thus in the structure of thought which they admit. The Italian sonnet begins with eight lines repeating only two rhymes, *abbaabba,* followed by six lines which may be arranged in any of a number of ways (*cdecde* and *cdcdcd* are probably the most common). The Shakespearean form allows more freedom in the rhymes — giving the poet seven rhyme sounds rather than five — and arranges them *ababcdcdefefgg.* Even from these schemata it can be seen that the Italian sonnet will regularly divide between the eighth and ninth lines — between, that is, the octave and the sestet — while the Shakespearean sonnet, though there may be slight breaks after any one of the quatrains, will have a major break between the third quatrain and the final couplet. This means that the Italian sonnet tends to divide into two more or less co-ordinate considerations (whether complementary or opposed) of its topic, while the Shakespearean tends to arrive at a forceful, epigrammatic affirmation or denial, in the brief couplet, of the topic developed through the three quatrains.

Here, to demonstrate this difference, are two sonnets, the first, in the Italian form, by Keats, and the second, naturally, by Shakespeare:

On First Looking into Chapman's Homer

Much have I travell'd in the realms of gold,
   And many goodly states and kingdoms seen;
   Round many western islands have I been
Which bards in fealty to Apollo hold.
Oft of one wide expanse had I been told   5
   That deep-brow'd Homer ruled as his demesne;
   Yet did I never breathe its pure serene
Till I heard Chapman speak out loud and bold:
Then felt I like some watcher of the skies
   When a new planet swims into his ken;   10
Or like stout Cortez when with eagle eyes
   He star'd at the Pacific — and all his men
Look'd at each other with a wild surmise —
   Silent, upon a peak in Darien.*

---

used in sixteenth-century English to describe many short lyrics that do not fulfill the strict requirements of the type of poem for which the name is now reserved.

   * l. 11. That it was Balboa, and not Cortez, who first saw the Pacific does not blunt the awe which Keats captures in his final image.

Farewell! thou art too dear for my possessing,
And like enough thou knowst thy estimate,
The Charter of thy worth gives thee releasing:
My bonds in thee are all determinate.
For how do I hold thee but by thy granting?   5
And for that ritches where is my deserving?
The cause of this faire gift in me is wanting,
And so my pattent back againe is swerving.
Thy selfe thou gav'st, thy owne worth then not knowing,
Or mee to whom thou gav'st it, else mistaking,   10
So thy great gift, upon misprison growing,
Comes home againe on better judgement making.
    Thus have I had thee, as a dreame doth flatter,
    In sleepe a King, but waking no such matter.*

Though some (though by no means all) of Shakespeare's sonnets
are, without doubt, among the best in the form that bears his name, it
is not a form he invented. Sonnets were first written in English in the
early sixteenth century by Sir Thomas Wyatt, translating and then
imitating Petrarch. Hence Wyatt's sonnets are primarily in the Italian
form, but among his experiments is one that rhymes *abababababababcc,*
a stricter version of the Shakespearean, while, within a few years of
Wyatt's beginnings, Henry Howard, the Earl of Surrey, was writing
sonnets in the usual Shakespearean form. Throughout the remainder
of the sixteenth century, sonnets were immensely popular, and many
variations of rhyme were tried: Italian octaves rhyming *ababcdcd,*
Shakespearean quatrains rhyming *abba,* and Italian sestets with all

* l. 3 *The Charter of thy worth gives thee releasing:* your worth is an authorization
for your release from me. Throughout the quatrains, Shakespeare, with a degree of
irony (see the second line), is using impersonal legal metaphors for personal relations.
The true feeling is therefore rather implied than stated.
    l. 4 *determinate:* beyond their set limits (usually of time, but here of the beloved's
value), and hence forfeit
    l. 6 *that ritches:* those riches
    l. 7 *cause of:* sufficient reason for
    l. 8 *my pattent back againe is swerving:* the right to you which I have had is re-
turning again to you
    l. 11 *upon misprison growing:* upon the growing of misprison; due to the in-
creasingly evident error
    l. 12 *making:* acting, proceeding

possible permutations of two or three rhymes. In general the Italian form remained more popular than the Shakespearean.

In the middle of the next century, Milton, in a number of his sonnets in both Italian and English, experimented with the form, attempting to free it from the strict insistence that the breaks in the thought correspond with the natural pauses in the rhythm of the rhymes. Thus, in his sonnet on his blindness, for example, which we quoted in Chapter II, no major pause comes at the end of the octave, or even at the end of the first quatrain. These are, in fact, insistent run-on lines. Except for the breaks at the ends of lines 6 and 13 (which themselves do not correspond with the natural rhyme-units), the main pauses occur *within* lines. Again, Milton is not the first, but rather the best and the best known, to have attempted the variation associated with his name. Though this driving on through the normal rhythmical breaks does, perhaps, make for a better-unified poem — one sweep of thought rather than two divisions — the Miltonic adaptation of the sonnet (which Milton used in only half of his sonnets, the rest being regular) is one that attempts to deny the sonnet's normal rhythm rather than to take advantage of it. The purpose of such an attempt would seem to be to create a "tension" between the form from which he has departed and the statement, comparable to the tension between accent and stress discussed earlier.

Though the sonnet in English has never regained the popularity it held in the sixteenth century — and has in fact been openly scorned by some poets in our own — it has remained a persistently attractive form. Its firm mold has perhaps been seen as a kind of insurance by too many poetic novices, but its actual difficulties have challenged most of the best poets. For the fact is, of course, that one can fulfill the apparent formal demands and write a very bad poem. And one can tamper with those demands and write a very fine sonnet, as does Milton. Or consider Gerard Manley Hopkins' poem "The Windhover" which — except for a certain freedom with the iambs which allows as many as sixteen syllables in some pentameter lines — is a formally perfect sonnet and a very moving poem indeed.

Then too, so many poets, good, bad, and indifferent, have used the sonnet to compliment their beloveds — in general, or detail by delicate detail — that it has become a challenge to write a love-sonnet which does not sound trite. There is even an old tradition of the anti-sonnet, which attempts freshness either through denying the usual images, as in Shakespeare's "Sonnet 130" ("My Mistres' eyes are nothing like the Sunne"), which we quoted in Chapter III, or through adopting supposedly shocking directness, as in Edna St. Vincent Millay's sonnet beginning "I too beneath your moon, almighty Sex, / Go forth at nightfall crying like a cat."

There is, in fact, however, no particular subject matter that must, or must not, be handled in a sonnet. It is a form that, just because it is definite and brief, has been very popular and, just because it has been so popular, has been subject to great abuse. The abuses should not be counted against it; when it has been well handled, the form has produced some of the finest brief poems in English.

MEANING AS FORM

The rhythmical patterns of sound that we have been discussing, especially such regular patterns as rhymes, meters, and stanzas, are often called *formal,* both in the sense that they are likely to be conventional, and in the more important, direct sense that they are formative: they create, or constitute, *form.* "Form" here, like its related words "shape" and "structure," is a spatial metaphor. Using it, we speak as though the elements of a poem, which in fact must occur in a temporal order, occurred simultaneously and in space. Such a metaphor, in prose as in poetry, is the common — or even the only — way of communicating an understanding; it conveys the idea because it *is* the idea. We speak of the form or the structure of a poem because that is our way of conceiving the final unity of whatever diverse elements may occur within its total pattern.

The danger in thus referring to sound patterns as formal is that we slide too easily into thinking in terms of the separation of form and content; we think of the ideas of the poem as having been fitted into the form, as though hot lead had been poured into a mold. In understanding poetry, however, it is crucial to recognize, as we have attempted to demonstrate again and again in this book, that form and content are infrangible. They may sometimes (and all too easily) be abstracted and separated mentally, for purposes of discussion, but only at the cost of modifying and falsifying them. In the experience of poetry they are not merely "interwoven" or "interdependent" or "simultaneous" or even "fused"— for each of these words suggests a duality. They are indivisible. They are so completely intercreative that they are not "they" but "it."

As we have seen repeatedly, the rhythmical patterns of sound in a poem inevitably control the rhythms of thought. Refrain, for example, is not merely a formally repetitive sound pattern; the structural outline it creates is one of repeated ideas as well as of repeated sounds. In fact, an adequate reading of the ballad "Edward" requires that the actual sound of the repeated refrains be modified by the developing context — by our understanding of the situation portrayed — so that the first and last refrains, though constituted of the same words, will not only have different meanings, but will not even be inflected in the same way. Idea controls sound just as sound controls idea.

We fall too easily into thinking of the "thought content" of a sonnet, for example, as having been forced to fit the strict demands of the form, whether it be the more evenly balanced Italian form or the more pungent Shakespearean. It is, of course, true that the sonnet pattern makes formal demands, and that if these are neglected the result will not be a sonnet. But it is nevertheless also true that — however the poet may have proceeded in conceiving it — the final sonnet, if successful, so integrates idea and sound pattern that neither can be distinguished as having been more or less determinative of form. Thought, no less than sound, is a formal element.

Consider once again how, in Bridges' poem "Nightingales," which we discussed in our first chapter, the images and thoughts of the second stanza parallel and contradict the first, and then how the ideas in both stanzas are modified by the repetitions and developments in the third and last. There is form here — the Hegelian form of thesis, antithesis, and synthesis, to be precise — form which *is* the content of the sound patterns. Or consider again the almost syllogistic form of Marvell's "To His Coy Mistress," a form which is implicit in the simple words introducing the three stanzas: "Had we . . . ," "But . . . ," "Now therefore. . . ." Logic is clearly a formal element.

Nor need the logic be as categorical as is suggested by such terms as "synthesis" and "syllogism." Any simple plot or narrative has its own logical, formal coherence. Or there may be an "emotional logic," a linking of ideas and images, in a lyric for example, on the basis of associations rather than argument or plot.

In fact, all the elements of poetry are formative: not only the sound patterns and the logical structure of the ideas, but the metaphors and the images, which both literally create forms in the imagination and also — through repetition and development or, without those, through coherence with other images — give unity to the poem. Not only sound patterns and logic and images, but the more elusive element of tone, which yields a formal unity of mood or point of view. Not only these but the syntax, which gives precise form to the sentences, themselves the structure of the thought. And not only the syntax but the very words, which *are* the sounds and the images and the thoughts and, through connotations as much as denotations, create *this* poem rather than another. If one wishes to distinguish the elements of a poem, therefore, it would be better to think, not in terms of form and content, but in terms of the interaction of simultaneous forms, such that each word determines, and is determined by, the whole poem.

And so we come back to our word "interaction." But even this word, as helpful as it may be in analysis, falsifies experience through maintaining the plurality of what is in fact single. In comprehending poetry, this crutch too must finally be abandoned as inadequate. No analysis or paraphrase can substitute for the experience of the poem itself. Every poem makes its own, individual demands, and these cannot be met by the application of any particular formulae. There is no ultimate "system" for reading poetry; there is only sensitivity to the demands of each poem. All our instruments of analysis have the single purpose of clearing the ground for the most meaningful interaction: that which occurs between a worthy poem and a worthy reader.

Index to Authors

Inclusive references to all quotations or discussions of the author or of individual works by him.

Index to Titles

Inclusive references to the quotation of any complete poem or extract of five or more lines. For originally untitled poems, either the popular title (in brackets) or the opening phrase is given.

Index to First Lines

References to three varieties of first lines: first lines of poems quoted completely; first quoted lines of extracts of five or more lines; first quoted lines of any extracts not identified in the text, with author and/or title supplied here, as needed.

Index and Glossary of Terms

This list includes most of the technical or literary terms used in the text, with brief working definitions. Page references are to the main appearances of the terms, particularly those offering explanation and examples.

AMPHIBRACH, *see* ROCKING FOOT 311

ANALOGY — a resemblance between two different things, or, more commonly the statement or pointing out of the comparison (*cf.* METAPHOR, SIMILE) 163 ff.

ANAPEST — three-syllable metrical foot with accent on final syllable (x x *l*) 311

APOPHASIS — a rhetorical device or figure which speaks of something while denying that it is doing so 189 f.

ASSONANCE — repetition of vowel sounds, usually a form of near-rhyme 280 ff.

AUDITOR — the person assumed to be listening to the speaker or singer within the poem (as opposed to the reader or audience outside the poem) 110 f.

BALLAD — a story-song, originally a folk form, commonly in a four-line stanza 101

BALLAD STANZA — a four-line stanza with alternating lines of iambic tetrameter and trimeter, the short lines rhyming (*abcb*), common in folk ballads, adapted for literary ballads and for other lyric forms 316

BLANK VERSE — unrhymed iambic pentameter 101

CAESURA — a relatively long pause within a line of poetry, often but not always marked by punctuation 306

CATALECTIC LINE — a line of poetry from which one or more unstressed syllables, according to the metrical pattern expected, are missing from the final foot 313

CLICHÉ — a trite or commonplace expression, usually figurative, which through overuse has lost its force 167n.

CONCEIT — an extended figurative comparison, tending toward the ingenious, in which more and more details of the thing being compared (A-term) and that to which it is being compared (B-term) are found to be congruent 215 ff., 234 f.

CONNOTATION — the meaning or meanings that a word suggests or implies, as opposed to what it states (*cf.* DENOTATION) 52 ff.

CONSONANCE — repetition of consonant sounds, usually a form of near-rhyme 280 ff.

CONVENTION — a commonly or traditionally accepted literary form or device 123 ff., 198

CONVERSION — rhetorical or logical figure in which subject and predicate of an expression are reversed to form another expression 140

COUPLET — pair of consecutive rhyming lines (usually in the same meter) 306 ff.

HEROIC COUPLET — pair of rhyming lines in iambic pentameter 307

CRETIC — a three-syllable metrical foot in which the first and last syllables are accented (*l* x *l*) 311

DACTYL — a three-syllable metrical foot accented on the first syllable (*l* x x) 311

DECAMETER — a line of ten metrical feet 312

DENOTATION — that meaning which a word names or points to, as opposed to what it implies or suggests (*cf.* CONNOTATION) 51 ff.

DIMETER — a line of two metrical feet 312

DRAMATIC MONOLOGUE — a poem in which a single character — not the poet or his persona — speaks to an implied auditor or auditors 99

DRAMATIC POETRY — those poems resembling plays in which the story or events take place in the "now" of the poem and are presented by or through one or more speakers within the poem 99

ELLIPSIS — the omission of a word or words necessary for completion of the grammatical construction but understood in the context, usually by the prior appearance of a completed but otherwise parallel construction 25

END-STOPPED LINE — a line which ends with a syntactical pause, usually but not necessarily marked by punctuation

ENNEAMETER — a line of nine metrical feet 312

EPIC — a long narrative poem, usually about a hero and written in lofty or elevated style 101

EPIGRAM — a short witty poem, usually with a turn or barb at the end 141 f.

FALLING METER (or RHYTHM) — meter characterized by feet in which the accented syllable appears first (*e.g.,* trochees and dactyls) and emphasis then "falls away" to the following unaccented syllables (*cf.* RISING METER) 311

FEMININE ENDING — a line ending with an unstressed syllable

FOOT — a unit of meter consisting, normally, of one accented and one or more unaccented syllables 301

FORM — sometimes, the *sound* of a poem, as opposed to its *sense;* properly, a spatial metaphor (like "shape" and "structure") to express the relations of elements (statements, images, rhythms, etc.) to each other within a poem, the result of their total interaction 157 f., 329 ff.

FREE VERSE — poetry without regularized meter, regularized sound pattern, or other patterned form 309 f.

FRICATIVES — a sound-family of consonants produced by air being forced through an opening — *f, v, h,* both *th*'s (*cf.* NASALS, PLOSIVES, SIBILANTS) 289

HAIKU (HOKKU) — three-line poetic form, originally Japanese, in which the first and third lines have five syllables each and the second line seven 182

HEPTAMETER — a line of seven metrical feet 312

HEXAMETER — a line of six metrical feet 312

HOMERIC SIMILE (or EPIC SIMILE) — an extended, explicit figurative comparison developed from what is often only a single point of similarity, the figurative (B-term) element at times constructing a little scene or story of its own with only tangential relevance to the literal (A-term) element that served as the point of departure 213 ff.

HYPERBOLE (OVERSTATEMENT) — a rhetorical figure in which the statement is an exaggeration of the intended meaning (*cf.* MEIOSIS) 119 ff.

IAMB(US) — a two-syllable metrical foot accented on the second syllable (x /) 311

IMAGE — the "picture" or other sense impression called up by a word or phrase, or, more usually, the word or phrase calling up such impressions 174 ff.

IMPLICATION — indirect hint or suggestion of meaning 80 ff.

INFERENCE — the act of drawing conclusions from indirect hints or (apparent) suggestions of meaning 81

INFLECTION — the changing of the form of words to indicate grammatical function 16 f.

INTERPRETATION — the rendering into the terms and structures of the reader the full meaning, explicit and implicit, of a work (cf. PARAPHRASE) 99

IRONY — VERBAL or RHETORICAL IRONY — a rhetorical figure in which tone, context, or other elements suggest contradiction, reversal, or serious qualification of the direct or literal statement 119, 132 ff.

DRAMATIC IRONY — a character's unwitting foreshadowing of his fate 119

ISOCHRONOUS LINES — lines which are or are intended to be of equal duration in reading time 309

JUXTAPOSITION — the placing of words, phrases, or other elements of meaning next to each other or in relation to each other in such a way as to create meaning beyond that of the words or elements taken individually and beyond that added by the syntactical relationships 136 ff., 168

KINESTHETIC IMAGES — words eliciting the sense of bodily tension or muscle movement 177

KINETIC IMAGES — words eliciting the sight or sound but not the feeling of motion 177

LIMERICK — a five-line anapestic poem, usually humorous, rhyming aabba, with the first, second, and fifth lines trimetric, the third and fourth dimetric (occasionally printed as one tetrameter line with internal rhyme) 296 f.

LOOSE SENTENCE — sentence in which modifying or other grammatically nonessential elements occur after the sentence is essentially complete (cf. PERIODIC SENTENCE) 20

LYRIC POEM — originally, a poem meant to be sung; now, any brief poem primarily concerned with evocation of emotion 101 f.

MEANING — full, final import of a statement, its implications, and its interpretation (cf. SENSE, STATEMENT) 13, 19, 99

MEIOSIS (UNDERSTATEMENT) — a rhetorical figure in which the statement is of less significance or intensity than the intended meaning (cf. HYPERBOLE) 119, 129 ff.

METAPHOR — an implicit figurative comparison of terms essentially unlike, usually in the form of a statement that speaks of one object, quality, or action (A-term) as though it were another (B-term) 165 f.

METER — a normative rhythmic pattern, though the term is usually confined to accentual measures 296 ff.

METONYMY — a rhetorical figure in which the name of one thing is used to designate another to which it is related (cf. SYNECDOCHE) 257

MOCK HEROIC (or MOCK EPIC) — poem in which the high epic form and style are used to ridicule a common or unworthy subject 101, 124 f.

MODULATION (VERBAL RHYTHM, CONSONANT AND VOWEL RHYTHM) — slight shifts of consonant or vowel sounds, usually within a pattern of repeated sounds 288

Pun — the (usually humorous) use of a word which has two meanings both of which may be applied to the context, or of two words that look or sound alike; a play on words 54

Pyrrhic — a two-syllable substitute metrical foot without accent (x x) 311

Quatrain — four-line stanza or unit of a poem 315 f.

Quintain — five-line stanza or unit of a poem 320

Refrain — a line repeated, often with slight variations, at regularly spaced intervals within a poem, usually at a fixed position within a stanza 145, 277 f.

Reordering — rearrangement of the words of a poem to approach the word order of normal prose 15 ff.

Rhyme — repetition of final accented vowel sound and following consonant sound(s), if any 264 ff.

    Masculine Rhyme — single-syllable rhyme 272

    Feminine Rhyme — rhyming accented syllable followed by one or more identical unaccented syllables 272

    End Rhyme — rhyme occurring at the ends of lines 274

    Internal Rhyme — rhyme in which either rhyme word is within the line 274

    Near-Rhyme — approximate rhyme, a general name for the relations of words with such sound-repetitions as assonance, consonance, or half-rhyme 269 ff., 281

    Half-Rhyme (Slant-Rhyme, Off-Rhyme)—rhyme in which the final consonant sounds, if any, are identical, while the vowel sounds are similar but not identical 269 ff., 280 ff.

    Eye-Rhyme — words which appear to rhyme (though they do not) because of similar spelling 274, 281

Rhyme Royal — seven-line stanza of iambic pentameter rhyming *ababbcc* 316

Rhyme Scheme (or Rhyme Pattern) — the pattern of rhymes within a stanza, poem, or unit of a poem, usually indicated by representing the sound-ending of each line by a letter, repeated letters indicating rhyme 268

Rhythm — any repeated occurrence of elements separated by unlike elements, as in meter 142 ff., 277 ff.

    Verbal Rhythms — repeated words, often with slight variations 142 ff.

    Consonant or Vowel Rhythms — repeated sounds, with slight shifts or variations (*see* Modulations) 288 ff.

Rising Meter (or Rhythm) — meter characterized by feet in which the accented syllable appears last (*e.g.,* iambs and anapests), the unaccented syllable(s) "rising" toward the accent (*cf.* Falling Meter) 311

Rocking Foot (Amphibrach) — a three-syllable metrical foot in which only the middle syllable is accented (x / x) 311

Run-On-Line — a line in which the absence of end-punctuation and the incompleteness of sense reduce to a minimum the normal end pause 110

symbolically has no apparent relevance to that which it symbolizes 244 f.

CORRELATIVE SYMBOL — a symbol in which there is a fitness between the word used and the thing or concept symbolized 244 f.

UNIVERSAL SYMBOL — a correlative symbol in which the relationship between the terms fits so well as to seem basic to human experience; natural phenomena that have inescapable metaphorical relevance to human experience, especially to concepts of time 246

SYNECDOCHE — figure of speech in which the part stands for the whole (*cf.* METONYMY) 178 n.

SYNESTHETIC IMAGE — an image demanding the exercise of some sense not literally capable of responding; mingling the senses 177 f.

SYNTAX — the arrangement of words within a sentence which reveals their relationships

TANKA — five-line Japanese poetic form often written as a kind of game, one person writing the first three lines (the *hokku* or *haiku*), the other topping it with a two-line conclusion 182 n

TERZA RIMA — a three-line stanza with rhymes interlocking from one stanza to another — *aba, bcb, cdc* . . . 316

TETRAMETER — a line of four metrical feet 312

TONE — a complex of contextual relationships (including some elements, such as historical attitudes, from outside a poem), which normally complement but sometimes qualify the explicit statements in a poem 115 ff.

TRIMETER — a line of three metrical feet 312

TROCHEE — a two-syllable metrical foot accented on the first syllable (/ x) 311

UNDERSTATEMENT, *see* MEIOSIS

VANTAGE POINT — the position of the speaker of a poem with relation to the events or details of the poem (*cf.* POINT OF VIEW) 112 ff.

VERSE-PARAGRAPH — a group of lines in a poem set off by indentation or a space, usually representing a unit in the thought and not a repeated metrical pattern (*cf.* STANZA) 318

VILLANELLE — a nineteen-line poem in which the first line is repeated as lines 6, 12, and 18; the third line, rhyming with the first, is repeated as lines 9, 15, and 19; the remaining lines either rhyme with these or use a second single rhyme 149

VOICE — the speaker or singer, usually, who is implicitly or explicitly purported to be delivering the words of the poem to the reader or listener 99 ff.